THRIVING AT WORK

What They Didn't Teach You in School

By

MICHAEL DAM

Best Wishes,

Editor: Linda Chau and Orion Dam

Cover layout and design: Ninh Dam

Thriving At Work: What They Didn't Teach You in School

ISBN 978-0-9994609-0-0

Printed in US, November 2017

Praise for

THRIVING AT WORK
By Michael Dam

"If you want to get a great head start in your career, this book is for you. The author shows you powerful solutions for handling work challenges and effective ways to fast track your career. Insightful, practical and interesting read with lots of real work examples. I highly recommend it."

— Mari Young, Category Management Senior Director, Fortune 100 Company

"Wish I'd had something like this when starting out. Concise, well organized and practical insight into work environments. Like having access to a personal career coach."

— Chris Bennett, Retired Vice President, NetApp Company

"With 'THRIVING AT WORK,' you don't have to learn the hard way to succeed at work and fast track your career. This book shows you how."

— Raj Das, Senior Director, Seagate Technology

"This book should have a prominent place on the book shelf of every person entering the workforce. One of a kind book with lots of real work examples, insightful and valuable suggestions to manage your career successfully."

— Loretta Li-Sevilla, Senior Director, Fortune 100 Company

"Among the many great topics covered in this most useful book, I found the chapter on 'How to Achieve Financial Independence' to be a wonderful premier on a subject that is often overlooked. Starting from the most basic, and often least followed, savings concept of "spend less than you make" to the more nuanced use of REIT's to achieve wealth, the information presented here will certainly help in planning one's wealth creation."

       – John E Sharpe, Chartered Financial Consultant (ChFC)

"In the many years Michael and I worked together, I was very impressed with his ability to communicate, build consensus and lead in any situations. The insight I learned from Michael has been valuable to my career growth. It's great that Michael is sharing his lifelong career wisdom, learnings and insights through this book. If you can put half of what's in this book to practice, you will do very well in your career."

       – Paul Chou, Vice President, Foxconn

Acknowledgments

This book is a brainchild of countless hours of discussion with my extended family members, friends, colleagues and students. I am grateful for the interesting, insightful and engaging discussions and the many thought provoking questions and topics that lead me to take the journey of writing this book. The wisdom and advice in this book is a result of wonderful relationships built and nurtured over many years with my colleagues, managers, consultants, educators and mentors. I am grateful for the many hours they engaged in conversations with me on work and career topics and the tremendous insight and wisdom they contributed to the writing of this book.

For the development of this book, I am grateful:

To Linda, for the thorough and excellent initial editing work and the wonderful ideas to keep the content up to date, especially in this fast changing world.

To Thomas for the great insight and suggestions from the millennial's perspective.

To Orion for the tremendous final editing work and for your dedication and labor of love.

To A. Ninh for the countless hours helping me with the book cover design and marketing graphics.

To the many colleagues, friends and students for reviewing the book's content and giving me valuable feedback and encouragement.

To the executives for taking the time from your busy schedule to review the book and sharing your valuable insight and wisdom.

To Joey for your creative ideas, loyalty and generosity. You are my inspiration.

To all my extended family members for your boundless love, advice and encouragement.

And most of all, to my lovely wife - Loan, and our wonderful son - Christopher, for loving me unconditionally, sacrificing and accommodating the many work demands in my career, and for being my tireless cheerleaders.

Thank you all, from the bottom of my heart.

Table of Contents

Introduction

"Technical" skills + **"Soft" skills** = Work and Career Success

After graduating from college, I started my career as a hardware engineer with an aerospace company. On my first day, my manager showed me to my desk, introduced me to the team, gave me my assignment and told me to go to him if I have questions. I did not know about the work environment, the ways things get done, decision process, key people to know and work with, and how to do my job effectively. My boss was inaccessible most of the time and I did not have a mentor and didn't know enough to ask for one. I had no idea how to get off to a good start, not to mention how to get myself noticed and stand out at work. Worse yet, two months into the job, I was transferred to another department that needed more engineers, and was given a completely new assignment to write code for a digital mapping system. Not only did I not know the lay of the land of the company, I also had to learn how to write software programs from scratch. In a nut shell, I was completely lost. I had to learn the hard way through trial and error, and after many months, I slowly found my footing. Looking back, if I had a mentor or a "how to" guide to help me get up to speed, I could have shortened my learning curve greatly, navigated the organizational dynamics better, and put myself in a position to be more productive, to contribute more to the company and make a name for myself much sooner.

My goal for this book is to share the skills and tools I learned, developed and observed in my career with the young people who are beginning to dip their toes in the professional world as well as current professionals. This book provides a proven roadmap for you to achieve immediate success and to fast track your career. The soft skills discussed in this book will enable you to get a head start, anticipate and navigate the many changes and challenges in the workplace as well as throughout your career. These are the skills not usually taught in school and can otherwise take years to learn.

What This Career Handbook Is About
It is a comprehensive collection of the best practices and skills to help professionals succeed throughout their career. I learned them during my

twenty five year professional career as well as from working, observing and interviewing successful professionals, from individual contributors to high-level executives. This book covers a broad career spectrum, from starting out after college to transitioning into management roles.

I discuss different situations in the workplace that employees will likely face and suggest ways to handle them effectively. In addition, I cover important skills required to succeed at work and to manage different career phases, including transitioning from an individual contributor to a first time manager.

Although I focus primarily on private industry, many of the skills are also relevant to employees in public sector workplaces such as federal, state and local government agencies. In addition, I focus on specific topics relevant to non-management professionals (individual contributors).

Why I Wrote This Book

I have found that people have a real thirst for knowledge pertaining to handling different situations at work and managing their career transitions, from the beginning to the end. From my five years of teaching and conducting workshops at colleges, I see many students lack the "soft skills" needed to succeed in the workplace, such as the ability to work effectively with people to solve difficult business issues. Students have many questions about work and career, such as "How do I get the job I want?", "How do I make a good first impression?", "What typical challenges will I face at work?", "How do I stand out?", "What do I need to do to succeed in my job?", "How do I deal with surprises or unexpected changes at work?", etc. If you have some of these questions, this book is for you. Colleges, for the most part, focus on teaching students academic and technical skills in their field, and fall short on teaching students the "soft" skills to complement their academic/technical training.

While mastering academic and technical discipline is fundamental to a student's profession, it's not nearly enough to guarantee them success in their career. According to a recent survey released by Payscale (PayScale, 2016), the majority of new college graduates are not ready for the workplace. Sixty percent of all companies said new graduates lack critical thinking skills, writing proficiency, attention to detail and inadequate public speaking ability.

During my management years, many employees and co-workers frequently asked me for advice on how to handle work issues. Moreover, many people coming from other countries are especially at a disadvantage at work due to cultural differences, not to mention the language barrier as well as the nuances of the English language.

I believe that much of the success a person achieves in their profession comes from the ability to communicate and work effectively with people to solve different challenges. I call these "soft" skills (whereas accounting skills are "hard" skills). I have seen many people who only have above average technical competence get promoted repeatedly thanks to their "soft" skills. I learned this the hard way and it took many years for me to develop the "soft" skills needed to thrive in the professional world. I spent my time in college focusing on engineering classes and little time on anything else; if I had learned and developed more "soft" skills, I truly believe my career growth path would have been more accelerated.

After giving this subject a lot of thought, I tested the idea of writing this book with students, colleagues and managers, and to my pleasant surprise, I received overwhelmingly support and endorsement to start this project.

Whom This Book Is Written For
- College graduates getting ready to enter the workforce for their first professional job. This book helps these graduates get a head start in their new career with practical guidance on writing resumes, preparing and conducting interviews and starting their job on the right foot.
- New employees who recently joined the workforce. This book helps these employees get off on the right foot from day one and deal effectively with potential work challenges and career transitions.
- Professionals who are struggling and want to be more effective at handling work challenges. This book provides the best tools and practices to help them work effectively with co-workers, manage up successfully and improve their standing in the company.

How This Book Is Organized
This comprehensive handbook provides the best practices and skills required to effectively manage various challenges throughout one's career. I cover a wide range of topics, with each topic covering a particular skill or situation. I organize these topics into 7 categories:
1. Starting out: writing resumes, conducting interviews, searching for jobs, and starting your job on the right foot.
2. Communicating: communicating verbally/written, presenting persuasively, and speaking to specific audiences.

3. Collaborating: facilitating meetings, resolving conflicts and challenges, earning people's trust, and getting people's attention.
4. Negotiating: negotiating skills, negotiating job offer, asking for a raise, and saying no smartly.
5. Taking care of yourself: promoting yourself, managing time and prioritizing, preventing and managing stress, exercising smartly, and planning for financial independence.
6. Managing your manager: managing up, working effectively with managers, dealing with difficult managers, working with HR, and preparing for performance review.
7. Managing your career path: building network, exploring career options, considering management paths, and transitioning to management.

How To Use This Book

I designed this book for you to read any specific topic of interest at any time as well as to be able to refer back to any topic throughout your career.

- This book covers a wide range of relevant topics (chapters). Each topic contains specific and practical solutions, and you can read one or more topics of interest at any time without having to read the whole book.
- Throughout your career as you encounter different situations, refer back to this book and read the topics applicable to your situations. I design this book for you to use as a reference throughout your career.

If you have the time, I would recommend reading the whole book since many topics complement each other and the book will give you a more comprehensive view over your career cycle.

Visit my website www.careeratwork.com for additional and complementary materials to the content in this book – including sample resumes, financial tools for budgeting and analysis, market updates, new topics and insight from the reader community.

Happy reading!

THRIVING AT WORK

Part 1

Starting Out

People are afraid of the future, of the unknown. If they face up to it and take the dare of the future, they can have some control over their destiny. That's an exciting idea to me, better than waiting with everybody else to see what's going to happen.

John H. Glenn, Jr.

Chapter 1

How To Search For Job Opportunities

In today's private industry world, you are unlikely to stay with the same company for your entire professional career, even if you want to. Company's loyalty to employees was real at one time, but not so much. Throughout your career, prepare to change jobs a few times, whether by choice or not. Make it a practice to keep your eyes open for better opportunities, to be proactive, and take control of your career. When you want to search for job opportunities, your networking contacts are a great resource and can also be a great reference for you. The best way to get the job you want is through referrals and recommendations from people you know. These people can help you expedite the applying process by connecting you directly to the hiring manager. However, this option may not be available to you all the time. In this chapter, I will cover the different sources and ways to search for job openings.

Job Search Using Your Network Sources
At the point you're looking for a job, hopefully you already have a significant network of contacts you've built and grown over time. Now is the time to tap into this network to help you with your job search. If you have not focused on building your network, start as soon as possible. It's better late than never.

- **Classmates.** This also includes members in school clubs, sport teams or other school organizations you joined and built relationships with. Many of them may be on social media sites such as Facebook and LinkedIn. Contact them using what you think are the most effective ways to reach them: social media, email, phone or if possible, face to face.
- **College or University Alumni Association**. All schools maintain an extensive list of alumni. Alumni members are encouraged to stay in touch, share information and provide assistance to each other. They

present a big exposure to potential job and career opportunities all over the world. If your school's alumni have a website offering a platform for alumni to stay in touch, this would be a convenient way to let people know about your job search. Through the contact list from your college directory, you can reach out to these people as well.

- **Co-workers.** These include people you're currently working with as well as former co-workers whom you have developed good relationships with, earned their trust and gained credibility. They are a fantastic resource for finding and getting job opportunities and can also be great references for you. Your former managers are great contacts to reach out. They obviously knew you and if they had a good working relationship with you and valued your work, they could be your meal ticket. From the companies you've worked at, you should already have a list of contacts. If you don't, you can put a list together using your phone contact list, email list and from social media sites, etc. Contact them and let them know what you are looking for. If they are local and possible, meet with them in person.

During a lunch I had with a former student, Samantha, she told me she had recently left her old company to join a financial services company. When I asked her how she got the job, Samantha told me a former colleague who went to this new company recruited and recommended her. Her colleague arranged a lunch meeting for her with the hiring manager. At the end of the lunch, the manager offered her the job on the spot. Although Samantha had a good working relationship with her colleague, she did not know her well. When she left the company, Samantha asked for her contact information and kept in touch periodically. And she was very glad she did. This is not usually how the hiring process works, but it shows the power and benefit of networking.

- **Professionals connected to your company**. These include suppliers, service providers, contractors you worked with on behalf of your company, or in some cases, even your company's competitors. You should have a list of the people you had good working relationships with. They are a good resource because they have a lot of visibility of the industry and know a lot of the key players. Reach out to them via whatever avenue is most convenient and effective for them.
- **Industry organizations**. There are many professional associations in different industries, such as the IEEE for electrical engineers, American Association of Finance and Accounting (AAFA) for

accounting and finance professionals, and American Marketing Association (AMA) for marketing professionals. If you are a member, you can get useful, relevant information specific to your field through the organization website postings and newsletters. Through the website, you may also be able to post your job inquiries and have access to many people in your professional field.

- **Head hunters and recruiting firms**. Throughout your career, you will likely receive calls or email messages from head hunters trying to recruit you for one or more job opportunities. You also find them on career and job sites such as LinkedIn, Monster and CareerBuilder. Head hunters want to add to their professional contact list and would be interested in talking to you even if they don't have any opportunity matching your interest and qualifications at the moment. In addition, they are a good source of information since they often have visibility to your industry, key companies and employment outlook.
- **Friends, family members, neighbors and social groups**. They often are the best ways to learn about opportunities and excellent resources to help you find the right job. Many of them have their own networks and by extension, can get your word out to many more people.

Job Search Using Additional Sources

- **Companies you're interested in**. Companies post job openings as they become available. You can search on their website for job openings and submit your resume with the job you're interested in. All the openings should have a fairly detailed job description including key responsibilities and requirements. Some may list recruiter contact information but most do not. If you know someone from the company, that person can help find out the recruiter's contact information or even better yet, forward your resume to the hiring manager. Especially in a difficult employment environment, you increase your chances significantly if you can reach out directly to the hiring manager. Many companies hire contractors to handle recruiting and screening, but unfortunately, because of the high turnover rate for recruiters, your resume may fall through the cracks. It's a good idea to follow up periodically to make sure the company still has you on file.
- **Professional and job search sites**. These include Monster, CareerBuilder, LinkedIn, etc. These sites have a large number of members, including professional employees, employers and

headhunters. Here you can post your profile/resume. Companies also advertise and post their job openings on these sites. They provide great exposure to many job openings as well as employment contacts. From these sites, some of which offer additional features to enhance your job search but may require a premium membership fee, you can customize your search for the specific type of job you're looking for as well as set up automatic search to receive reports on a regular basis.

- **Government**. This includes federal, states, counties and local agencies. Government agencies list employment opportunities on their websites. Many of my friends and family members have discovered job openings through these sites and secured jobs with state and local government agencies. Depending on the profession, these agencies typically use a formal hiring process, and although some maybe different than others, many do require you to submit your resume, cover letter and complete an application. Many also require you to take an online test. From the test results, they narrow down the list of candidates for the interview process. This formal process can take a long time to complete, sometime months. For high level positions, from Director and above, the hiring process may be more expedited.
- **Classified ads** in newspapers, magazines and trade publications, including online ads. While these are not as common and popular, they still are a useful source of job opportunities. Local newspapers are especially good sources to search.

Additional Tips

- Hopefully, you have been proactively managing your career on an ongoing basis, including building your network and keeping your resume up to date. If you are new in your professional life and have not built up your network, start one and keep growing it. Don't wait. If you don't have your resume or have not updated one recently, put your focus on creating the best resume possible. After all, your resume is your initial communication vehicle to potential employers. Since they will likely read your resume before deciding to interview you, don't shortcut your resume writing effort. Before you start or at least during your job search, make sure you have a resume ready to go. Refer to the "How to write a compelling resume" chapter for the best way to go about this.

- There are online resources such as glassdoor.com that provide you useful information in your search for the right job and company. Information you can find includes reviews of salary compensations for specific job titles, benefits, cultures and management teams.
- Once you apply for a position, you may get a phone call any time. The phone call could be to set up time for a phone interview or it could be the interview itself. As a result, assume the phone call you get will be a screening interview and be prepared. Your success in the screening interview will get you face to face interviews with the hiring manager and other people in the company. You don't want to get caught unprepared for the phone interview because that might be your only one with that company. If you're not prepared, ask to schedule a time soon after so you have time to prepare.

Chapter 2

How Companies Hire

Many college students and even professionals who have been employed for some time don't really understand how employers conduct and manage the hiring process. Understanding this process helps you better prepare for your job search, interviews and job offer negotiations. While companies may differ somewhat in their hiring process, their approach and procedure are similar. I'll describe in this chapter a typical hiring process.

How Companies Conduct Staffing And Hiring

- **Staffing decision**. Companies begin working on next year's operating plan a few months prior to the next fiscal year with the goal to have final approved plan by the start of next fiscal year. Once approved, each department has its specific budget plan showing how many additional positions can be added for the coming year. The additional headcounts include the number of new college graduate hires as well as experienced hires. The new college graduate hiring process is normally completed by May with offers extended to candidates in Feb or March. Because of this schedule, company's college recruiters usually visit colleges and participate in job fair events for graduating students much earlier. The experienced hires can occur throughout the year.

  It's important to remember that the annual operating budget is subject to be revised quarterly. The number of hires for each quarter may increase or decrease, depending on the company's business performance and market conditions. An exception to this planning process happens when a manager needs to replace an employee who transitioned to another job or left the company. This replacement hire must be approved by appropriate management levels. One additional note - the company at any time can decide to freeze all hiring and open positions. Timing also plays an important factor and dictates the manager's hiring process. Due to fiscal calendar constraint of end of fiscal quarter or year, all managers may be given a deadline to complete their hiring or lose their head count allocations. As a result, managers may shorten the hiring process in order to beat the deadline.

- **Posting job openings**. Once the manager knows how many additional employees to hire, he writes a job description for each position. The job description includes job title, main responsibilities and qualification requirements such as college degree, number of years of experience, technical skills, etc. In addition, the job description may also list "desirable" qualifications. To start the process, an HR staffing recruiter meets with the manager to confirm the position's job level, review criteria for selecting candidates, decide whether to use external head hunter and how to proceed with the interview process. Then the manager submits the job positions to be posted on company website and on external sites as appropriate.
- **Screening and interviewing**. The company staffing recruiter screens resumes, verifies candidates' qualifications and sends qualified resumes to the hiring manager. The manager or recruiter conducts phone interviews to select candidates for in-person interviews. The manager also puts together an interview team consisting of people from his team and other teams who will be working with the new hire.

Regarding interview methodology, many companies use behavioral interview method where the interviewer describes certain work scenarios and asks the candidate to respond to each situation. This is an effective method to gauge the candidate's qualities and skills. For example, if the interviewer wants to probe for teamwork ability, she may say: "Give me an example of a time you had a conflict at work with a colleague and describe how you handled it." Or if the interviewer wants to probe for problem solving skills, she may say: "Give me an example of a complex problem you had to solve and explain how you solved it." In terms of organizing the interview team, some managers are more organized and assign a specific area for each member to probe, such as teamwork, communication, job skills and creativity. Other managers are less structured and would leave it up to the interviewers to decide how they want to conduct the session.

Some companies also have a practice of hiring for a functional area, Supply Chain for example, without focusing on any specific job.

They may not have specific jobs defined yet or may want to re-organize the job positions in the organization. After the hiring process is completed, the manager places the employee in a specific job position.

- **Hiring decision**. After all the interviews are completed and feedback collected, the manager narrows the list down to a few finalists and either decides to hire one of them or bring them in for final interviews with high level executives. Before making the final hiring decision, he checks out references and HR conducts background check on the finalists. During this final stage, the manager stays in touch with the other finalists to update them on his progress and to affirm their availability and interest in joining the company.

- **Job offer package**. Once the manager decides on a candidate, he and his HR manager put together an offer package which includes base salary, stock incentives, sign on cash bonus, etc. Some offer items are firm per company policy while others are negotiable. HR manager informs the candidate and sends the offer out. The candidate is given a certain number of days to formally accept or reject the offer. This period can be a few days for an experienced hire or as long as two months for college hires due to their college's job accepting policy. During this period, the hiring candidate can ask to clarify unclear items and negotiate the offer. Since time is of the essence, the manager will push the candidate for a decision as soon as possible. He likely also has a backup plan in case the offer is rejected. If this happens, he'll quickly move to make the offer to the second finalist.

- **On-board preparation**. Once the candidate accepts the formal offer, the manager will complete the necessary paperwork and take steps to prepare for the new hire's arrival. This preparation includes procuring IT equipment, setting up the employee in the company HR and IT system, as well as lining up key people for the new hire to meet.

Although companies tend to have a similar hiring framework, they may have differences in specific hiring procedure, depending on the company size and industry. Start up and small companies may have simpler hiring process than large employers. For example, instead of a few rounds of interview, it may take one and instead of a team of several interviewers, it may just be a couple of people, including the hiring manager. The budget planning process for smaller companies may also be less formal and managers have more discretion over when they can hire. Moreover, since smaller companies do not have a fully staffed HR department, they may outsource much of the recruiting and screening tasks to outside head hunters or recruiting firms. When contacted by the company recruiter, ask for information on the hiring process so you can prepare appropriately.

How Public Sector Organizations Manage Hiring Process

These organizations typically have a different hiring process than private sector. They are dictated by agency regulations. You should do a thorough research on the organization you want to join to make sure you understand the application process and hiring requirements clearly. Below is a summary of a typical process.

- **Job postings on organization's website**. Government agencies, which include federal, state and local agencies, post job opportunities on their websites. You should start with the website to search for job openings, along with detailed job titles, descriptions, salary levels and required qualifications. These sites also provide details on how to apply.
- **Submittal requirements**. Depending on the position, these agencies typically require you to submit a resume along with a cover letter and a completed application. They may also require you to take an online test to score your job skills. As you can see, this is different than the process used by private companies who usually don't require a cover letter or taking a test as the initial steps in applying for employment.
- **Interview and hiring process**. Based on the test results, a certain number of candidates with the top scores are selected to proceed to the next step. They either will go through one-on-one or panel interviews. This hiring process can take many months. However, for high level positions such as Directors and higher, the process may be more streamlined. No test is required of the candidates and the hiring process is similar to private sector's practice.

Chapter 3

How To Explore Job Options

This chapter may be a little more relevant for new graduating college students. When you start your job search, you may be asking yourself what job you should pursue. While this is an important question, there are other key questions you need to consider as well, such as what department/organization in a company you like to work in. This chapter helps you think through these questions, provides visibility and ways to explore your job options so you can make the best decision for you.

For every college major, there are a number of different job positions where you can utilize your skills. As importantly, there could be a number of organizations within a company that have relevant positions for your college degree. When you explore the different job options and organizations in a company, get as much information and as clear a picture as you can to determine if they fit with your interests and goals.

Refer to Table 1 example below. For each college major, Table 1 shows: 1) a sample list of possible organizations in a company you can join and 2) a sample list of job positions in each of these organizations. I'll discuss each of these in detail.

Considering Different Job Positions

As you begin to search for job openings in the market place, you should know all available job positions related to your college degree. You need to understand what the positions entail, differences between them and which ones best fit your strengths and interests.

- Let's look at an engineering example from Table 1 below. For our discussion, let's assume you graduated with a Computer Science bachelor degree (BS degree). Some of the relevant job positions for this major include Software Design Engineer, Test Engineer, Quality

13

Assurance/Quality Control Engineer, Application Engineer and Customer Support Engineer. Each of these positions has its own specific responsibilities. For example, responsibilities of a Software Design Engineer include designing overall solution for a project or a part of a project, defining clearly inputs and outputs and writing code. On the other hand, a Test Engineer has the responsibilities to test for software bugs and any problems between the different SW programs within the project. The SW Design Engineer position normally offers a higher salary than the Test Engineer position due to the skills required. Depending on your skill level and experience, you may find one of these two Engineering positions a better fit for you.

- Let's look at another example from Table 1 – Finance/Accounting. Similar to Engineering, there are a number of positions applicable to the Finance/Accounting major, such as Finance Analyst, Financial Reporting Manager and Cost Accounting Specialist. These jobs have different responsibilities. One responsibility of a Finance Analyst is performing an ROI (Return on Investment) analysis of a project whereas a responsibility of a Finance Reporting Manager is gathering key business results and creating a report for company management. The former requires more finance analysis skill while the latter requires the ability to understand business metrics and organize data in a logical manner.

For your reference, there are online resources that provide comprehensive lists of job positions and titles for each college degree. One example is www.payscale.com.

Considering Different Organizations

In addition to the job positions, you should research to determine which organizations in the company are best suited for your career goal and interest.

- With the Computer Science degree, there are several organizations offering job positions relevant for the degree, including Engineering, Customer Support, Sales/Field Operations and Manufacturing Operations. In the Customer Support Organization, you focus on providing technical support to customers, working with customers to design specific solutions, or providing technical training and support to sales people. In addition, you generally interface more frequently with customers and salespeople than if you work in the engineering organization. If you have an interest on the technical as well as business side and like interacting with customers, you may want to consider the Customer Support Organization.

On the other hand, if you want to be a Sales Representative in the future, you may apply to work in Sales Operations where you will have opportunities to work closely with the sales team and have firsthand knowledge of how salespeople work with customers.

- For Finance/Accounting major, organizations having relevant positions include Finance Department, Corporate Finance Department, Product Operations, Sales Operations and Customer Support Organization. While you may perform similar duties in these organizations, whom you work with is different. In Finance Department within Product Operations, you interact with engineering teams whereas you work with sales people if you're in Sales Operations. Working in Sales Operations gives you exposure to the external business world. On the other hand, working in Product Operations gives you more in-depth view of the internal business workings of the company.

One other factor to consider is which organization may offer opportunities that align with your goal. If you like to gain international experience, working in Sales Organization may present opportunities for you to work in a sales office overseas in the future.

Small and medium sized companies may have multiple functions combined into one organization or department. For example, Technical Support is within the Engineering department. In addition, employees in smaller companies may perform more than one job function. For example, if you work in the Marketing department, you job duties may include marketing communications, product launch, sales training and public relations. Or if you work in the Finance department, your job duties may include business analysis, program management and business reporting. Working in a smaller company offers you an advantage of learning and developing different skills in multiple areas whereas you tend to develop a specialized skill in a specific job with a big company.

When you explore the different job options and organizations in a company, get as much information and as clear a picture as you can to determine if they fit with your interests and goals.

Table 1. Example of mapping between job positions and organizations in a company. This is for illustrative purpose only and not meant to be a complete list. There are available online resources providing more comprehensive lists that match different careers to college degrees. One such resource is www.bigfuture.com.

Degree/Major	Organization	Job Position
Electrical Engineering; Computer Science	Engineering Group	Design Engineer Test Engineer QA/QC Engineer BIOS/Firmware Engineer Document/Technical Writer
	Manufacturing Operation	Production Engineer Process Engineer QC Engineer Test Engineer
	Technical-Customer Support Organization	Technical Marketing Eng. Technical Support Engineer Application Engineer
	Field Sales; Sales Operation	Solutions Architect Application Engineer Professional Services Eng. Sales Engineer
Math	Finance Dept.	Finance Analyst Business Analyst Business Planner
	Corporate/Headquarter	Merger & Acquisition Mgr Investment Specialist Business Strategist
	Engineering Group, Quality Control Dept.	QC Process Specialist Product Quality Specialist Business/Cost Analyst
Finance; Accounting	Finance Dept.; Corporate Finance Dept.	Finance Analyst Finance Reporting Manager Business Analyst Budget Analyst
	Accounting Dept.	Cost Analyst Business Analyst Accountant
	Field Sales; Sales Operation	Finance Analyst Finance Reporting Manager Business Analyst Customer Billing Specialist

Business	Finance Dept.	Business Analyst Program Manager Business Planner
	Marketing Organization	Business Analyst Program Management Specialist PR/Communication Specialist
	Field Sales; Sales Operation	Sales Support Specialist Order Administrator Program Management Specialist Salesperson
	Engineering Group; Customer Support Operation	Project Manager Business Analyst Customer Returns &Escalation Manager
Marketing	Marketing Organization	Program Manager Marcom Specialist Outbound Marketing Specialist Marketing Event Coordinator
	Filed Sales; Sales Operation	Program Management Promotion/Advertising Specialist Event Planning Manager Salesperson
	Customer Support Operation	Customer Service Rep Event Coordinator Program Manager Training Program Manager
Communications	PR Dept.	Financial Analyst Liaison Industry Analyst Liaison Marketing Communication Specialist Program Manager
	HR Organization	Training Program Manager Department Liaison Employee Development Manager Benefit Administrator

	Marketing Organization	Marketing Event Planner Program Manager Marcom Specialist Business Development Specialist Industry Partnership Manager

How To Research Job Positions And Organizations

If you are in college, meet with as many company recruiters as you can when your school holds Career Fair events. Ask the recruiter about the different positions in the company that match your degree, to describe the different duties from one position to another, and provide you copies of the job description. In addition, talk to the recruiter about the different organizations in the company that have positions where your degree is applicable and to explain to you the differences among these organizations. Contact an HR manager or any manager in the companies of interest for an informational meeting where you can pick their brain. This takes time but be persistent and you may be able get some managers willing to meet you or at least talk to you over the phone. If you have friends or know people in the company, ask them to refer you to the HR manager or other managers for you to meet. LinkedIn is a good place to locate HR staffing personnel and other recruiters. Explain to them that you are exploring different positions to help you consider the best fit as you start out your career. Also use your network of contacts who work in different jobs and in different organizations.

Although these efforts require a significant amount of time, it's worth the investment. As a new graduate, it's easier to obtain an entry-level job position from a list of several job openings as well as organizations in a company. Companies are more willing to train new college hires. On the other hand, if you are an experienced professional in a particular job, it's more difficult to move into a different position since the new position would more likely require someone with experience.

Chapter 4

How To Write A Compelling Resume

A resume enables you to get your foot in the door. While a resume does not get you a job offer by itself, it can get you an interview opportunity which can lead to a job offer. Unless the employer already knows you, a prospective employer will review your resume to determine if they want to interview you. While your ultimate objective is to get a job offer, it's not the goal of a resume. In all my professional years, I have not seen or heard of offers being made from just reading a resume, no matter how compelling. The resume's key objective is to generate enough interest for potential employers to want to interview you. You have a much better chance of getting an interview if you produce a compelling resume that matches well with the job's requirements and makes you stand out against other candidates. In this chapter, I'll show you how to write such a resume by focusing on two areas - style and content development. In addition, I'll discuss the type of content to include in your LinkedIn profile.

Creating Resume Style
This is creating the looks and feels for your resume, including how to format, how to organize and how to make it easy to read and follow.
- **Keep a resume to maximum two pages**. If you are a new graduate without much work experience, one page resume may be sufficient. Focus on quality instead of quantity. The person reviewing your resume could be HR (Human Resources) staffing recruiter, outside recruiter, or a hiring manager. Due to the sheer volume of resumes to review, I would typically only spend a few minutes on each resume. I would look to see if you meet the required qualifications and how you stand out against other resumes. So if your resume is longer than two pages, I probably would scan through your resume even quicker, which would increase the likelihood of missing important information you want me to know.

Moreover, a long resume indicates a possible lack of discipline to be succinct and lack of ability to prioritize key information about you. A four-page resume listing everything you have done in your career will likely create a negative impression even before the manager begins reading it.

- **Keep the format simple**. Since you will likely submit your resume online, PDF or text format is appropriate. Some employers use programs to scan for certain keywords on your resume to determine your potential fit. Use normal font size for the body content (10-12 point) and no need to use fancy fonts or colors.

- **Make the resume easy to read and follow**. Use "bullet" point format instead of long sentences. Try to keep each bullet point to one or two lines. If the manager has a few minutes to read your resume, you don't want him to have to re-read over certain things because he wasn't clear what you meant to say. Moreover, using bullet point format encourages you to be succinct and to the point.

- **Make your resume come alive**. Use active, "power" words as appropriate. For example, use "I lead" instead of "I was involved," "I initiated" instead of "I assisted," and "I delivered the project results ahead of schedule" instead of "I was able to finish…"

- **Check for spelling and grammar errors**. Misspelled words or grammatically incorrect sentences can turn a good resume into a mediocre one and the mistakes could negatively cloud the reviewer's opinion of you. It also indicates laziness and lack of attention to details. So it's worthwhile to spend a few minutes running through spell and grammar check.

Developing Resume Content

The objective of a resume is to generate interest for potential employers to want to interview you. To start off, focus on developing a great "foundational" resume that highlights your skills, experience, education, qualities and accomplishments without focusing on any specific company. In addition, be creative and use any relevant and factual information that will help you stand out and put you in as good a position as possible. Then as you find a specific job you want to apply for, you can tweak this foundational resume for that job. If you did a good job creating the resume, tweaking your resume to match the requirements should be quick and without a lot of effort needed.

The general structure of a resume includes:

1. Contact information and job objective.

2. Summary of skills/qualifications.
3. Education summary.
4. Experience summary.
5. Relevant hobbies/interests/other technical skills.

It's not necessary to include a Reference section. If the employer wants to check for references, they will ask you at that time. The order between Education Summary and Experience Summary can be interchanged. If you have a fair amount of experience, you may want to order your experience before education.

1. **Contact information should be straight forward.** For your contact information, use a phone number that you can be easily reached. Usually this is your cell phone. Don't list a phone you use infrequently. Since managers are usually busy, they would like to be able to talk to a candidate live on the phone when they call. If they need to leave a message, you run the risk of playing phone tag since it's a good possibility they will not be available when you call back. Also use an email account you check regularly. If the employer sends you an email message regarding your job interest and doesn't hear from you in a few days, they'll assume you're not interested.

    For job objective, reserve a line to fill in the job title/description when you want to apply for a specific job. For example: "Seeking a challenging and interesting Business Analyst position that will enable me to use my skills and growth with the company. (Job Requisition# 123REQ)." Remember to include the job requisition number if there is one so you can ensure the resume will reach the right person.

2. **Summary of Skills/Qualifications**. This is the most important section of the resume. This is where you can summarize a few key points you want the manager to remember about you because he's not going to remember everything on your resume. The analogy here is similar to writing a thesis paper where you put your theme and main points at the beginning of the paper. Instead of having the manager try to come up with what to remember about you, why not make it easy for him by stating it upfront. This section should include a short list of 4-5 skills and accomplishments that best match the position's requirements and put you in the best possible light. Here are some example bullet points for graduating college students:
    - Strong technical skills and experience that match very well with the position's requirements;

- Track record of successfully leading different groups of people on multiple school projects;
- Exceptional communication skills developed through communication classes and internship at ABC company;
- Dean's list for 3 consecutive quarters;
- Demonstrated ability to get up to speed quickly, solve problems and go above and beyond to get things done right and on time.

You need to support these skills and qualifications by providing "proofs" in subsequent sections of your resume. If you have difficulty writing this section first, skip it and work on the last three sections. After you have completed those sections, pick out key nuggets and include them in your Summary of Skills/Qualifications section. You may find this method more helpful in writing this summary section.

3. **Education Summary**. Many graduating students don't make full use of this part of the resume. They simply list their college major and a few classes they completed. As a result, they miss an opportunity to reveal special accomplishments or unique skills they have learned. It's not enough to just list out your major and classes taken. This does not separate you from others. Focus on pointing out and highlighting any excellent results you achieved with your education. Some specific suggestions:

- Include College Major(s), degree, high GPA. If you have a Minor degree, list it as well.
- Include relevant and successfully completed classes as well as results and accomplishments from significant research projects, group projects or other completed papers. Also highlight the skills you developed. For example, learning leadership skills from leading a group project, developing analytical skills from research projects, writing skills from publishing papers, etc.

    If part of your education program involved working with a real company on a specific project where you/your team delivered tangible benefits to the companies and at the same time, learned and developed concrete skills, you should definitely highlight this experience. This is especially useful in situations where a company requires a certain amount of work experience which you don't have. However, this kind of "school" experience can serve as a good substitute for the lack of "real world" experience.

In a business class I taught, we had a business plan group project. Students formed in teams of four and their objective was to create a business startup that serves an unmet need in the community. They developed a complete business plan with detailed marketing strategy, operational plan, financial analysis and forecast. Upon completion of the project, each team gave a presentation on their business plan. As a member/leader of the team, this would be a great experience to include in the resume – highlighting skills the students developed including leadership, communication, collaboration, analytical and presentation skills. This would be viewed positively by the hiring manager.

- Include key awards and accomplishments during your educational years such as Honor Roll, Valedictorian, Dean List, top 10% of class, scholarships, etc.

4. **Experience Summary**. I want to emphasize two important points here. First, focus on highlighting your positive results and accomplishments on each of your jobs. Many people only provide a list of job responsibilities and activities they performed. While it makes sense to describe the job, it's not enough and is only a small part of what you should include. You want to make yourself stand out as much as possible. Just listing your job responsibilities does nothing to highlight you. Pointing out good results and accomplishments will separate you from others. Secondly, think about your paying as well as non-paying jobs and volunteer work experience. Work experience is not limited to paid positions only. The experience and skills you gained in your volunteer work are as meaningful and valuable, and in many cases, create better impression to hiring managers than a paid position.

If you have a long work history, put more focus on recent employment experience (within the last 5 years). If you limit your resume to 2 pages, you will not have enough space to cover every job in detail. Here is how to develop the content for Experience Summary section:

- For each position, list job title, company's name, location and employment duration.
- Describe briefly your job and key responsibilities. Keep to one or two lines.
- List successful results and key accomplishments. Think about how your results helped contribute to your team or your company's success. Excellent results include finishing a project ahead of schedule or below budget, helping sales to exceed target, saving company cost, increasing customer satisfaction,

23

and improving quality of product and services. It's best if you can show quantitative results. For example, finishing a key project two months ahead of schedule or reducing the defective products by twenty percent is a tangible result. When I was a product manager working on a new computer product, we completed the project three months ahead of schedule. This allowed the company to launch the product in a peak buying season and as a result, the company gained an advantage in the market. You bet I included this in my resume. One more point, you need be able to support your claims and explain them in details if you're asked about them in the interview.

- Think about examples that demonstrate your value and standing in the company, such as bonus awards, excellent job review/ranking, praise from managers, company recognition, customer/partner appreciation, employee of the month/year award, significant salary raises and stock grants. Don't forget to include anything that makes you look good and separate you from the crowd. This is not the time to be bashful.

- Another way to show your skills and qualities is highlighting the times you were a leader or played a leading role in motivating people and driving the team to get the job done. This shows you were a skilled, dedicated leader and not just an average employee. Companies don't want to hire average employees.

5. **Relevant hobbies/interests/technical skills**. Use this section to highlight yourself in other areas you have not covered in the resume. Many people give this section little focus, no more than just a cursory attempt to add the same hobbies most people put on their resume which don't convey anything unique about them. Here's what you should do:

- Include hobbies or interests that enhance your appeal to the position or provide even more support for the qualities you highlighted. For example, if you are a long distance runner and have participated in long distance races, including this hobby demonstrates your self-motivation, dedication and discipline. If you play a musical instrument, including this hobby shows you have creativity. If you participated in competitive events in sports, technology or arts, including this shows your passion, competitiveness and motivation to succeed.

- If you hold professional certificates, even ones not in your related area, including them demonstrates your range of interests and curiosity. If you belong to the IEEE association or have a professional accounting certificate, highlight it. Although I was a product manager for a high tech company, I also had a real estate license. I included this in my resume to highlight my people skills, negotiation skills and communication skills– all important qualities for my product management job.

- Organizations you belong to and hold a key position such as Treasurer, Finance Analyst and Marketing Specialist. All this goes to show your ability or at least, your motivation to develop and improve key skills required in the workplace.
- Any other technical skills that highlight you even more, such as expertise in certain technology areas, Web Design for example, or deep knowledge about specific and unique accounting audit processes.

Creating Your LinkedIn Profile

LinkedIn is a popular online networking site for professionals. It's a platform where they can stay connected, share information, stay current on their field, research for job opportunities, and advertise themselves. The good news is you can use your resume's content for your LinkedIn profile. With LinkedIn, you have an opportunity to personalize your resume and tell more of a story about you. Below are a few things to keep in mind when creating your profile.

- You can expand on your resume's specific content. While I advocate keeping your resume content succinct, you can use your profile space here to add more color to your bullet points. If you mentioned a great accomplishment in your resume, you can tell a story behind that result. For example, during your internship, you delivered a proposal that impressed company management so much they decided to implement it. On your profile, you can elaborate on what made the proposal compelling and go into more details about your role and contributions.
- With your LinkedIn profile, you don't need to be as narrowly focused on your professional skills as you do in your resume. You should include other skills and areas of interest and expertise to demonstrate your versatility, curiosity and aspirations.
- Another excellent LinkedIn feature you can use is posting endorsements and recommendations. A powerful way to promote yourself is to have other people endorse you. Solicit your co-workers, managers, professors and others to write you a recommendation on LinkedIn or endorse your specific skills or expertise. It's also a great way to back up your claim. For instance, if you claim that you have excellent leadership skills and ability to

25

work with people to get things done, having your manager or colleague's testimony is a powerful proof.

- Sharing photos, posting videos or articles is an effective way to stay connected with people as well as highlight your unique skill or expertise. You can keep your profile fresh by posting professional or personal updates as often as you like. Through LinkedIn, you can greatly expand your network of contacts. It provides and suggests people you either have a direct or indirect connection to link to your network. Through LinkedIn, I was able to stay connected to people who I would have otherwise lost touch with years ago.

- Take your profile as seriously as you take your resume. Be thoughtful and careful about what you include in your description. Since anyone can look at your profile, you don't want to post anything that could affect your image negatively or show you in a bad light. This advice applies to your LinkedIn account as well as all your other social media platforms. Employers will check your social media postings and anything that raises a red flag can potentially hurt your employment chances.

Additional Tips

- Don't include a cover letter unless you are asked to provide one. This is not a common practice. Most managers only have time read the resume to determine your fit for the position.

- Don't include references on resume. This is not needed. If you get far enough into the hiring process, the employer will ask for references at that time. So use the extra space on your resume to promote yourself.

- Don't use slang, jargon or acronyms that are not easy to understand, unless the acronym is common and widely understood (such as IEEE). If you need to, spell out the acronyms. Slang may not be easily understood, especially by people whose native language is not English.

- Don't include personal information that may negatively affect your chance of getting an interview, particularly if you don't know who will be reviewing your resume and whether that person has any biases. You need to use your judgment here; there is no right or wrong answer. For example, I was asked by a student whether he should include in the resume his membership in the National Rifle Association (NRA). Since neither he nor I know if the potential reviewer has any strong opposition to people owning guns, I advised him to use his judgement and to think whether this detail is relevant and helpful to the position and whether it is worth taking the risk.

- Don't lie. While you definitely should promote and make yourself look as good as possible, be sure that every fact or claim is accurate and can be supported. In today's world, your records can be easily verified. You probably have heard of famous people losing their jobs because they lied on their resume. On a consulting service project with a high tech company, the prospective employer did a background check on me before I started the job. When I received the report, it provided a detailed record of the last ten years of my life.
- Visit my website www.careeratwork.com for sample resumes.

Chapter 5

How To Prepare And Conduct Interviews With Confidence

The key to having a successful interview can be boiled down to one word: preparation, as emphasized by Martin Yate, author of the "Knock 'em Dead Job Interview" book (Yate, 2012). What is a successful interview? You may think a successful interview is one that results in a job offer. While that is the desired result, you can have an excellent interview without getting a job offer. That may sound contradictory and illogical, but let me explain. The fact of the matter is you don't have much control over the hiring decision. You don't know how many other people also interviewed for the job or what factors the hiring manager considered in making his decision. You may not receive a job offer even though you felt you did well in the interview. For instance, I had seen in one case where there were two qualified candidates, each with different strengths. The manager ended up choosing one person over the other due to experience level. Or in another case where there were three equally qualified candidates, one female and two male candidates, the hiring manager, wanting to have a more diverse team, decided to offer the job to the female candidate.

However, do not despair. In my mind, a successful interview is one where you were prepared, gave your best effort answering questions, engaged the interviewer fully and were satisfied with the information you learned about the company. Your goal for the interview is to do so well you make it easy for the manager to want to hire you. Managers have to juggle many balls at work. When they need to hire a new employee for their team, they have to squeeze the time into their schedule. It takes a lot of time to conduct hiring process, including writing job description, completing the required paperwork, posting the job opening, reviewing resumes, interviewing candidates and negotiating job offer.

Let's take an example. A manager has five candidates going through the in-person interviews and it takes a total of three hours to spend on each candidate. That takes almost two work days, not including the time the manager had spent reviewing other resumes or the amount of time the interview team spends interviewing. If the manager is really impressed with you and satisfied that you are an excellent fit, she has a great incentive to hire you quickly because would save her a lot of time. It's in your best interest to do your best to make it as easy as possible for the manager to make the hiring decision.

However, even if you did not get the job but did well in the interview and left a good impression, the manager will remember you and would likely recommend you to other managers who have openings. I had seen this many times in my career. When I was looking to hire a forecasting specialist, I had two qualified candidates but could only hire one. Even though I did not hire Ted, I kept his resume. When I learned two weeks later that Doug, a colleague, was looking to hire a demand planner –a different position but has similar skillset requirements, I recommended Ted. After interviewing him, Doug offered him the job. This example illustrates the importance of being thoroughly prepared and giving your best effort to impress the hiring manager and interviewers. If you achieve that, be satisfied with your effort, regardless of the outcome.

In this chapter, I will explain how to best prepare for your interview and how to conduct yourself in the interview. I will cover two main areas: what to do before the interview and how to conduct yourself at the interview.

Before Interview

How you prepare for an interview is extremely important as it determines how well you will perform at the interview.

- **Know the company**. Inevitably one of the interviewers will ask why you are interested in working for this company. If you are stumped by this question, you just hurt your chances of getting a job offer. After all, why should I hire you if you cannot tell me why you are interested in joining my company? Another key reason to know about the company is for you to determine whether this is the company you want to join. Company information is widely available publically. Its website provides most of the relevant information - its products, services, reputation, culture, etc. Other online websites such as indeed.com or glassdoor.com also give good insight about the company's culture, reviews from employees, etc. Let's say you find out company ABC is known for offering innovative products, has been growing faster than its competitors and is rated one of the top places to work. When asked, you can tell the interviewer you are impressed with the company's innovative products, its reputation as a great place to work, its leadership in the industry and you would like to be a part of this growing company. Take a little time to research and learn about the company. It'll be worth your time investment.

- **Know the job details**. Knowing as much about the position as possible will help you prepare for the interview, both in the potential questions you may get as well as the information you want to find out. Before the interview, you should have a copy of the job description describing the main responsibilities, people you will be working with, your role in the overall organization and the job requirements. Usually the job description is listed on the company's website. If you don't have a job description, ask the company representative to email you a copy. Sometimes you can find out useful information by asking the representative for any specific qualities or requirements the hiring manager is especially keen on. Be sure to read the job description carefully to help you anticipate questions about the position and formulate your answers.
- **Know the interviewers**. This is not a must but will help you feel more at ease at the interview. Many companies have a team of people to interview you. These tend to be people you will be working with. Ask for the interview schedule if you did not receive one. It should show each interviewer' name and their title. This reveals their job level status and the function they work in. Today, many professionals are on social media sites, such as LinkedIn, where you can get relevant information on them. Knowing something about the interviewers helps you think about what questions you want to ask them. For example, if a person has been with the company for several years in a few different positions, you can ask this person about the company's support in developing employees and providing different opportunities. At the very least, when you meet with the interviewers face to face, your knowledge about them will put you at more at ease and help you establish a rapport with them.
- **Prepare a list of potential questions and your answers**. Different companies may have some differences on what they want to find out about you. However, I find that there are some common categories companies want to focus on.
    1. Job skills.
    2. Problem solving skills and creativity.
    3. Teamwork – how effective you are working with people.

4. Communication skills – your ability to listen and understand people's viewpoints as well as express your thoughts clearly and compellingly.
5. Dedication/commitment – your willingness to take the extra step, to go above and beyond to get the job done.

Many companies use behavioral interview method when they interview you. Simply put, instead of asking you if you have the ability to do something, such as: "Are you good at presenting?" the interviewer gives you a specific situation and asks you to respond. This type of open ended question enables the interviewer to glean greater insight about you because it requires you to think on your feet, consider things thoroughly and give well thought out answers. For example: "Give me an example of a situation where you had to present to a large group of unhappy customers and how you managed it." Regardless of how the interviewer asks questions, preparing the interview as a behavioral interview will help you do your best.

I will describe these categories in more detail. For each category listed above, think of a few questions and your own answers to them. Also, for each category, think of a couple of specific examples to strengthen your answers and highlight your qualifications. Why examples? Your examples add "meat to the bones" to your answers, personalize you and make you unique. Before we dive deeper into these areas, take an example of two answers to the question: "Are you a good communicator?"

- Answer 1: "I consider myself a good communicator with good verbal and writing skills. I've always been able to express myself clearly and persuasively."
- Answer 2: "I consider myself an excellent communicator with strong verbal and writing skills. For example, during my previous job at XYZ, I lead a major product launch where I developed the marketing materials, provided training to sales people and presented to many customers. I received excellent feedback on my communication skills."

The second answer is by far a better one. The first answer is so general anybody can give the same answer. It does not distinguish you from other candidates. Answer #2 demonstrates your ability with a specific example.

Now let's look at the categories in more details.

1. **Job skills.** This is simply to find out if you have the technical skills to do the job. If you are applying for a position in the accounting department, you must have good accounting and finance knowledge. The job description I mentioned earlier should list specific job responsibilities and tasks you will be doing as well as the job's requirements. This is a fundamental category. If you cannot demonstrate you have the knowledge and technical skills to do the job, you won't get the job offer regardless of how well you do in the other categories. The questions here are specific to your field. If you are a software engineer, you may be asked to write a short program using a specific programming language. If you are a finance analyst, you may be asked about cost/benefit analysis. If you apply for a job as a marketing analyst, you may be asked about conducting customer survey or return on investment methodology. Make sure to study the job description because it will give you a good idea on how to prepare and brush up on your technical skills.

2. **Problem solving skills.** Practically any job will involve business problems and require the ability to solve them. The problem may include a range of issues, from customer, sales to quality issues. Demonstrating your ability to solve problems will help you stand out among the candidates. While most people can follow instructions, people who take the initiative to solve problems are viewed as high performers and valuable assets to the company.

   The question you get could be a general question such as: "How do you go about solving a problem" or you could be given a specific problem situation and are asked to solve it. For example: "You are working in the customer support department and the customer's level of satisfaction has been declining for the past two quarters, what would you do to improve customer satisfaction?" Many fall into the trap of jumping to solutions. That is a wrong approach. Since you have not worked at the company and don't have much insight, the interviewer doesn't expect you to give specific solutions. Whether it's a generic question or a specific one like this example, the interviewer is looking to understand your approach to problem solving, your thought process on how you would go about arriving at the answer. A smart approach to solving problem is: 1) understanding the problem, 2) finding out the root causes of the problem, 3) brainstorming and identifying possible solutions, 4) weighing the pros/cons and benefits/costs of potential solutions, and 5) deciding the best solution.

For the "customer satisfaction" example above, this is how I would answer the question: "First, I will go about finding out the root causes of the problem by analyzing customer data, customer feedback reports and by talking to customers and salespeople if possible. Once I identify the root causes, I will engage with the appropriate experts inside and outside the company to brainstorm specific ideas to improve customer satisfaction. Then I would analyze the pros/cons and cost/benefits of these ideas to determine the best one for the company and then make the appropriate recommendation." And if you have time, give an example from your previous experience where you solved a problem successfully. This will strengthen your answer even more.

3. **Teamwork.** This is to find out how effective you are at working with people or more specifically, how you handle difficult situations working with others. For the vast majority of the time at work you will be working with other people on certain projects. The ability to work well with people to get things done is highly valued and companies examine this quality closely in deciding which candidate to hire. This skill or lack of it determines how effective you will be at your job. Consider this question: "You are a leader working on a project where one of your team members is not meeting his deadline and putting the team's project at risk. How would you handle this situation with this individual?" With this kind of question, avoid jumping to the answer. When I used this question in interviews, I have heard candidates say they will try to get the person off the team or fired. While removing the person from the team may ultimately be the answer, it's more important to try to understand why and then come up with the appropriate plan. After all, it's difficult to address this situation with the team member if you don't you know why he was not meeting his commitment.

Early in my career I faced a similar situation with Joy, a team member. Fortunately, a more seasoned colleague advised me to go talk to her to find out why. Joy told me she had some recent family medical issues that required her to leave work unexpectedly and early sometimes. As a result, she missed a few team meetings and fell behind her work. Once I heard this, I offered to help take on some of her tasks and she accepted. She was very appreciative and felt bad she didn't come to me sooner. She was embarrassed about her situation and didn't want to reveal it.

The moral of the story here is that there could be a number of reasons for this situation and it's prudent to find out before taking action. If asked this question, this is how I would answer: "First of all, I would let him know the team depends on him meeting his commitment in order for the project to stay on track. Then I would tell him I'd like to know why so I can find ways to help. Once I know the reasons, he and I can brainstorm potential solutions. If we reach a dead end, I'll escalate to the manager for help and, at the same time, let him know I'm taking this action to ensure that the project stay on track." My answer shows that I am a team player who goes out of my way to work with people to resolve issues and get things done. At the same time, I understand the team goal and, if I need to, I would escalate to make sure the project stay on schedule. While the team member may not like my escalation, he would respect me for being straight with him. This also enables me to build trust with him for any future project we may work together.

4. **Communication skills.** This is to probe your ability to listen and express your views clearly and persuasively. Regardless of what the job is, you will likely be working with other people, people from your team, from other functions in the company as well as outside the company. The ability to communicate effectively is critical to your success and that of the company. You will be tested for this skill in the interview. I covered this important skill in details in the "How to communicate effectively" chapter. Think of a couple of examples from your experience where you used your communication skills successfully to persuade a colleague or manager to go with your view, or where you gave a strong presentation to a new audience. The interviewers will judge your ability in this area by watching to see how you come across and listening to your answers. A lot of this is about your style – do you come across confidently, persuasively and

engaging? Here are some examples of questions you may get:

- Your manager gives you an additional project and you feel that your plate is already full. How do you handle this situation and how do you say no?
- How do you rate your communication skills? Which part of your communication skills needs to be improved the most?
- Describe a situation where you had to give an important presentation to a new group of audience and how you handled it.
- The company creates a new exciting project that many people, you included, want to lead. I am in charge of selecting a project manager for this new project. Convince me you are the best person to lead this project.

5. **Dedication/commitment**. We want to know about your work ethics and your commitment to get the job done. Think of a time when you took the extra steps and went above and beyond your duties to help out co-workers to ensure the team project is completed successfully and on time. Also think of an example where you identified a need that was not being addressed and took the initiative to work on it. This shows you have the company's best interest in mind and you are a team player willing to do what it takes to help the team succeed. Possible questions you may get include:

- Give me an example when the project you worked with other people was at risk of missing an important deadline and describe what you did to get the project back on track and complete on schedule.
- Give me an example where you show initiative to take on a task important to the company even though that was outside of your job responsibility.
- You have a situation where your manager asks you to work the next weekend in order to meet project deadline but you already had other personal plans. Describe how you would handle it.

- **Prepare a list of questions you want to ask the interviewers.**
  Think of the interview as a conversation. Although most of the time you will be answering questions, you will have time to ask questions. It's an opportunity to find out information you want to know about the company, about the job, about people you will be working with.

This helps you determine whether this is the right company and the right job for you. Since time is limited, be selective about which questions you want to ask. Here are some potential questions:

– What would be my specific duties in the first 90 days? This is a specific question for the hiring manager.
– What are the key success factors in this job?
– What are the key challenges in this job?
– What are the key characteristics of successful people at this company?
– What experience and growth opportunities will I be able to gain from this job?
– What do you like about the company and what are the challenges you see for the company in future?
– What are the next steps in the hiring process? This is a specific question for the hiring manager.

At Interview

You have done your homework in preparing for the interview. Now you are at the interview with the opportunity to show how qualified you are and why the company should hire you. To accomplish this, you need to know how to conduct yourself. The key word here is "how." A lot of it is about optics - your personality and the way you carry yourself. In all likelihood, the interviewers don't know you and they're meeting you for the first time. Therefore, the impression they form of you will be what they remember. Following these guidelines below will help you perform your best and help you come across as confident, energetic and engaging.

- **Speak clearly**. If you have a soft voice, this is an area you need to pay attention to. If the interviewer has to strain to hear you or have to constantly ask you to repeat, it doesn't make for a good conversation and it brings into question your ability to communicate. Also, when we are nervous, we tend to speak faster than usual. If you need to improve in this area, practice and focus on speaking clearly and loudly enough for the person sitting across the table from you to hear comfortably.
- **Maintain eye contact**. It's a good way to establish rapport and to show you are engaged in the conversation. Imagine what impression you would create if you're looking at your feet while answering questions. You give out the impression of being disengaged, timid and not confident.
- **Show energy and enthusiasm**. When I have other people interview my candidates, their initial feedback on the candidate oftentimes is

about their energy level – whether the candidate had good energy, showed enthusiasm and was excited to be there. If you maintain eye contact and engage in the conversation, your energy will show. You don't have to jump up and down to show your enthusiasm.

On one occasion when I was interviewing a candidate, Kelly, for a position on my team over lunch, I asked her when she would like to start. I expected a typical answer of two weeks after offer acceptance. Instead, she answered: "How about after lunch?" I knew Kelly was joking and it made me laugh, but her answer showed her energy and excitement about joining my company.

- **Buy time when you need to**. When you get a question you're not sure how to answer, don't get rattled or feel you have to give an answer immediately. You can buy some time to think about it and come back to answer later in the interview. You can buy time by saying: "That's a good question. Let me give it some thought and get back to you in a little bit if that's okay?" Then while you're answering other questions or talking about other topics, you can think about it in the back of your mind and when ready, re-engage the interviewer on the question.

- **Ask for clarification**. If you get a question you're not quite clear on, don't hesitate to ask for clarification. It's important that you understand the question clearly so you can answer appropriately. The interviewer would be happy to elaborate on the question and this may also give you some clues on what the interviewer is looking for. You can say something like: "I just want to make sure I understand your question, would you mind repeating it for me?" or "I want to make sure I understand, you're asking ABC. Is my understanding correct?" After giving your answer, you can also ask a follow up question to determine if you were on the right track of what the interviewer was looking for, such as: "Did I address your question?" or "Is there anything else you would like me to cover?"

- **Turn negative/tough questions to your strengths**. You may get questions such as: "Tell me about your biggest weakness" or "Tell me a major mistake you made." The weakness question is intended to understand if you are objective in your assessment of yourself and what you are doing to address it. Don't answer: "I have no weaknesses." You come across as arrogant and not having self-awareness. The way to answer this question is to give a weakness trait that shows your desire and effort to mitigate it, and at the same time, can be seen as having upsides. One such trait is "impatience." If you are a "go getter" type of person who drives to get things done right and as soon as possible, you tend to have less patience with other people. However, you recognize that other people may work at a different pace and you are consciously working to give them more space and assistance to get their work done. Moreover, the "impatience" trait also reflects positively on your motivation, dedication and commitment to complete the job. The mistake question is intended to determine what you had learned from your mistake and what you have done differently going forward. Think of a work mistake you made that you learned from and worked to rectify.

- **Get contact information**. Thank the interviewers and ask for their email address at the end of interview. This helps in case you have a question you want to ask but didn't have a chance during the interview. You may run out of time before you get a chance to ask your question. This also is a good way to build your network of contacts.

Additional Tips

- Show up five minutes early. Don't be late. Remember what I said earlier about making a good impression. Also bring a copy of your resume and a pen to take notes.
- Dress business professional unless you are told otherwise. If you're not sure, ask your contact if the company has a preferred dress code.
- Turn your phone off or put it on silent mode. You want to eliminate any potential distraction during your interview.
- Take notes as needed. This helps you to ask follow up questions and may give you additional clues on what the interviewer is looking for from their questions.
- Don't ask about salary, vacation days or benefits during interview. When you get a job offer, you will know what the offer includes and then you will have an opportunity to negotiate the terms of the offer. You have limited time in the interview so ask questions that are most relevant and helpful to you. In addition, you want to avoid giving the impression that you care most about the money and benefits.
- Never talk bad about your current/previous company or your manager, whether they deserve it or not. It may create a suspicion in the interviewer's mind about your professionalism.
- Don't get rattled by the question. Think about the category of the question being asked and refer to your mental list of answers and examples. Also remember that you can always buy time.

- If you have an interviewer who is not disciplined and rambles on instead of interviewing you, don't be confused or think you don't need to say much. If the interviewer finishes the interview without knowing much about your qualifications, it's a lost opportunity. Find opportunities to ask questions that will help you talk about your qualifications. You can accomplish this by asking, for example, about the qualities that will enable you to be successful. By listening to his answer, you can then highlight your own qualities with relevant examples. Or you can ask for his opinions on the challenges he sees with this position and prepare to respond appropriately to his answers.

- Be aware of posting things on social media sites. Don't post things that may reflect negatively on you. I have seen examples of people not getting the job offer because of comments or things they posted on their social media page. On one occasion, I interviewed a candidate for a management position on my manager's team. She was very qualified and seemed a good fit for the company. As part of the background check, my manager learned of insulting remarks on her Facebook page about a previous manager. This raised a red flag to my manager and made him reconsider his decision.

- Attend the interview alone and don't take anyone with you to the reception area or worse, to the interview room. You may find this tip unnecessary and amusing, but it had happened. You want to come across as independent and a self-starter who doesn't need hand holding.

- When you receive a job offer, you have an opportunity to negotiate for the best offer you can. Refer to the "How to negotiate your job offer" chapter for details.

Additional Tips For Phone Interviews

In addition to the discussion above, there are a few specific things to keep in mind when doing your interview over the phone.

- Have the information you want with you to refer to, such as your examples and answers. However, do not read from them. It's easy to notice if someone is reading instead of talking. Have the materials there as references, but talk normally on the phone.

- Your voice is the only instrument to show your energy and engagement level. It's even more important to make sure the interviewer can hear and understand you clearly. So be sure to speak clearly and loudly enough. Don't mumble or whisper. Think of the interview as two-way conversation. Engage the interviewer by asking clarifying questions, asking about the job, and giving examples in your answers.

- Don't hesitate to ask for clarification if you're not sure about the question before answering. If you don't, the interviewer will assume you understand and judge your answer accordingly.
- If English is not the interviewer's native language, gauge to see if you need to speak slower. Check to see if he has any questions or needs clarification regarding your answers.
- Some companies use a different interview format to screen candidates. For example, instead of interviewing over the phone, the interview is conducted online without a live interviewer. You may be videotaped for this session. Through an online website, you are given a series of questions, one at a time, to answer verbally. After reviewing your recorded interview, the company representative or the hiring manager will decide whether to invite you in for an in-person interview. With this interview format, you need to be even more thorough in your preparation since you cannot ask for clarification or buy time to think about the answers. Even though it may seem awkward talking to a computer screen, you need to make sure you stay engaged as if you were talking to a live person. Smile, stay relaxed and keep your eyes on the screen as you answer the questions. If you're looking down or away, the reviewer would see your head instead of your face.
- Last but most important, practice your interview and role playing with a friend or someone you're comfortable with. This will give you confidence and put you more at ease when you're at the real interview.

Potential Interview Questions

1. You are given a business problem. Our sales this quarter were below target. What steps would you take to increase sales?
2. Tell me about your last job.
3. What accomplishments are you most proud of?
4. What are your biggest strengths? Biggest weaknesses?
5. Tell me about a major mistake you made.
6. How do you resolve a conflict with a co-worker at work?
7. If you're working on a team and the project's going to be late because a member of the team is not meeting his commitment, what would you do?

8. Your manager gives you an additional project and your plate is already full. You can't take on any more responsibility without jeopardizing your work. How would you handle this situation?
9. What did you like and dislike about your last job? And why?
10. What classes or projects did you like/dislike in school? And why?
11. What drives you? What motivates you? How do we help you do your best work?
12. Where do you see yourself 3 years from now?
13. Describe a difficult challenge you faced and how you handled it.
14. Describe a situation where you had to give an important presentation to a new group of audience and how you handled it.
15. The company creates a new exciting project that many people want to lead. I am in charge of selecting a project manager for this new project. Convince me you are the best person to lead this project.
16. Why are you interested in joining this company?
17. If you had a chance for a do over, what would that be and why?
18. Tell me a time when you were under a lot of pressure to meet a tight deadline and how you handled it.
19. What did you like and dislike about your last manager?
20. Tell me a time you had to multi-task and how you prioritized and handled the tasks.
21. What salary do you expect to get?

Chapter 6

How To Start Your Job On The Right Foot

The initial weeks when you start your job provide you a good opportunity to take advantage of the "honeymoon" period to learn the lay of the land, to get up to speed and make a good first impression. Given the pace of work these days, new employees have less time to learn the ropes and are expected to contribute quickly. Employees who prove to be quick learners and contributors will make a great impression, gain credibility and confidence with co-workers and management. You need to have a plan to hit the deck running on the first day and this chapter will show you how.

What To Do Before You Start Your First Day

Before your start date, there are a number of tasks you can do to put you in a position to be productive from day one on your job.

- Work with your new manager to make sure all your IT equipment and services will be in working order and ready for you to use on the first day. Submit all your IT needs soon after you accept the offer to give the IT department time to order equipment and set up. A few days before you start your job, follow up to make sure things are on track and in case of any issues, you have time to resolve. Don't just trust that everything will be there in working order the day you start. Your manager may forget to follow up due to his busy schedule and he would appreciate a reminder from you. Moreover, ask your manager for a buddy – someone with a good reputation at work and is valued by the manager. This person is a valuable resource for you to learn the ropes. Ask the manager to set up a one-on-one meeting with your buddy on the day you start.
- Obtain approval and permission to access company services you need for your job. Your manager can help you with this and get the

approvals needed. Double check with your manager and don't assume it will be taken care of. For example, meetings conducted over video or audio conference are quite common. If you schedule these meetings, you need to have the system access code to use the equipment, or if you will need to access and use company sensitive data, you need to receive permission and the passcode since accessibility is restricted to certain employees. It's frustrating and a waste of time when you start your job and have to wait a few days to be able to access the data.

- Familiarize yourself with company materials. Ask for company materials relevant to your job that you can read before you start. This may be your manager's annual team plan, status reports on current activities or projects, product or project plans, last quarter's CEO presentation, etc. Reading these ahead of time will give you a feel for the current state of the company business and insight about your job. Your manager should be aware of company policy on confidential materials to determine which documents you can have access to.

- Get settled in if you are relocating. When moving to a new town, you will need to take care of your living arrangements and other personal tasks. Try completing them before you start your job so you don't have to spend time and energy trying to settle in a new place and do work at the same time. These tasks can consume a lot of time and if you have to take time out of work to attend to them, that will slow you down. When you start, you want to focus your energy and time to get up to speed as quickly as possible.

What To Do When You Start Your Job

Use your first couple of weeks to get a good picture and feel for the lay of the land as it relates to your job. Understand the ecosystem in the company – how things get done, how people work and communicate, important processes, key people you will be working with, decision makers and influencers, and how decisions are made. In addition, spend your time to obtain knowledge and insight on company products and services. Having a good understanding of company's ecosystem is paramount to your job's success. Imagine this ecosystem as the Global Positioning System (GPS) of a new city you just moved in for the first time. This smart system shows you the different routes to get from place A to place B, with all the variables that can affect which route you're going to take, including speed limits, traffic flows and road closures. Moreover, these variables can change at any moment, depending on the time of day, weather condition and traffic flow changes. The smart GPS helps you determine the best route to take and navigate through these unpredictable obstacles. Without the knowledge of the company's ecosystem, it would be similar to driving without a GPS in trying to get to your destination and not having a clue how to get there.

- Create the ecosystem map. With help from your buddy and manager, start putting together an ecosystem map pertinent to you and your job. This is a chart of important people whom you will be working with, key influencers, decision makers and potential executives who could be your champions. This group includes people in your organization as well as other functions. Make notes of their title, organization, job responsibilities, keys to working with them, and if possible, their reputation in the company. Then get to know them because your success depends on how effectively you work with them and help them be successful in their job. A second key part of the ecosystem is to capture how things are done in the company – decision making process, communication method, operational processes, project management, teamwork dynamics and unwritten "rules." Your buddy and manager are great resources for this.
- Meet with your buddy and spend a good amount of time with this person on the first day. Ask him to share with you how things get done, how people work and communicate, key people you will be working with, how decisions are made, and who the influencers, decision makers and potential advocates are. Use the information to help complete your ecosystem map. Find out the best ways to do things at work, major issues and "elephants in the room" you should be aware of. In addition, get your buddy's thoughts on your manager – the best ways to work with him, his hot buttons and his strengths/weaknesses. Also ask your buddy to show you how to access and use the company IT system, and take you on a tour of all the facilities so you can be familiar with the buildings and the people working in them.
- Use your computer and IT systems to go through the login process to make sure the systems are in working order and you have access to the services you need. If you run into any issues, call the helpdesk. You should also get into the company's internal website and familiarize yourself with company's services, including Human Resources, market research and IT support. In addition, through the company internal website, you can learn about other organizations and their role in the company.
- Meet with your manager. Talk with him to understand his expectations, how best to work with him, his hot buttons, how he wants to be updated, and his key challenges and priorities. Also ask the manager similar questions you ask your buddy, especially the

important co-workers and managers you need to be on their good side as well as people who can be your advocates. If time permits, discuss with him about your annual plan. Otherwise, schedule a meeting for this. Typically, every company requires the manager to have a yearly plan for each employee. This plan is critical to your performance review and it includes the objectives/goals, expected results and timelines.

- If you are working remotely and will not have regular face to face interactions with your manager, make sure you and your manager work out a way to stay connected and to keep you in the loop. The most common feedback I hear is that remote employees feel disconnected from the rest of the company, don't know what's going on and don't receive real time information. Since you and your manager will not be able to touch base frequently, commit to having regular one-on-one meetings. Moreover, discuss how to keep you in the loop. Some managers are not on the ball when it comes to sharing information, especially sending a message out to their team. It's not top of mind and they tend to share information verbally and often, informally. This doesn't work for you. I would suggest using a portion of your weekly one-on-one meetings for your manager to update you. In addition, find out if your manager uses or would consider using a trusted onsite employee to help him disseminate information to the rest of teams, especially remote employees.

- Schedule one-on-one meetings with key people you will be working with, including project lead, team members and other managers. Try to meet with them in the first two weeks. Your goal is to get to know them, find out their needs, expectations, priorities, any issues or concerns they have, and how you can best work with them. If possible, meet with them over lunch where they'll have more time to talk with you. Finally, since it's not feasible to meet everyone, especially people who work remotely, send them a greeting email to introduce yourself.

- If your company offers product and/or service training, take them as soon as you can. Other types of classes may also be available, including meeting facilitation, public speaking, project management and time management. This is the time to take advantage of these classes. You get the knowledge you need and gain the confidence to do your job. In addition, attend the company orientation and meetings set up for new employees with company executives. This is an opportunity to hear directly their thoughts and ask them questions.

- Attend team and other company meetings to get a feel for how the company works, key issues and challenges it's dealing with and its decision making process. The people you work with will let you know what meetings you should attend. Ask your buddy and manager for suggestions on meetings that you can tag along to observe even though you're not required to be there. In addition, find out about customer visit and briefing events where customers meet and talk with company representatives about a variety of topics. Contact the company speakers for approval to come and observe. Even if your job doesn't require you to interact with customers directly, this is a good way to learn about company information being shared with customers, their issues and needs, and observe how the company representatives interact with them.

- If there are data mining and analytic programs you need for your job, learn and practice using these programs during this time. Moreover, if there are external services available to the company from industry service firms, request access to these services if they are relevant to your job. These services include industry reports, research projects and consultation.

- Keep your regular work hours when you start your job, or better yet, stay a little later at work. Since you probably have a lot to learn, it's a good idea to use the extra time to get up to speed. Coming in late or leaving early leaves a bad impression.

- Familiarize yourself with the company "look and feel" guidelines for creating media and other materials. For example, when you create presentation slides for a meeting with company suppliers, you need to use the company's content and style guidelines. It helps you present a consistent company image and saves you the headache of hearing from the "brand" police.

THRIVING AT WORK

Part 2

Communicating

Half the world is composed of people who have something to say and can't and the other half who have nothing to say and keep on saying it.

Robert Frost

Chapter 7

How To Communicate Effectively – Verbal And Written

If I had to pick one skill that separates a star performer from an average employee, it would be communication. Communication is the ability to convey information to other people effectively and efficiently, is how you articulate your views and opinions clearly and persuasively, either verbally or written. From my experience, it is the number one factor that determines how successful you will be in your job.

Why It Is Important To Be A Good Communicator

When I was a Senior Director at a Fortune 100 company, I had an opportunity to promote one of my employees and I had two talented candidates who had been delivering excellent results - Robert and Timothy. As part of the process, I solicited input from people who had worked with each of them. Their feedback was consistent that both were dedicated team members who worked hard, met their commitments and delivered excellent results. However, I received very different feedback in the area of communication. For Robert, his peers said he needed to improve his communication skills. Often, he wasn't clear in expressing his points and they had to ask him to repeat or elaborate. Due to this weakness, the team couldn't work very efficiently at times since they had to spend more time clearing up any confusion. In addition, two company executives commented that, when doing a presentation, Robert came across a bit timid and unsure of his recommendation. Timothy, on the other hand, received rave feedback for his communication skills. He expressed his views clearly and persuasively, and asked for and welcomed feedback from other people. Executives commended him for his presentation skills and his ability to get his point across and handle questions.

Based on the feedback I received, I decided to recommend Timothy for the promotion. He deserved it and my recommendation was easily approved. If I had recommended Robert, I would have gotten strong push back from my boss and company executives who favored Timothy more. I committed to get Robert the necessary resources to help him work on improving his communication skills.

Being a good communicator also enables you to be more productive and efficient. Time is precious and having more time to do your work is a big plus. Moreover, if you are recognized for your communication skills, you will get more opportunities to present to company executives, to represent your company at industry events and customer meetings. Taking advantage of these opportunities is a natural way to promote yourself, gain visibility and enhance your standing in the company.

In today's work environment, both verbal and written are common communication methods. In this chapter, I will cover the best approach and practices for both. While a successful professional must have both strong speaking and writing skills, I would rank verbal communication above written skills. The main reason being that the business world focuses on visible optics – how we look, how we appear, how we carry ourselves, how we speak, how we respond, etc. However, I want to emphasize that mastering both verbal and written communication skill is the best way to achieve success and advance your career.

Verbal Communication

I believe verbal communication is a more difficult skill to master than written. In speaking, we often have to think on our feet with little time to formulate and articulate our thoughts. Once the words leave our mouths, they are gone and we cannot really take them back. In this section, I'll focus on the skills and techniques to help you gain confidence in speaking up and getting your point across. We'll focus on group settings - team meetings, project meetings, meetings with management, customers and partners. By mastering communication skills in group meetings, you will easily be able to handle other settings, such as one-on-one meetings.

Verbal Communication Techniques And Best Practices
- **Listening is a key part of communication**. Excellent communicators I know and have observed over the years are good listeners. Chloe, a friend of mine who is a great listener, told me of a

dinner meeting with a client. Through the entire dinner, she spent most of her time listening and maybe ten percent of the time talking. When they said goodbye after the dinner, her client thanked her for an enjoyable evening and commended her for being a great conversationalist, even though for most of the dinner, she just sat back and listened. Most people like to talk about themselves. By listening, we understand their views and issues, and that will help us respond more appropriately. In addition, if you are new to a meeting, asking questions and listening to the responses are good ways to build rapport. Oftentimes, we may be listening but not really hearing what the other person is saying. It's a good practice to ask clarifying questions to make sure you understand clearly.

- **Know objectives of the meeting**. This helps you ask the right questions and keep everyone in the meeting focused on the right business issue if and when a discussion goes off track. Sometimes we don't spend enough time making sure the objective is clear with everyone on the team. When problems arise during a project, as they inevitably will, the best way to get the project back on track is to reset and get everyone to focus on the objective the team is trying to achieve.

- **Seek to understand before you respond**. Use your listening skill here. When you don't understand what someone is saying, ask them to clarify. Something like: "Could you elaborate for me? I just want to make sure I understand your points," or "What I heard you say is XYZ. Is my understanding accurate?" When you want to respond or add to someone's comment, having a full understanding of their comment will help you respond appropriately. I would be a rich man if I got a dollar for every time I heard someone giving a response to another person, only to have that person say "That's not what I meant."

- **Build rapport**. Asking for clarification and rephrasing others' comments are also good ways to connect with your co-workers because it shows you are interested and engaged in the conversation. This also helps other people feel comfortable engaging with you and giving you feedback on your work. If you're new to the team and are hesitant to ask "dumb" questions, you can preface your question with: "I'm new to this; sorry if this is redundant, but I was wondering if you could elaborate on that point for me."

Acknowledge and add to other people's comment. For example: "That's a good point, John. I also would like to add to that…" Again, this shows your interest, engagement and willingness to share feedback and add value to the discussion.

- **Contribute by speaking up**. Find out the purpose of the meeting before hand and ask questions relating to the topic. This helps you formulate your thoughts ahead of time so you can contribute to the meeting meaningfully. Having well thought out comments gives you the confidence to speak up and helps you gain credibility. One more point – it's important for you to speak up in meetings. If you don't, people tend not to notice your presence. If you don't think you have any valid points to add, ask someone to clarify their points. At least this allows people to see you, hear you and helps you to feel more comfortable speaking up later. Make a habit of speaking in any meeting at least twice, especially when you are in a meeting with your boss or company executives. Since you may not get this kind of opportunity often, it's your chance to be recognized, get visibility and make a good impression with the management team. You may not want to take the risk of looking bad; however, preparing and thinking beforehand on how you want to contribute to the meeting will give you more confidence speaking up in these situations.

When I taught business leadership classes to college students, I invited one of the country's youngest mayors to speak to my class. Rob was a 28 year old serving a second term. Since he wasn't much older than the students, they could relate to him. When he started his political career, speaking was not natural to him and he had to learn to master his communication skills. One advice he gave to the students was to speak up in meetings in order to be noticed. He said: "You must speak up when you're in a meeting with other people. If you don't, nobody knows who you are."

- Focus your comments on the meeting topic. Avoid making your comments personal. Express your disagreement in a professional manner and base your comments on the topic at hand. By focusing on co-workers' actions and not who they are, they will more likely have productive discussions with you. For example: "I believe your analysis needs more supporting data" as oppose to: "You are clueless." This is a bit extreme but you get my point. Acknowledge their comments before expressing your viewpoints. For example: "I understand and appreciate your perspective, but I see the issue a bit differently. Here's why …." Avoid saying: "That is the most stupid thing I've ever heard."

Don't take people's criticism personally. Ask for examples. Even when someone gets personal with you and makes condescending remarks, resist the temptation to lash back. Put the spotlight back on that person by making them focus on the topic and the facts. For instance, if Debbie says: "Your analysis is horrible," you could reply with: "Debbie, can you give me specific details on the part of my analysis you think is bad." This forces Debbie to be specific. If she was putting you down for her own enjoyment, she looks bad in front of others and probably will not repeat that behavior next time. You put her on notice that she will not be able to get away with such a behavior. If she gives you specifics, you can thank her and follow up by asking for suggestions on how to improve your analysis.

If the discussion is getting heated and distracting the meeting from its purpose, propose to take the issue offline and discuss later. For example: "Let's not take more time in this meeting. How about we take it offline and talk afterward?"

- Avoid using American slang and jargon when communicating to people from different ethnic backgrounds whose native language is not English. Sayings such as "between a rock and a hard place," "half a dozen in one and six in the other" and using American business jargon could be confusing to them and can come across as disrespectful.
- Speak clearly and loudly enough, especially if you have a soft voice. This is particularly important in a phone conference or in a meeting with people from different countries whose native language is not English. It's helpful to ask follow up questions to make sure everyone understand your comment, such as: "Any question?", "Is that clear?" or "Anything you would like me to clarify?"
- At the end of the meeting, ask for a summary of the meeting's outcomes and next steps. In addition, if you did not run the meeting, ask the meeting facilitator to send out a summary email to everyone after the meeting. This helps ensure everyone is on the same page and if there were any confusion or miscommunication, this provides a chance to resolve the issue right away.
- Staying actively engaged in meetings is more challenging if you're working remotely and calling in. You're not able to read people's reaction in the room and if there are side discussions, you probably can't hear them. Moreover, because you're not physically present, people tend to not notice you. To avoid feeling disconnected from the meeting, make sure you speak up at least a couple of times. Ask people to repeat or clarify their comments to make sure you

understand clearly. Sometimes people are looking at a picture or a graph specifically related to their discussion and you're lost because you can't see what they're talking about. They don't mean to exclude you. They just aren't cognizant of you because you're not physically there. Don't hesitate to interject and ask them to describe it or email it to you; if you wait, the discussion will pass you by and it's too late to revisit later. To avoid interrupting the discussion, make a point of asking the meeting facilitator to send you the materials to be discussed prior to the meeting.

The next best alternative to attending the meeting in person is via video conference. When you receive the meeting schedule, ask the facilitator to set up a video conference if possible. The meeting will be more productive and easier for you and people from remote locations to participate.

Written Communication

I believe written communication is easier to master than verbal because we have time to think about what to write, review what we wrote and make changes as we wish before sending out. However, you should not have any doubt about the importance of writing skills. Capturing key notes from a meeting is critical to ensure everyone is on the same page. All contracts and agreements are written documents. Even the presentations you deliver include written content. Every strategy plan, product plan or marketing plan is a written document. In addition, people we interact with outside our company or co-workers in other countries may prefer to communicate in writing. In this section, I will discuss useful techniques for written communication.

Written communication includes emails, texts, tweets, memos, slides, marketing materials, social media content, etc. A common method of communication in the workplace today is email, especially when discussing business topics. However, given how busy work is, no one has enough time to read through all the emails and memos they receive daily. When we send out a message, we need to be aware of this and make smart use of the recipient's time.

Best Practices And Techniques For Writing
- Professional etiquette I discussed in the verbal communication section applies here as well. You should focus on the topic at hand and not get personal. Avoid being sarcastic, condescending or

insulting to the person you are addressing. Even if you send out a critical message, focus on the action that person did and not on their character. Absolutely avoid calling people names. While it may make you feel better temporarily, it can and often will come back to hurt you.

- If you are writing a message when you're upset, do not send it immediately when finished. Wait until you're calmer. Take a short break and then go back to read your message over to see if you want to make any changes. Chances are you will want to modify your original message before you hit the "Send" button.

- Keep your message brief and to the point. People are busy and have short attention spans; each day they probably have to sort through and read hundreds of email messages, not to mention reports and memos. You need to get their attention quickly, so state the objective and key points of your message up front. If the message addresses a complex topic, explain briefly and let them know you will set up a meeting to discuss. You will lose their attention with a lengthy message.

- After an important meeting, write a summary of key points, decisions, next steps to send to the meeting attendees and other appropriate people. This will offer them a chance to bring up and clarify any unclear issue right away. The written message serves as proof of the decision or agreement, and to prevent unnecessary revisiting of the decision. This helps everyone to be more efficient with their time.

- As explained in the "Verbal Communication" section, avoid use of slang, jargon or acronyms.

- Re-read your message to make sure you're satisfied with the content. Without fail, whenever I re-read a message, I inevitably find a way to make it more succinct or that I had forgotten to include some key information that would strengthen my message. It's worth your time to re-read your message.

- Similarly, double check for spelling and grammar errors. Having spelling errors or grammatically incorrect sentences is sloppy. Take a few minutes to run a spelling and grammar check. If you have spent a lot of effort writing a strong message, don't risk weakening it by having some careless errors.

- Double check the "To" list to make sure the recipients are the people you want to send your message to. I have made the mistake of copying and pasting a list of email addresses I thought I wanted to send to. However, after sending the message, I discovered, to my embarrassment, there were people on the list I didn't want to read the message. This creates an embarrassing situation or worse, ill will, especially if your message is not a pleasant one.

- Don't burn bridges or insult people in your message. Getting even may bring you short-term satisfaction but usually has long term consequences, especially with people you need to continue to work with. Even if you take it back, it makes little difference since the damage was already done. Keep in mind your emails can have a long life. Even if you delete your messages later, copies of your messages are stored and can be shared or forwarded without your knowledge.

- When writing to external parties, follow the company's policy and guidelines. Every company has procedures, policies and format for written documents to external parties. Make sure you are familiar with and follow them. There could be legal or ethical issues if you don't adhere to the guidelines. If your message has potential legal implications, have legal personnel review your message before sending it out.

Chapter 8

How To Organize And Develop Presentation Content

How well you create and organize your slides plays an important role in your presentation success. The structure, flow and organization of your content are a reflection of your thought process. If the content flow is difficult to follow and the structure is confusing, you will be hard pressed to keep the audience engaged. In this chapter, I'll discuss strategies to organize your presentation slides and to make them compelling.

How To Organize Your Presentation

Since slides are commonly used visual materials in presentations, we'll use slides as the presentation format in this chapter. However, there are other formats, such as video, visual props, or just verbal presentation. Regardless of the format you want to use, the basic fundamentals for organizing your presentation are the same.

- **Know your audience**. You absolutely should know whom you will be presenting to – your co-workers/peers, company executives, and other workers from different departments in the company or external parties. This will help you tailor your content as well as your style for the target audience. For example, if you present to customers, the look and feel of your slides must be professional and adhere to company standards, and the presentation content is geared to be more selling and persuading.
- **Determine your goal of the presentation**. Knowing the goal of your presentation helps you focus on developing the right content and helps you stay on topic during your presentation. Is your purpose to share information, persuade, educate or seek approval? If your presentation is a proposal to management and your goal is to get

their approval, your slides will be about why the proposal is good for company business, what the expected results will be and what you need from the executives. On the other hand, if your purpose is to inform, your slides will simply contain the information you want to share, relevant explanation and data you believe your audience wants to know. If your goal is to persuade a customer to be interested in your company products, your slides will focus on highlighting the benefits the products will provide and how they will solve the customer's problems better than the competitors. This customer will be front and center of your slides and your presentation.

- **Be clear on the topic**. You need to be clear about the topic as well as making sure the audience knows. This seems basic, but don't assume the audience has knowledge of the topic before they sit down to hear your presentation. If you present new product technology, make sure this is clear at the beginning of the presentation. This helps you keep the presentation on track. When the audience discusses something else or asks questions not related to the presentation, you can draw them back to your topic. For example: "That's a good question. Since it's about a different topic, I don't want to take time away from today's presentation. But I'll happy to discuss that after the meeting. Would that work for you?"

- **Organize the presentation into three parts** - introduction, body, and conclusion. Remember the presentation adage "Tell them what you're about to tell them. Then tell them. And when done, tell them what you just told them." This is similar to how you would structure writing an essay. In the introduction, you tell the audience your goal for the meeting, the topic you present, set expectations and give any request or expectation you have for the audience. The body is the meat of your presentation. This is where you provide details, explain, expand and support your points. And the conclusion is a chance for you to summarize the key points you would like the audience to remember.

How To Make Your Slides Compelling

Your slides should be easy for the audience to follow, yet intriguing enough for them to want to listen to you. These steps will show you how.

- **Plan for the right amount of content**. Plan to fit your presentation content with the amount of time allocated to you. Plan for an average of four minutes per slide to account for audience questions. For example, if the presentation is for one hour, plan to have no more than fifteen slides. People tend to have too many slides for the allotted amount of time. What usually happens is the presenter spends a lot of time on the first few slides and either rushes through the rest or cuts the presentation short because they were running out of time. The audience ends up missing a significant portion of the presentation, and the presenter misses a chance to summarize the key messages he wants the audience to remember. That is not a successful presentation, and it happens more often than not.

- **Prioritize your content**. If you have a lot of content to cover, prioritize on the most important content and put the rest in backup slides that people can review on their own after the meeting. Also put most of the supporting data in backup slides. This will help you manage and pace your presentation better.

- **Keep it simple**. Ideally, you should have one key message and no more than five bullet points for each slide. The slide should get the audience's attention and allow you to expand your point. Using examples to illustrate your points is an effective technique. However, some companies, such as consulting firms, use the practice of putting all the details on the slides. Their reason for this practice is to ensure the audience does not misunderstand or forget any information. This practice is ineffectual due to the sheer amount of information that saturates one slide. If your main priority is to give the audience every detail, write a memo and send to them. It does not serve a useful purpose if you just read to the audience the content on the slide. If you have a lot of information to give to the audience, prioritize and put the secondary or supporting information in backup slides, and let the audience know the details are available for them to refer to.

- **Save wordsmithing for later**. When writing content on the slides, don't spend too much time trying to wordsmith. You want to keep your creative juices flowing and put your thoughts on the slides. Afterward, you can read the slides over and decide what to include, delete or put in backup slides. Then you can wordsmith to get your points across clearly. Since there is limited space on the slide, be succinct and focus on using only appropriate words to convey your points. Don't write sentences as they take up too much space and may confuse the audience. Bullet point format is very effective for slides as it forces you to be succinct and clear.

- **Use animation**. If you have several bullet points on your slide and you want to go over each point at a time, animation technique is an excellent way to manage this. You can show the bullet point one at a time and "hide" the rest. This gets the audience to focus on each bullet point, your comment about it and not get ahead of your presentation.

- **"A picture paints a thousand words."** Displaying graphic icons or pictures on your slides is a powerful way to demonstrate your message. They can also help make your slides more lively and dynamic. Slides that only have words can be dull and look uninteresting. However, use your judgement to balance the use of graphics, because too much of them can distract the audience from the message you want to convey. The use of font colors, size and format can help highlight and emphasize your key messages. However, excessive use of formatting dilutes your message and even distracts the audience from paying attention to your presentation.

- **Show graphs instead of numbers**. If you have a lot of numbers in your presentation, create graphs instead of showing tables which put too much burden on the audience to read and draw their own conclusions. Trend lines, pie charts or bar graphs make it much easier for the audience to understand your message. For example, having a line graph with a trend line showing increasing sales for the past few quarters is much more preferable to a table full of sales figures. It's better to help the audience see your point than requiring them to try to figure it out and risk having them form the wrong conclusion.

- **Include agenda and takeaways**. The first slide should clearly show the purpose of the meeting and the topics you plan to cover. The last slide should have a summary of the key takeaways and if appropriate, a list of the next steps.

- **Run spelling/grammar error check**. More often than not, I've had spelling or grammar errors when creating slides. Taking a few minutes to double check will save you from potential embarrassment when you discover the errors in the middle of your presentation or even worse, having the audience point them out to you. The errors may also lessen the quality of your slides and make them look sloppy. Since you have invested a lot of time in making your slides as clean as possible, spending a few extra minutes running a spell and grammar check is easy and worthwhile.

Common Mistakes In Creating Slides
- **Unreadable or confusing graphics**. At the most, the audience will spend too much time trying to make sense of your graphics and determine what you are trying to say instead of paying attention to what you are actually saying. At the very least, it's distracting and does the opposite of what you want to achieve with using graphics.

- **Over-Animated slides**. As discussed above, animation is a great way to accentuate a slide. However, too much is distracting. Also avoid using sound effects in a professional meeting environment unless there is a good reason to do it. Make a mental note to test your animated slides before you actually present to make sure they work the way you want them to. Avoid dancing or lots of movement animations. They might be entertaining but ultimately detract from your presentation as a whole.
- **Failure to proofread**. As suggested earlier, use spelling/grammar check to correct errors. In addition, make the font size large enough so the audience can read easily, especially for people in the back of the room. Don't try to squeeze in more text on the slides by reducing the font size. If people cannot read your slides, you will lose their attention. Moreover, if you use color text or a background, make sure the text is easily readable. Proofread your slides when you are done and run the slides when you practice presenting to make sure the slides show the way you want and there is nothing abnormal you didn't catch earlier.

Chapter 9

How To Present Persuasively

Presentation skill is an integral component of your overall communication. Regardless of your field of work, you either had or will have opportunities to present many times in your career. Whether you feel comfortable or not, giving presentations and speaking publicly provides you a great opportunity to shine and get noticed by your co-workers and management. Depending on the size of your company and your job position, you may not get a chance to speak or present in front of company executives often. When the opportunity presents itself, take full advantage and make the best of it. Your goal is to make a great impression on these people. The impression you make, or the perception the executives have of you, is based on your presentation performance, good or bad. While this may not seem fair because this could be one of just a few times they see your work, their impression plays an important role in your next performance review and standing in the company.

Moreover, speaking in public is important in a number of activities, including conducting meetings, training sales people, interviewing with the press, meeting with customers, negotiating with company suppliers and representing your company in industry conferences. As a result, being perceived as a good communicator/presenter will open doors to opportunities and serve you well in your career. If you have aspirations to be a high level executive or run a company someday, keep in mind that most, if not all, executives or people in powerful positions have excellent communication skills, especially public speaking.

Some people are natural speakers. Presenting and public speaking seem to come easy to them while others struggle. From observing many outstanding speakers, I firmly believe that this skill can be learned and anyone can be a good speaker, regardless of their personality. I cited Mayor Rob in an earlier chapter, one of the youngest mayors in the US, who came to speak to my students about his career path and public service. Before Rob became a seasoned politician, he was not great at public speaking. He was a bit shy and tended to be quiet in meetings. Through a lot of work and the coaching he received, he gradually improved his communication skills and became an accomplished speaker. If you see him delivering a speech today, you would think he was a born natural.

Even if you don't think you're a good or natural speaker, embrace the challenge and train yourself to improve. This chapter will show you the techniques and best practices to deliver a great presentation. The goal here is to have confidence in yourself so when an opportunity arises, you will be excited to volunteer instead of waiting to see if you will be asked to do it while secretly hoping you won't have to. As you continue to improve your public speaking skill, you will feel free to explore future job opportunities without feeling limited by your lack of confidence in your presentation skills.

Regardless of your audience – whether it is co-workers, company executives, internal partners or external parties, there is a set of best practices you can follow to deliver a successful presentation.

How To Conduct Your Presentation

Equipped with a well-organized and compelling content package, now the time comes for you to present. It is natural to have butterflies in your stomach. The key to handle nervousness is **confidence**. You must believe you are the content expert and you know more about the topic than anyone in the audience. They should not have more knowledge about the topic than you. Otherwise, you shouldn't be presenting. This belief will give you confidence and also motivate you to prepare the presentation content thoroughly and to practice your presentation until you feel fully prepared. If you are prepared, your confidence will enable you to deliver an outstanding presentation. Below are the best practices you can use.

- Start the presentation by telling the audience what you will cover, then proceed to tell them and then wrap up by telling them what you just told them. Wrapping up allows you to summarize the main ideas you want the audience to remember.
- Maintain eye contact with the audience and engage them. This can be accomplished by asking questions to get the audience to participate. Start the presentation with a light hearted joke to break the ice or a quiz question about your presentation to have the audience take a stab at the answer. During the presentation, when

you finish making a key point or before transitioning to the next point, ask: "Is this clear? Do you have any questions?" This offers the audience opportunities to comment. If you have a colleague in the audience, a good technique is to have them ask a question which allows you to elaborate. Many people don't want to be the first one to ask a question but once somebody does, they tend to follow. Moreover, don't just read from the slide. Use the slide as a guide for you to expand on and give examples. If you spend most of your talk looking at the slides, you disengage from the audience and create an impression that you may not know your materials well.

- Speak clearly and loudly enough for everyone to hear. Make it a practice to ask the audience before you start if they can hear you. When speaking publicly, speak louder than your normal voice so people can hear clearly without having to strain to hear. In addition, when we are a little nervous, we tend to speak faster than usual. Be aware of this and slow your pace down a bit. A good technique to maintain your voice and speaking pace is breathing. We sometimes forget to breathe under the excitement or pressure, and that can negatively affect our ability to control our voice.

- Maintain your poise and don't let questions rattle you. If you're not clear on the question, ask the questioner to repeat: "I just want to make sure I understand your question, can you repeat it for me?" If you don't know the answer to a question, no need to panic. You can say for example: "I don't have the information off the top of my head. I'll find out after this meeting and get back to you." If you're not ready to give your opinion on a question, buy time by saying: "Good question. I'd like to give it some thought and get back to you." This allows you time to think in the back of your mind while maintaining your composure. When you're ready to answer, you can then get back to that person.

- Remember to acknowledge the audience's good questions or comments. For example: "That's an excellent question" before proceeding to answer. This connects you to the audience and motivates them to participate.

- Put unrelated issues in the "parking lot." If and when other topics come up during your presentation, resist diving into them, even if your audience wants to, because these issues will distract from the purpose of your meeting and take up valuable time from your presentation. A good technique to handle this without offending your audience is to "park" the issue – capture them on the whiteboard for offline discussing. Your audience is satisfied the issues are noted and will be addressed later and you are happy to continue with your presentation.

- Wrap up the meeting by summarizing the key points. If there are action items, summarize them with the names of the people responsible for those action items. If the objective of the meeting is to get approval, confirm if you have the approval. If the management team is not ready to make a decision, ask for a timeline you can expect to hear from them or the next step.

- Remember to practice giving the presentation in front of the mirror. Speak as if you're presenting real time. It may be a bit awkward at first to see yourself, but you can get useful feedback on what you need to improve. You can also practice in front of your friends or family members who can give you direct feedback. Don't rush into the meeting without rehearsing your presentation. You have worked hard to create your slides and develop the content, so don't leave it to chance on the most important step – delivering your presentation. Even practicing just once is beneficial. Some people prefer framing their presentation as a "story" for practice and having a conversation with their friends instead of actually presenting to them. I find that rehearsing my presentation as if it were real works better for me. Use whatever technique works best for you, and remember: you are the expert. Be confident.

- Get feedback on your presentation performance from your manager or co-workers who are good presenters and were present at the meeting. Consult with people who will give you objective feedback. Ask what they liked and didn't like about the presentation, what else they would have liked to see and where you can improve.

- If your company offers presentation classes where you can be videotaped, take advantage of the opportunity. Given your busy schedule, it can be inconvenient to take time out from work, but make this a priority and it will provide a long lasting benefit to you.

- If you are presenting to a remote audience over the phone, there are a couple of additional key points to remember. If you cannot see the audience's reaction, you have to use your verbal skills to gauge the audience's response and feedback. You need to pause more during your presentation to check for audience's understanding and solicit questions to avoid misunderstandings. If you manager is in the audience, ask him to be your eyes and to help getting the audience to engage. Moreover, he can help reset the meeting and pull people back to the topic of the presentation if they get off on a tangent. Before wrapping up the meeting, confirm the key takeaways, next steps and address any disconnects that may arise. If there are open issues, make sure you assign owners for these action items and deadlines to resolve.

Common Presentation Mistakes

- Lack of professionalism. Failure to dress professionally or appropriately. If you are presenting to customers, don't come in jeans and t-shirts unless that is what the customers are comfortable with. When in doubt, dress businesslike to show respect. This goes without saying, but you must avoid exhibiting unprofessional demeanor such as appearing intoxicated, making off color jokes, being sarcastic or condescending to the audience. These are not only unacceptable but can get you in serious trouble.
- Distracting gestures or movements. Gesturing during a presentation is a good thing, but dancing, or repetitive, distracting gestures and movements detract from your message. Again, recognizing your audience and remembering the purpose of your presentation will help you act appropriately.
- Distracting filler words such as "and," "um," "ah" and "basically." Everyone uses these sometimes and it is fine to use them from time to time, but try to limit the frequency. When it's repetitive, it becomes a distraction.
- Reading to your audience. If you put everything you have to say on your slides and just read to your audience, you can just email them the slides and they can read them on their own time. Moreover, try not to use notes or note cards because they encourage reading and discourage eye contact with your audience.
- Misunderstanding the purpose of your presentation between you and the decision makers. Make sure everyone is on the same page on the topic and objective of the meeting before you deliver your presentation. This happens more frequently than we think. To prevent this, send an email confirming the purpose of your meeting to the audience prior to your presentation date so any misunderstanding of the meeting objective can be cleared up immediately.

Chapter 10

How To Communicate And Present To Specific Audiences

Before proceeding with this chapter, read the "How to organize and develop presentation content" and "How to present persuasively" chapters first if you have not, since that content complements the materials here. While the techniques described in those chapters are relevant to all audiences, specific audiences also have their own unique characteristics you should be aware and tailor your presentation to. This chapter covers different audiences you may have opportunities to present to, their differences and how best to address them.

Communicating And Presenting To Executives

I have had many opportunities presenting to company executives as well as observing firsthand how they conducted themselves in meetings. I also have heard from well-known CEOs of multinational companies talk about their expectations when attending a presentation. Here's a summary of what I learned.

- **Limited available time**. Company executives normally have a tight schedule. Usually you have a short amount of time (30-60 minutes) to meet with them, depending on the topic and objective of the meeting. They are unlikely to extend your meeting time because they typically have other meetings scheduled already. As a result, you must prepare your content to be able to finish your meeting within the allotted time while also achieve your meeting goal, especially if it's a meeting where you need a decision from them.
- **Possible interruptions and meeting time reduced**. It's not unusual for your meeting to be shortened due to the executive team getting interrupted with other matters or if they decided to extend the

meeting prior to yours. This can be a real time decision you need to make just before your meeting begins or worse, during your meeting. Therefore, you need to be prepared to handle these unexpected situations and still be able to accomplish your goal.

- **Impatience**. Patience is not their strong suit, given the demand on their time and attention. They don't tolerate unclear meetings if they don't know the meeting's purpose and what is expected of them. They tend to lose their patience if the meeting gets sidetracked or if they're not getting answers to their questions. The irony is that sometimes the executives can get the meeting off track by their own discussion with each other. While they like to see a well-run, disciplined meeting from you, they sometimes are not disciplined and need to be guided back to the topic at hand. You need to be aware of this and prepared accordingly.

Here are the keys to preparing your content and conducting presentation.

- **Organize your content to be able to adapt on the fly**. Since you likely will have more materials to cover than the time allowed, prioritize on the relevant content executives care most about. Also, allocate time for questions and discussions from the executives. Keep in mind the rule of thumb of having one slide for every four minutes of meeting time. If it's a sixty-minute meeting, have no more than fifteen slides. Put other more detailed slides in backup in case you need to refer to them. In addition, organize your presentation slides into modules so if you need to, you can prioritize and use the most important modules first and leave other details for the executives to review later at their convenience.

- **Keep your content succinct, clear and at the right level**. How well you do this determines how likely you and the executive team can stay on track and finish the meeting as you hope. Adhering to having one slide for every four minutes will help you accomplish your meeting goal. However, this doesn't mean you should cram as much detail as possible into every slide. We have a desire to show how extensive our work is and are afraid we may leave out something important that executives care about. Avoid the urge to do this.

You should have one key message for each slide you want your executives to remember. Many executives are data driven and the more data you show, the more likely they will drill down and not able to see the forest from the trees. If this happens, your meeting is at risk of becoming derailed. Moreover, you don't want your analysis to be questioned since it is your job to make sure it's thorough and to deliver the key conclusions you want the executive to keep in mind. If they question your analysis, it brings your credibility into question and will cloud your overall meeting goal.

There is one story in particular I would like to share with you that still brings a smile to my face whenever I think about it. As a manager leading a team of marketing professionals in my company's server business unit, I normally review my team's presentations before they present to the management team. Before one important business review meeting with our General Manager and Marketing Vice President, I reviewed the presentation slides from my employee, Elaine. Elaine had done an extensive and thorough analysis, but put a great deal of detail on already crowded slides. I suggested to Elaine to "dumb it down" and simplify her slides so the executives could understand. Well, during her presentation, our GM, a brilliant executive who had a tendency to drill down on numbers, started asking detailed questions and getting into a rat hole with Elaine. After getting a few questions too many, she stopped her presentation and said to him: "Well, I had all the details on the original slides to show you, but Michael told me to keep it really simple because otherwise you won't get it." I felt like hiding under the desk. Fortunately, I had a good enough relationship with the GM and he laughed it off because he recognized his data driven tendencies. He understood that we wanted to highlight the key points for him and the Marketing VP to make decisions instead of using their valuable time to talk about the numbers.

- **Be clear on your meeting's objective**. When you start your meeting, this is the first thing you should cover. You need to state clearly the purpose of the meeting and more importantly, what you want from them. Do you need them to make decisions on your proposal? Do you need them to provide their input and guidance on your project? Or are you there to only give them an update and share information? This will prepare their mindset for the meeting since they probably have not seen your presentation materials.

- **Confirm on the amount of time you have**. Confirm this at the beginning of the meeting even if you had been told earlier how much time you have. If you learn you have less time now, adjust in real time to make sure your meeting agenda fits into the time constraint. And even if you have confirmed the time at the start of meeting, your time could still be cut short by unexpected events. However, if you had organized your content as we discussed above, you are prepared to handle these unexpected interruptions.

- **Balance between executive discussions and achieving your meeting goals**. In your meeting, the executive team may become animated and get into lengthy discussions with each other. While it's important for them to talk and think through the information to help them make decisions, you need to determine whether the discussion focuses on the meeting topic or on another unrelated topic. I have seen numerous meetings where the discussion evolved from the original topic to something completely different. Also keep in mind some executives may not be disciplined about staying on topic. Moreover, be aware of the politics at play because some of the executives may be trying to score points with the CEO.

  If you see the discussion getting off track, look for an appropriate time to interject and remind the executive team to get back on the topic. A good time could be when an executive finishes her thought. You can be polite but firm by saying: "Sorry to interrupt, but we only have twenty minutes left in this meeting and we have quite a bit of materials to cover. Can I continue?" Or if they seem to be in the middle of some serious discussion, you can suggest: "Sorry to interrupt, but we only have twenty minutes left in this meeting and we have quite a bit of materials to cover with you and I would like to continue, or would you like me to schedule another time?" Chances are they will ask you to continue. You may need to do this a couple of times throughout your presentation to keep the meeting on track. This is also a good way to show your leadership ability.

- **Have a champion to support you**. This can be your manager if he is high enough on the management chain relative to the executives, or this can be one of the executives you and/or your manager have a good relationship with. With this executive, try to have a little bit of time beforehand to give her an update, your recommendation and most important, to ask for her support. She can play a pivotal role in providing you support and air cover during the meeting. Because of her status and credibility, she can help placate other executives who may have concerns about your recommendation. If you have an important decision making meeting, try your best to meet with the key stakeholders prior to meeting to get their buy in or at least to understand what issues they may have. This will help your meeting go smoother and minimize surprises.

- There will be times when you're attending a meeting but not presenting, and in these cases, you don't need to be as prepared as the presenter. However, since it's not often you get a chance to be in a meeting with key executives, you should view the meeting as an opportunity for you to participate intelligently, contribute to the discussion and gain visibility. In order to do this, yes, you guessed correctly - you need to spend a little time to prepare.

o   Know the purpose of the meeting. This provides you some ideas for your participation. If the meeting is to make a decision, you can play a role in making sure there is closure – a decision is made or clear next steps are understood. In certain meetings, especially difficult ones, people are reluctant to make decisions and the presenter or meeting facilitator is hesitant to push the executives for an answer. If you see this situation, you can speak up to remind everyone the objective of the meeting and the importance to reach closure – one way or another. People will respect you for your assertiveness. No one wants to come out of a meeting confused or unclear about the outcomes or next steps.

o   Know your role in the meeting. If you are responsible for the content of a particular agenda item, prepare to provide insights even if you're not presenting or to answer potential questions from the executives. If you don't have the agenda, ask the presenter/meeting facilitator so you can anticipate potential areas where you can speak up and add value to the meeting.

o   Be ready to provide support to the presenter or other team members. This is a natural way to gain credibility and visibility at the same time. Presenting under the spotlight can be stressful and rattle anyone, especially when facing tough questions. This is where you can help. If the presenter seems unsure about the answer or doesn't seem to have the information to a question and you do, you should volunteer and give your answer. The presenter will appreciate your help and the executives will be impressed with your knowledge and teamwork. You do need to keep in mind the balance between stepping in to help out and showing up the presenter. If you repeatedly chime in, you come across as overbearing, especially since you're not the focus of the meeting.

o   Asking questions to get the presenter to elaborate on certain points is another way to provide support. Oftentimes in the heat of presenting, the presenter or meeting leader may forget to elaborate certain important points. By asking them to elaborate, you help them slow down and stress the key points. Something as simple as saying: "To the point you just mentioned, can you elaborate and provide more detail" would serve as a trigger for the presenter to expand their point. Throughout my career I have used this technique many times with my peers and my team members and they very much appreciated my gesture. Many of them have asked me to play this role for them when they have important presentations.

○ Speak up once or twice even if you have no visible role in the meeting. Obviously you should make comments relevant to the meeting and not something out in "left field." Many times we don't speak up because we're afraid to ask stupid questions or say something silly. However, asking for clarification is a good and safe technique to use. For example, if an executive makes a comment that's unclear to you, you should ask the executive to elaborate. For example: "Can you elaborate on that point a little more? I just want to make sure I understand" is a perfectly acceptable response. Some people in the meeting are likely to have the same question but were afraid to ask and would appreciate that you did.

Communicating And Presenting To Customers

If you have a chance to meet and interact with customers, take advantage of the opportunity. You can gain great insight about the customer's business and their challenges. You can read reports about customers but nothing hits home quite like meeting them in person and hearing first hand.

- **Customers like to be heard**. Customers frequently have business challenges they need to address in order to improve their company's performance. When they meet you, they like to talk to you about their challenges and look to you as a source of information that potentially can help them. Moreover, if customers have some issues with your company's service and products, they will definitely want to let you know.

- **Big investment of time**. Whether they come to visit at your company's site or vice-versa, it's a significant investment of their time and resources, and as result, they have specific objectives and expectations in meeting you. You probably also have specific needs you want to get from them. Therefore, it's important to understand their objectives and balance those with yours to make sure both parties get what each wants from the meeting.

- **You are your company**. When you meet the customer, they see you as representing your company. They don't see you as an engineer in the engineering department or customer support representative or a product manager. They don't look at you as only having specific responsibilities for your job. When I visited and presented to customers, they didn't see me as a Product Management Manager responsible for hardware products. They saw me as my company's representative and would feel free to discuss anything relating to their business with my company. When you meet them and if they have a request or demand, they will ask you and expect you to follow through.

Here are the keys to preparing your content and conducting presentation:

- **Be clear about the objective of your meeting with the customer**. As with meeting with executives, find out the customer's objectives for the meeting, their issues, topics they want to discuss, etc. The customer Sales Representative (SR) or Account Manager (AM) is a great resource to find out. Most SRs or AMs will contact you to let you know ahead of time about the meeting details. They have a vested interest to keep their customer happy and to make sure they get what they come for.

  If you don't hear from the sales team, get in touch with them prior to the meeting to get all the information you need so you can properly prepare. As importantly, when you meet with the customer, confirm the agenda and topics with them. Ask questions to find out what is top of mind, what issues they are facing, what they want to discuss and what their expectations are. Between the time of your meeting with the sales team and your meeting with the customer, they could have met with other competitors and learned about new information they want to discuss with you.

- **Know who you are meeting with**. Different companies may have different representatives meeting you, including technical people (IT managers, system administrators, CIO) and business people (purchasing managers, business line managers, CEO). Knowing whom you will meet and what they have in mind helps you determine if you need to invite other experts from your company to cover topics that you don't have the expertise on. In the course of briefing with the sales team, you can also learn if there is someone from the customer company who is a champion for your company - someone you can count on to support you in the meeting.

- **Balance being company advocate and projecting honesty**. While customers understand you are there to advocate and promote your company, they do not expect you to be just a talking mouthpiece for your company. You will earn respect and credibility if you can be objective about the strengths and weaknesses of your company products or services while at the same time, promote your company. They don't expect your products or services to be perfect but they do want to know about any product issues and how your company is addressing them. In particular, if they hear from one of your competitors pointing out the weaknesses of your product or services, they would definitely want to validate the credibility of the competitor's claims.

A common place where customers want objectivity is in comparing your company versus your competitors. Customers realize every company wants to differentiate themselves from others, but what they look for is whether the comparisons are credible and can be validated. As a result, you will earn the customer's trust and gain credibility by balancing between being an advocate for your company and being objective in your assessment of potential solutions to solve their problems. However, before you give your opinion, make sure you listen and ask a lot of questions so you have a clear understanding of what they heard as well as their own perception. I have seen instances where my company's presenter turned off the customer and lost their interest by being in complete selling mode regardless of what the customer was saying.

- **Be cautious with confidential information**. Customers are interested to hear about your company's future strategy and product roadmap so they can plan accordingly. Since much of your company's future plan is confidential, exercise caution. Customers typically sign a non-disclosure agreement (NDA). However, even with an NDA, proceed with caution. If the customer is a loyal customer and has a good track record with your company, it may be fine to share confidential information with the confidence they would not divulge it to your competitors. My rule of thumb is, especially with customers you're not sure about, assume that whatever information you share, confidential or not, will get into the hands of your competitors.

- **Be careful about making commitments**. Oftentimes customers will take advantage of the opportunity to ask for certain commitments – for example, commitment for a date to fix a problem, to deliver a replacement product, to provide a new software upgrade, to provide longer support to discontinued products, or to give special pricing. Unless it is within your power and you are sure it's the right thing to do and you can deliver on your promise, do not commit. Although you may feel a lot of pressure to agree to the request, especially if you have an unhappy customer, resist the urge. It's worse if you cannot deliver and, trust me, the customer will hold you to it. Instead, commit that you will take the request back to the company to have the right person work on the request and get back to them. You must follow through on this agreement.

- **Maintain your professionalism when facing an upset customer**. Sometimes you may get blindsided by an unhappy customer with issues you were not aware of. On one of my customer visits, I wanted to discuss with the customer about our future printer technology. Prior to the meeting, I had a briefing with the account Sales Representative and no issues or concerns came up. When a co-worker and I arrived at the customer site to meet them in a conference room, they proceeded to lay into us about the problems they had and their dissatisfaction with our company. We sensed their frustration and anger as the volume of their voices got louder. We were caught completely by surprise and worse, the SR was nowhere to be found as he never warned us about the customer issues.

We were clueless because their issues were related to the computer business unit and not our printer business unit. However, we realized that we represented our company, not just the business unit we worked in. There was only one thing we could do. We sat down and listened patiently. We did not even attempt to mention the reason for our visit. We asked questions to make sure we captured their problem accurately. When they finished venting and giving us a list of things they wanted answers on, my colleague calmly thanked them for their feedback. Then he explained that we were not aware of the issues beforehand, and although we were not directly involved in these issues, we will make sure that appropriate people will get back to them. We committed to them that we will personally let them know who their contact would be.

After the customers calmed down, I asked them if I could take a little bit of their time to show them a new printer technology and get their feedback to help us design the right product. They agreed, listened attentively and actively gave us feedback. They ended up talking with us for another hour. The moral of the story here is that when we meet customers, we are our company's spokespersons, we listen to their needs and concerns, and we take ownership to follow through with them.

Communicating And Presenting To Third Parties

These include suppliers who provide your company with materials to produce your products, contractors who perform services for you such as programming or creating marketing plan, partners who team up with your company to provide solutions, and the distribution partners who market and sell your company's products.

- While this relationship is different than that between your company and customers, the discussion points on customers are applicable here as well – confidentiality, understanding the other side's perspective, the need to listen, etc.
- One area I want to emphasize is regarding contract agreement and negotiation. Usually it takes many meetings to negotiate an agreement on how the two companies will work together and what to commit to. Refer to the "How to be a good negotiator" chapter for details. Don't rush or get pushed into an agreement. Take your time to understand the other party's issues and needs as well as explore all possible options in order to arrive at a win/win agreement. Moreover, don't commit to an agreement unless you have full authority on the final contract and you're confident about the terms and conditions. Review the terms with your manager and other experts in the company to ensure you have covered all the bases. Finally, have the legal department review the contract. This review process can be lengthy but it's better to take this step to avoid any legal issue or liability in the future.

Communicating And Presenting To International Audiences

This applies to company employees, customers as well as partners in other countries who have different native languages, customs and business cultures. The points we've discussed in this chapter apply to these audiences also. In addition, I'll focus on the unique characteristics of these groups and how to prepare and present to them.

- **Be aware and sensitive to their differences**. These include languages, business cultures and customs. The more you understand the unique differences and how to work effectively with them, the more successful you will be. For example, if English is your native language but not theirs even though they can converse in English, be aware they may not understand the English business jargon or slang, and they would appreciate it if you spoke a little slower so they can understand clearly. Culturally, people in other countries may not be as direct as Americans. For example, Japanese customers are polite and tend to listen and not ask a lot of questions in public. Moreover, they're not comfortable saying no, even if they cannot commit to your request. Silence does not mean yes. It's prudent to confirm in writing all agreements before proceeding. It's beyond the scope of this book to cover this subject in-depth, and there are many resources for you to research in this area to help you work effectively and have a good working relationship with international audiences.

- **Speaking at a pace that works for your audience**. Speak a little bit slower and louder to make sure your audience can follow you. This is true especially if you are a fast speaker or have a soft voice. After every key point, pause and ask for understanding and anything the audience wants you to repeat or elaborate.

- **Learn to work with translator**. In your speaking engagements, you may have a translator to interpret for the audience. This can be a bit awkward since it doesn't promote a smooth presentation. However, you should plan your presentation to accommodate the translator if there will be one. Meet with the translator prior to your talk to brief her on your topic and give her a quick overview of your presentation. Also work with her on how to coordinate the presentation, including where you should pause for the translation. Some translators prefer short sentences or one message at time while others can handle multiple points at a time. Syncing up and coordinating with the translator will make your presentation more seamless to the audience.

- **Avoid using American jargon, slang and acronyms**. While people who are used to working in the US may not have any problem understanding, people from different countries can be confused or even offended by your use of jargon or slang. Even a common phrase can throw them off. For example, when I travel to Asia on business, I often present to customers. In my presentations during my early visits, I would forget about the audience and ended up using phrases like "six in one and half dozen in the other" or "at the end of the day" and I would see confused looks on their faces. Now I think people in general understand most common phrases we use here in the US, but we should avoid using them.

- **Use of graphics or visual aids**. This is a good way to make your presentation easier to understand and get your point across. For example, when my team presented to a Chinese audience about our new computer, we would have the actual computer in the room. We opened the computer to show the key sections and components inside. The team used the computer as a visual aid to demonstrate their key points and it was also an effective technique to get the audience engaged. While your customers may not feel comfortable asking questions in the room, they can inspect the product first hand and get many of their questions answered.

- **Offer one-on-one meetings after the presentation**. Because the audience may not feel comfortable asking questions publically, they may welcome a chance to speak to you one-on-one. Remember to allocate time after your presentation and invite them to talk with you and discuss any questions they may have.

THRIVING AT WORK

Part 3

Collaborating

The amount of meetings I've been in - people would be shocked. But that's how you gain experience, how you can gain knowledge, being in meetings and participating. You learn and grow.

Tiger Woods

Chapter 11

How To Collaborate Successfully

According to dictionary definitions, to collaborate means to work jointly with someone or a group of people on an activity, especially to create or produce something. Regardless of your profession, it's rare when you work alone. You spend most of your time working with people in your company as well as external parties, including customers, suppliers, partners and consultants. These people play a key role in determining how successful you will be.

Why Having Good Collaboration Skills Is Important

Before we delve into the strategies, let's first understand the benefits of being a good collaborator.

- You normally spend a lot of time working with other people on a team project. Everybody needs to do their part and deliver on their commitment in order for the whole project to be successfully. Because a project is only going to be as strong as the weakest link in the chain, team members are dependent on each other and need to work together closely. Collaborating effectively is the key to a successful project.

- Effective collaboration enables you and the team to work more efficiently. Teams who don't collaborate well often have miscommunication, confusion and conflicts – all of which result in loss of critical time. For example, I have been on teams where we had multiple meetings rehashing the same topic, revisiting decisions or clarifying unnecessary confusion. Teams who work well together only meet as needed and use meetings to set goals, review project status and resolve issues. If you have good collaboration skills and use them to help your team work effectively together, you not only help your team but also yourself by saving time to work on other important activities.

- How you perform on a project and how you work with other people is a major factor in your yearly performance review. Your team members and other managers' feedback have significant influence on how you will be evaluated. Positive feedback along with delivering excellent results will earn you good performance reviews, salary raises and consideration for promotions. I consistently noticed during my career that high performers share one common trait – the ability to work with people to get things done successfully.
- In collaborating with people, whether in a leading role or as a team member, you have a great opportunity to grow professionally, develop leadership skills, enhance communication skills and improve your ability to work effectively with others. Moreover, demonstrating good collaboration skills is a great way to make you stand out at work and get the attention of company executives.

Companies spend a significant amount of money to train their employees on teamwork. I once had an employee, Mark, who was an expert in his field, knew his stuff inside out but was not good at working with people and getting people to do what he needed to complete the project. If Mark could develop and improve this skillset, he would be a star. I sent him to a one week professional development training program in Florida at the cost of five thousand dollars, not including hotel, travel and food expenses. This not only cost the company a lot of money, but more importantly, five days of productive work from him. If you have or develop these skills early in your career, you will have a leg up in your career and a great head start over other people.

In this chapter, I'll cover how to effectively collaborate with other people and to get them to collaborate with you.

Skills And Qualities Needed For Effective Collaboration

I'll discuss three important skills and qualities – Adaptability, Communication and Negotiation.

- **Adaptability**. People you work with may come from different cultures, different backgrounds, have different personalities and work styles. Since there is no "one size fits all" approach to working with others and getting the most out of their effort, you need to be able to adapt to them. Invest your time on your team members to develop a rapport and understand how best to work with them - what motivates them, what work method they prefer, what makes them tick, etc. Investing your time with them will go a long way to gain their trust and set you up to work well with them.

- **Communication skills**. Having good communication skills goes hand in hand with collaboration skills. I covered this in detail in the "How to communicate effectively" chapter. Specifically, I talked about the importance of being a good listener. Moreover, I covered ways to communicate in different work situations. Lastly, I discussed the importance of maintaining professionalism, staying focused on the business issue and not react personally in difficult situations.
- **Negotiation skills**. This is the ability to influence people to achieve a mutually desired outcome. Even without being aware of it, we frequently negotiate. We negotiate with our manager on work assignments and priorities, with our project team members on project tasks and deadlines, with our suppliers on material cost and delivery schedule, etc. Negotiating with other people plays a key role in collaboration. Refer to the "How to be a good negotiator" chapter for details. I described a strategy and approach to use in any negotiation, the need to gather as much information as possible, to be creative, and most importantly, to achieve a win/win outcome.

Collaboration Strategies

Try these strategies for collaborating effectively on a team project.

- Start of a project. This is more applicable to the project manager, but even if you are not, you can play an active role in spending time in the beginning of a project to:
  - o Clarify the goals/objectives to make sure everyone is on the same page. If there is any confusion, this is the time to clarify and confirm project goals and objectives. If and when issues arise causing the project to get off track, going back to the project objectives is a good way to refocus everyone.
  - o Discuss and gain clear understanding of deliverables and timelines expected of the team. Moreover, it's important to align with management on the deliverables since they will hold the team accountable to these commitments. If the team cannot commit to the expected deliverables and timelines, they must negotiate with the management team.
  - o Clarify your specific tasks/responsibilities, negotiate and prioritize your deliverables and deadlines. Be thorough in assessing your tasks and schedules before committing. While you want to be aggressive, try not to over commit to action items

you don't have control over or confidence to deliver on time. All things being equal, it's better to under promise and over deliver.

o Understand your dependencies on other people and vice-versa. Know specifically whom you need to work with to make sure they deliver to you what and when you need for you to complete your job.

o Determine how team members prefer to work together – method of communication, frequency of meetings, forums to resolve issues/conflicts, etc.

- Spend time to figure out effective ways to work with your team members as discussed in the "Adaptability" section earlier.

- At the end of each meeting, make sure there is a meeting recap which summarizes decisions made, action items/owners, and next steps. This helps eliminate confusion among team members and prevent wasting time from having another meeting to clear things up. Confusion can easily happen when many topics were discussed at the meeting. To ensure team members have the same understanding, the project manager should send out a summary message after the meeting.

- Create a central online share work space for sharing information, work in progress, and capturing up to date changes and status. This enables everyone to see the same work being done as well as changes made in real time and ensures everyone has the same information at all times. There are many online share workplace tools available. Check with your company IT group (Information Technology).

- Lead by example. Meeting your commitment and completing your deliverables on time gains you credibility and trust from team members. Moreover, looking for opportunities to put the team above individual results is a good way to show your leadership skills. For example, offer your team members a hand when they need help.

- Identify problems/conflicts early and resolve as soon as possible. Refer to the "How to resolve conflicts and deal with difficult situations" chapter for ways to handle these situations. Focus on the business issue and not on personal matter is important to solving problems.

- Seek regular feedback from team members and give constructive feedback as appropriate. This enables any confusion between team members to get cleared up and gives everyone the opportunity to make improvements on their work.

- Keep your manager updated on the project status and your progress. This enables your manager to keep her manager up to date and allows you to seek help if and when you need it.
- Know when to escalate for help. You need to use your judgment here. While we may want to try to solve problems ourselves, sometimes we need help from our management. It's always better to ask for help than to miss your deadline. Your manager would much prefer you ask for help than hearing the bad news about the project. Her obvious question then would be "Why didn't you ask for help sooner?"
- Compliment and reward people for excellent work and teamwork effort. People appreciate being recognized for their work, so even a small gesture of sending an email to thank them for their effort and copying their manager goes a long way in building strong teamwork.
- Celebrate key milestones and accomplishments. Many of us put our heads down to finish our work and then move on to the next project without taking time to celebrate the team's accomplishments. It's an opportunity to catch our breath, enjoy each other's company and to recognize our own contribution to the success of the project. Moreover, it offers a great way to gain visibility and recognition.

Resolving Conflicts And Challenges

Inevitably, there will be conflicts or issues that arise during the project. The team's ability to stay on track and complete the project on time depends on the team members' ability to address and resolve these issues timely and productively. Here is a summary of steps to follow when a conflict arises:

- Recognize and identify issue early. Don't ignore and hope it will go away.
- Focus on the work issue and not personal issue.
- Identify the root causes of the issue – be honest and objective.
- Once root causes are identified, hold frank discussion to brainstorm potential solutions.
- Decide which solution is best to implement. If need to, escalate to management for help.

Let's take an example: a team member is not meeting his commitment and that is impacting your work. Because your specific project deliverables are dependent on his deliverables, you cannot perform your work without his output. As a result, the team risks not meeting the deadline. You are in a bind, what should you do?

- Seek to understand the root cause. Talk to this team member to understand why he's not able to complete his work and help him understand this is impacting the entire team's project. Don't make any assumption on why he is not delivering on his commitment and avoid making any accusations. Maintain your professionalism and focus on the business issue.

- Once you understand why, offer to brainstorm with him ways to help him complete his work so you will be able to do your work and the project can get back on track. Let's assume that he was late because he had to take time off to attend to a family matter. Knowing this was the reason and not his competence or motivation, you can offer to take on some part of his work so both of you will be able to catch up. This will earn you goodwill and trust which will be helpful in future projects. If you found out he was just lazy and not motivated to do his work or if he rejected your offer to help, you should escalate to the project manager to help resolve the issue. Before escalating, let him know the action you plan to take. While he may not like this, he should understand you have tried your best to resolve the issue with him, but you must put the team first and do what is needed to help keep the project on schedule.

While I have covered collaborating in the context of a team project, much of the same strategies and techniques apply to other situations such as working one-on-one's, working with people in other functions and even with people outside the company.

Chapter 12

How To Run And Facilitate Meetings

One of the most precious commodities we have is time. We value time. We usually feel we don't have enough time to get things done. This is especially true at work. We are rushing against deadlines and wishing we had more time to do a more thorough job. One of the most time consuming activities at work is attending meetings. There are many types of meeting: company meetings, staff meetings, project team meetings, one-on-one meetings with your manager and co-workers, meetings with customers and external parties, meetings to address unexpected crises or urgent issues, impromptu meetings, etc.

Majority of meetings are run inefficiently. They take longer than needed and oftentimes, little gets accomplished or worse yet, confusion arises and as a result, another meeting has to be called to revisit the issue. This wastes time and frustrates people who could have used the time more productively. One main reason for inefficiently run meetings is the lack of know-how from the meeting facilitator.

You will have opportunities to run meetings in your career. Knowing how to run meetings effectively will save you and your co-workers valuable time and foster positive working environment. In this chapter, I will cover the best ways to run an effective meeting and achieve the meeting's goals.

How To Prepare For The Meeting
- **Understand the meeting's goal clearly.** Is it an informational meeting where people share knowledge, a meeting to review project status and progress, a meeting to discuss and solve a problem, or a meeting to reach a decision? This helps you determine the right

people to attend the meeting, set the agenda, determine the length of the meeting and ensure people are prepared.

- **Determine the meeting's attendees**. For the meeting to be effective and productive, only people who have "skin in the game" should attend. Too often, a meeting has too many people including those who don't add any value. If these people like to talk, they can dominate the meeting and run the risk of ending it without accomplishing what you wanted. When you put the list of names together, ask yourself what their roles are, what value they add and what the impact would be without their participation in the meeting. This is especially important for working meetings where the team needs to make decisions, solve a problem or review project progress. When you schedule a meeting and send out the agenda, include a note to let meeting participants know to check with you if they would like to invite anyone else. You are the meeting facilitator and you have the final say on the attendees.

- **Have a clear agenda**. When you schedule the meeting and send out the invites, include a short but clear message stating:
  - Purpose of the meeting. For example: "Purpose of meeting is to finalize the project proposal to be sent to CEO Executive staff for approval" or "Purpose of the meeting is to finalize the XYZ project schedule."
  - Agenda items. List out the items you will cover with the team during the meeting. List the name of each person responsible for covering a specific item. Allocate amount of time for each item so the item's owner knows how to prepare. For example, if the meeting is to finalize the project schedule, your agenda could be as follows:
    - Product requirements – John S (15 minutes)
    - Design requirements – Betty J (15 minutes)
    - Quality plan – Manish T (15 minutes)
    - Manufacturing plan – Tom R (15 minutes)
  - Ask if anyone has a suggestion on the agenda to contact you before the meeting. Also ask the item owners to let you know if they will not be ready so you can revise the agenda accordingly.
  - Include the meeting location in your invite if possible. If you have people who will be attending on the phone or via video conference, make sure the meeting room has the IT equipment you need. Many meetings start late due to people scrambling to find out where the meeting was or missing IT equipment needed for the meeting.

How To Manage The Meeting

- Start on time. We are creatures of habit. If you set a hard start time and stick to it, eventually people will get the message and be at the meeting on time. You may want to allocate five minutes of at the beginning of the meeting to allow people leaving from a previous meeting to get to your meeting. But do not let five minutes become ten. Remember, you probably won't have the luxury to make up for lost time.
- Start the meeting by reiterating the purpose of the meeting and reviewing the agenda to make sure everyone is on the same page. If someone wants to modify the meeting or add to the meeting, you need to make a judgment call on whether their request is appropriate for the meeting and can be accommodated within the meeting's time. Normally, I would recommend no. Unless it was an exception, that person should have added it to the agenda prior to the meeting. If the request is important enough to the meeting's objectives and the person is ready to cover the new item, you may add to the agenda. Otherwise, ask that person to work offline with you.
- Monitor the progress of the agenda to make sure each item has the allocated time. If the discussion on a particular item is taking longer, you can check with the team to see if the remaining agenda items would take less time and allow this person to continue. Or you can ask them to wrap up and continue offline after the meeting. If someone asks a question that's not relevant to the topic, remind that person of the topic being discussed and ask them to discuss it after the meeting. For example: "Sorry Pat, we are tight on time and we're discussing topic ABC. Can you discuss that offline after the meeting?"
- Confirm the outcome of each major agenda item. For the example above, when a team member finishes his product requirement discussion and agrees to a timeline, capture the results and confirm with this person.
- If a conflict or debate occurs, let the discussion happen within the time allowed. However, make sure people don't talk over each other and each person is heard. If everyone is talking at the same time, you can interject firmly to remind people that one person should speak at a time. Make sure the discussion is focusing on the work issue and not personal. If someone is getting emotional and attacking someone personally, you need to interject immediately and emphasize the need to focus on the issue. Cut off that discussion and continue with the meeting's topic. You need to take control of the meeting.

93

- Monitor to see if discussions are related to the agenda topic. If a discussion is getting off track, stop the discussion and bring it back to the meeting's agenda. For example: "We are tight on time and need to focus on our agenda to finish our meeting. So let's get back on track."
- Before ending the meeting, summarize the outcomes and next steps. If some team members have a different understanding, they have a chance to raise the issue and resolve it right away.
- If you have people from different ethnic backgrounds and English is not their native language, be respectful to their needs. Remember to remind everyone to speak clearly. This is even more important if the meeting is over the phone. Also make a point to confirm their understanding. Moreover, avoid and remind attendees to not use American slang or jargon.
- Using humor is a good technique to enhance the working environment, promote teamwork as well as defuse unnecessary tension in the meeting. So be yourself and use your sense of humor at appropriate times in the meeting.

Common Mistakes In Facilitating Meetings

- Too many people in the meeting. As a general rule, the larger the meeting the less you will able to get things done. If you have a meeting with too many people, determine who are needed and disinvite people who are not. How many is too many depend on the context of your meeting. If the meeting is a working or decision making type of meeting, I believe less than ten is more conducive to having a productive meeting. If it is an informational meeting where no deep discussion or decision is required, a larger number of people can attend.
- Not keeping the meeting on track to be able to cover all the items adequately, potentially resulting in sub-optimal results and rush decisions. If you have to schedule another meeting because you weren't able to cover all the topics, you're taking more time out of your and other people's schedule. If you need to focus on facilitating the meeting and are not able to monitor the time, ask one of the participants to be a timekeeper for you.
- Failure to summarize key points, decisions, action items and next steps from the meeting. Forgetting or ignoring this important step can cause confusion or miscommunication. People are usually multi-tasking and probably don't remember all the details from the many

meetings they attended. Having a written summary that team members can refer to will help save headaches and precious time.

- Forgetting or ignoring to get full participation from the meeting participants. This is especially more common when you have meetings with people attending in person as well as people on the phone. Keep a list of people on the phone and remember to repeat key discussion points and confirm their understanding. Also remember to check if they have questions or comments.

- If you facilitate a meeting from a remote location and the attendees are either on the phone or gathered in a conference room, the above practices are also relevant. However, since you are remote, you need to be more assertive in running the meeting. Listen for side conversations and put a stop to them; they are distracting to the meeting agenda. If multiple people are talking and making it difficult to hear, intervene right away. In addition, make sure you have video systems setup to enable people to see the meeting materials. It's especially important to verbally summarize the takeaways, decisions or next steps to make sure any miscommunication can be addressed before the meeting ends. Once the meeting is over, send out the summary with clear outcomes and next steps.

Chapter 13

How To Earn Trust

E ven though we are in the digital world with plethora of social media tools, face to face interaction between people at work is still the most effective way to collaborate and build strong working relationships. If you work remotely and face to face interactions are not practical, having phone conversations is your next best alternative. Trust is another important factor in having a good professional relationship. Trust is defined as "firm belief in the reliability, truth, ability, or strength of someone." If your colleagues trust you, you are in a good position to work with them effectively and be able to get things done.

But how do you build and earn trust, especially if you are new to the team, to the organization or to the company? In this chapter, we will cover ideas you can apply to everyday interactions with your colleagues.

- **Meet your commitment**. First and foremost, you must do what you say. This demonstrates your reliability and dependability. It takes a sustained period of effort to earn trust but you can easily lose it. Regardless of how big or small your commitment is, if you commit to deliver a result or do something for someone, you must do your best to meet your commitment and follow through. If you realize that you won't be able to deliver on your commitment, let them know as soon as possible, fully explain and give an alternative option.

    My former manager, a Vice President, had a tendency to ask the same person on my team to complete a task for him. After seeing this a few times, I asked him why he did not ask other members on my team. He answered: "Because I know when Julie says yes to my request, I have complete trust that she will get it done on time, and more importantly, done right. I can go away and don't have to worry about it." One other thing to keep in mind before you commit is that you need to consider carefully whether you have the ability and resources to complete the task on time. If you're not sure about the deadline, give yourself some buffer in case unexpected problems occur.

- **Honesty**. Simply put, you can keep a secret, honor someone's confidentiality and tell the truth. When you say "Your secret is safe with me," honor it. Don't use someone's information shared in confidence against them. As a senior product manager working with my operational planning manager, Dan, on a production plan, I met with him to discuss my proposal. After our discussion, Dan agreed that it was a good proposal and he would support it. When I presented my proposal to the management team later, I received push back from the manufacturing executive about the proposal's feasibility. After listening to my explanation, the executive asked Dan for his opinion. Sensing his manager's hesitancy, Dan backed off his support and said he had concerns as well. Needless to say, I lost my trust and respect for him on that day. I confronted him afterward and he wimped out saying he wasn't very sure about his support in the first place. From that point forward, I avoided working with him and when I had to, I proceeded very cautiously.

  Having a hidden agenda is something to avoid as well. For example, proposing something that you say will be good for the team when it will only benefit you. As the old saying goes "Fool me once, shame on you. Fool me twice, shame on me." People don't want to look foolish or feel they have been taken advantage of. If your idea benefits both you and the team, explain how that will be a win/win. If you only highlight the benefits to the team, people will either see through it or will find out later. Either way, you lose credibility and trust. You may win this time, but in the long run, you'll find it more difficult to work with people and to achieve success for yourself.

- **Give credit where credit is due**. It goes a long way when you praise or give people credit when they have earned it. It makes them feel appreciated and demonstrates your honesty and trustworthiness. When you're leading a team or as a team member, focus on the team and not on you. It is better for a team member to have others recognize him for his work. When people see their work is recognized and appreciated, they're motivated and more willing to put their energy to the task at hand. Therefore, you should make a conscious effort to pay attention and recognize opportunities to reward your colleagues for the job well done. A small gesture goes a long way. Something as simple as complimenting them and recognizing their work publically during a team meeting or sending a message to their manager will do wonders to earning their trust.

When I was working on data analytics, I received a request from a Senior Vice President to develop an IT tool for him to be able to access any key business metric he wanted. I solicited a couple of strong IT experts to help me with the project. When we presented the tool to him, he was impressed. He knew me but not the two IT specialists. At the end of the meeting, I thanked the team for going above and beyond to help me. When I told the Senior VP that they were the architects responsible for the development of the tool, they were very pleased with the recognition, especially from a high level senior executive. I earned their trust and felt confident they would be willing to help me again in the future. Even though I did not publically give myself credit, the Senior VP later told me he appreciated my leadership in recruiting the right people and getting it done quickly and successfully. In this project, I also earned the executive's trust by delivering on my commitment.

- **Maintain your professionalism**. At all times, especially when under pressure, maintain your professionalism. This means you should stay calm, poise, focus on the business issues at hand and not get personal. This is particularly important when you're leading a team or working on a team. During a project, inevitably the team will run into unexpected problems that may cause people to react emotionally. When we are emotional, we tend to get personal instead of focusing on the task at hand, show our tendency to be condescending, sarcastic and to blame other people. If you feel you are getting too emotional, excuse yourself and take a break to calm down. Or if you see others behaving this way, call for a break.

I saw firsthand an episode in a meeting my former manager attended with his boss and his peers. As he got heated, he made some out of character insulting comments about another VP, even suggesting that this VP should be fired. Well, it didn't go over well with the people in the meeting and a few weeks later, he was fired. Although the reason given for the firing was "organizational change," my boss and I knew full well that that was not the reason for his firing.

- **Listen**. While I don't have any direct evidence to show the connection between listening skills and trust, I believe that if you are a good listener, people are more likely to trust you. This is because people feel you have taken the time to listen to them, to seek to understand and are empathetic to their situation. When we fully listen to people, we develop and nurture a safe environment where they can open up and be themselves without fear of judgement. If we honor their confiding in us and keep it confidential, we will earn their trust even more. Take the time and make an effort to listen by asking questions so you can truly hear them. In addition, before you give feedback, seek to understand fully and accurately so you can give specific feedback. And when you do give feedback, focus on giving constructive feedback instead of criticism. Refer to the "How to be give and receive feedback constructively" chapter for suggestions.

- **Striving to achieve team goal**. If you're leading a team, focus relentlessly on having your team achieve the common goals and persuading them that the team's success defines their success. If the team fails to meet the team goals, everyone fails. There is no room for anyone to feel they can deflect the blame for the team's failure by pointing fingers at other people. When your team sees that you don't have a personal agenda and you drive them to work together to deliver results, they will likely follow your lead. Even if you are a team member and not a leader, you can still play a significant role in helping your leader focus the team on achieving the team goals.

- **Good team player**. If you act and present yourself as a team player willing go out of your way to help team members get their work done, people are more likely to trust you. However, make sure you can complete your work before committing to help. Completing your work is your first priority. It's better not to commit than commit and not deliver. Knowing how to work efficiently will enable you to have time to assist your team. Being a good team player also means recognizing the team's weaknesses, bringing them to attention and finding ways to address them. The team is only as successful as the weakest link in the chain. By proactively addressing the weak spots – whether it's a specific area of the project or someone not delivering quality work, you help the team achieve the best results possible.

- **Seek first to understand**. If your colleague is delivering subpar work and that's hurting the team, seek to understand first and not jump to conclusions. Resist the urge to assume that he's a bad team player who's not fit to be on the team, especially if he has a good track record. There could be many reasons for this situation, such as personal or family issues, or too much work responsibilities that are spreading him too thin. Seek this person out to discover why he's not delivering his best work by listening and asking questions. Chances are he would be open with you if he knows you sincerely want to help. Once you find out the root causes, then you can explore possible solutions.

When I interviewed my former colleagues for this book, I heard an example from a person I worked closely with for several years. Mary said during a big project she was working on, there was a team member who was delivering mediocre work results. There were several unhappy team members who were afraid this would reflect negatively on them. Mary came to this person and expressed her desire to understand what was going on and to help. She came to learn that the team member did not know how to say no to his boss, and as a result, kept getting work added to his plate. He was spread too thin, felt overwhelmed and did just enough to stay above water. Mary helped him approach his manager to explain his situation. Together they helped the manager understand the risks and consequences to the team of not delivering on his commitment due to the heavy workload. The manager understood and removed some of the lower priority tasks. As a result, he was able to get back on track. He thanked Mary and from that point on, he was more open to confide in her and seek help before it was too late.

- **Socializing**. Get to know your colleagues. We spend so much time trying to get work done that we have little time for socializing, to get to know another side of the people we work with. I was guilty of this early in my career. I didn't spend enough time to build personal connections with my peers. Developing and maintaining relationships with my peers sooner would have helped me work with them and get things done more effectively.

Although time is valuable and we never seem to have enough time to finish our work, make it a priority to get to know your colleagues. Start by showing your genuine care for them as colleagues and as people. Learn about their interests and hobbies outside of work. If both they and you enjoy biking for example, invite them for a ride together from time to time. Make an effort to eat lunch with them instead of having it at your desk. Instead of taking a walk by yourself during a break, ask a co-worker to walk with you. And once in a while, organize a group happy hours after work where everyone can enjoy an hour or so of one another's company. This worthwhile time investment will enable people to feel closer and have more trust in you, and help you to work even better with them and get things done more effectively.

Chapter 14

How To Get People To Listen

A question I frequently get from my students, employees and co-workers is "How do I get people to listen to me?" Particularly in meetings, people have things to say and they get impatient when other people talk too much. They in turn, may react by interrupting and speaking louder, resulting in a lot of people talking over each other and nobody really listens. Moreover, when in a large group meeting, we feel hesitant to speak up for fear of saying "dumb" things and embarrassing ourselves. We keep quiet but wishing we could speak up and get people to pay attention. I'll cover in this chapter the qualities needed and best ways to get people to listen to you, especially in a group meeting setting.

Here are the qualities needed to get people's attention.

- **Build credibility with people you work with**. This doesn't happen on day one. This is something we earn over time. Credibility is earned by meeting your commitment, delivering results on time and being dependable to help out when needed. In addition, if you could develop a specific standout skill or an expertise in an area and use it to help people, you will go a long way to build credibility.
- **Earn trust by treating people with respect.** By being a good team player showing genuine care for your co-workers, they will tend to give you the benefit of the doubt because they believe you are honest and put the interest of the team ahead of your own. Respect what people say and genuinely seek to understand instead of being condescending. People in turn will reciprocate their respect to you. When you speak up, people will listen, take your words at face value and not have to wonder if you have any hidden agenda.
- **Being a good listener**. This is a key part of communication skill. When we listen to people carefully, we understand their issues better which will help us respond more appropriately. Moreover, it will encourage them to be more open to what you say. A good

communicator is also an excellent listener. If you are new to the meeting and don't know people there, asking questions and listening to them is a good way to establish rapport.

How To Get People's Attention In Meetings

I'll focus on a group meeting setting for this discussion.

- **Understand the context of the meeting**. Is it a meeting where you're there to receive information, review project's progress, solve a problem or reach a recommendation for management? Knowing the context of the meeting will help you prepare appropriately and identify ways you can contribute. If it's an informational meeting, you can participate by asking for clarification, praising the value of the information received and suggesting additional information needed. If it's a project status meeting, be prepared to review your own work progress, answer questions people may have as well as discuss your team members' work. If it's a meeting to address and solve a problem, you can play a mediator role to keep people on track, focus on the issue at hand and to offer potential ideas for people to consider.

- **Listen and pay attention to people's comments**. Before you speak, focus on listening to what people are saying. Is it clear to you? If not, ask them to clarify. Something like: "Could you clarify that for me. I just want to make sure I understand your points clearly." And if you want to respond or add to their comment, say: "What you're saying about XYZ is really helpful, and I would like to add to that."

- **Build rapport**. Ask for clarifications or rephrase their comment to avoid misunderstanding. This is a good way to connect with people and to show you are interested and engaged in their work. This will also help people feel more comfortable engaging with you. If you are new to the project and might feel hesitant to ask "dumb" questions, you can preface your question by saying: "I'm new to this and sorry if this is redundant, but I was wondering if you could elaborate on that point for me."

- **Seek opportunities to offer comments**. Once you know the purpose of the meeting and have prepared yourself, look for opportunities to chime in. Keep in mind that having well thought out comments will gain credibility and give you the confidence to speak up. As you listen to someone in the meeting and decide you want to respond, wait until that person finishes his thought. Acknowledging his point and offer your own comments. For example: "That's a really good point, John. I would also like to add to that……" or if you're having a hard time to chime in, raise your hand clearly for people to see and firmly state: "I'm hearing a lot of good points and I also have a couple of comments I would like to share with you." Then proceed with your comments.

- **Know when to interject**. If you are in a contentious meeting where people are speaking over one another, it's fruitless for you to interject with your comments. At some point, the meeting facilitator should step in and take control of the meeting. Then you can take advantage of this opportunity to raise your hand and say: "I have a comment I would like to add." Then proceed with your comment. If the facilitator is not taking control of the meeting, wait for a good time to interrupt with a friendly but firm voice: "We're not making progress here when everyone is speaking at once. Let's have one person speaking at a time." Then gesture to the meeting facilitator to resume running the meeting. Simple gestures like these show your assertiveness and also demonstrate your leadership quality.

- **Express your disagreement professionally**. Base your comments on the issue and not the person by focusing on what they do and not who they are. For example: "I believe your plan is missing some key details" as oppose to "You make no sense." Acknowledge their points before you express your opinions. For example: "I understand and appreciate your points and perspective, but I see the issue differently. Here's why …." When you're finished, you can ask for feedback: "Is it clear what I said? Any questions or anything you want me to elaborate on?"

- **Remember to speak up**. It's to your benefit to speak up in the meeting. If you don't, nobody knows who you are and what value you add. If you don't think you have any valid points to add, ask someone to elaborate on their points. At least this will allow people to see you, hear you and it helps you feel more comfortable speaking up later. Make a habit of speaking in a meeting at least twice, especially when you're in a meeting with your boss or company executives. This is your opportunity to be recognized, get visibility and to make a good impression with the management team. Thinking ahead of time about potential comments and insight that would be good to bring up in the meeting will make it easier for you to speak up.

- **Don't take people's criticism or negative comments personally**. Ask for clarification or specific details. Even when someone gets personal with you and makes condescending remarks, resist the urge to lash back. Put the ball back in that person's court by making them focus on the topic and the facts. For example, if Ted comments: "You don't make any sense with your analysis," you should reply with: "Ted, can you give me the specifics on the part of my analysis that didn't make sense to you." This puts the onus on Ted to give examples or risk looking bad with his colleagues.

- **Can you hear me?** When speaking, make sure you speak in a clear and loud enough voice for everyone to hear. In addition, look at the people you are talking to. This shows you are engaging actively and expressing your views confidently. Try to minimize the word fillers such as "um," "ah" and "and." They can make you appear timid and lacking conviction in your comments. If you have this habit, practice it in a safe environment with friendly people you're comfortable with. If you are nervous, take deep breaths. With practice and repetitions, you will be more comfortable speaking up.

Chapter 15

How To Give And Receive Feedback

Giving and receiving feedback is a regular practice in most if not all companies. Formal feedback takes place at annual or semi-annual employee performance reviews. This is when your manager solicits feedback from people you worked with throughout the year - your team members, co-workers, project managers, managers as well as people outside the company. Their feedback plays a significant role in how you will be evaluated. Delivering good results is only one part of your evaluation. How you work with other people is just as important.

As a manager, I was often puzzled when someone on my team expressed surprise at the feedback from their peers. If you have an open communication channel with people in the company and you pay attention to your working relationship with them, you shouldn't be surprised at the feedback you receive. Moreover, it shouldn't be that the first time you hear feedback is at your formal performance review. You should be asking for feedback from the people you work with and from your manager on a regular basis; this helps you address any issues that may exist, gives you a chance to clarify and take corrective actions when things are still fresh on both of your minds. In addition, if you are able to resolve these issues timely, chances are these issues will not reflect negatively on you when your peers give their feedback for your formal performance review. Better yet, they will more likely appreciate your proactive effort to reach out and improve your working relationships with them.

Moreover, other managers will ask you to give feedback on their employees who have worked with you over the past year. Well before the employee evaluation meeting, I would ask for feedback on each of my employees from people who have worked with them. Knowing how to receive and give feedback is an important skill and an important part of your communication skill. The good news is this skill is not difficult to learn. In this chapter, I'll share the best ways you can use to receive and give feedback, and have this skill as another tool in your toolbox.

Giving and receiving feedback is important because it:
- Helps your team members to be better at their job. We all want to improve our job performance and any help we can get to help us achieve this would be welcomed.
- A good practice to build and maintain relationships if giving and receiving feedback is done the right way.
- Effective way to ensure you and others are on the same page. Any conflicts are brought up and addressed timely.
- An excellent way to recognize someone for their good work as well as an opportunity to influence and persuade them.
- A great practice for you to continue to develop your interpersonal and communication skill.

Feedback Is Not Criticism
Many of us view feedback as unpleasant and associate it with criticism. However, it should be seen as a positive communication vehicle. Simply put, feedback is not criticism. Criticism is being negative, comes across as judgmental and even personal. Moreover, it tends to put the person on the receiving end on the defensive and as a result, prohibits productive discussion. Feedback, on the other hand, is positive communication with good intentions. It's constructive and collaborative. It's intended to recognize others for their good work and help them improve their performance.

How To Give Feedback Successfully
Follow these steps to help you prepare and give feedback constructively.
- **Think about what you want to give feedback on**. What were the specific issues that triggered your desire to give feedback? Is there anything you need to clarify? Do you need to check with anyone else to validate the issues? The more specific the issues, the more effective you will be able to give feedback.
- **Pick an appropriate place and time to meet.** When you want to give feedback, it's best to have this conversation between the two of you and out of other people's ears. This promotes an open environment for dialog, especially if you don't know how sensitive the other person will be. You want to avoid any risk of embarrassing

them in front of other people, even if that was not at all your intention. In addition, be aware of their mood and state of mind before you start. If they seem under a lot of stress, unhappy or on a tight work deadline, wait for another time. If you're not sure, check if this is a good time to talk: "Kelly, is this a good time to talk? I was wondering if I could have a few minutes to share some feedback with you."

- **Prepare the message**. The message should be constructive, not critical. Stay on the issue, on what that person did and not who they are. Bring specific examples to clarify your points. For example: "Tom, I've been thinking about your recent report on the team project. The report made some really good points. I also have some ideas and feedback to help make the report even stronger. Would it be okay for us to discuss them?" This focuses on the report Tom wrote and nothing about him personally. Of course, any smart person would accept your invitation to offer ideas and feedback. Contrast that comment with: "Tom, I don't know what you were thinking when you wrote that report. It makes no sense. You have a lot of work to do to fix it. I have some ideas." This is derogatory and insulting since it implies Tom is "stupid." Starting with this comment will not likely result in a good, productive discussion.

- **Listen.** A key part of giving feedback is listening to the other person. Allow them time to reflect on your feedback and to respond. Ask them if what you said was clear or if they need you to clarify. Listen carefully to their response. Don't get defensive if they're not taking what you said seriously. Don't get rattled if they're taking it personally and reacting emotionally. Try to understand their reaction. Ask: "I'm sorry you seem upset. Was there something specific about my feedback that made you feel this way?" Then listen. Affirm with them that your only objective is to be constructive and to help. Before you end the discussion, ask them for their opinions on the way you gave feedback and how you can give feedback better next time.

- This skill will prepare you if and when you become a manager. One of the responsibilities managers have is to coach their employees, which involves giving feedback. Your employees will want and expect to get feedback from you on a regular basis.

How To Receive Feedback
In addition to willingly sit down with your co-workers to receive their feedback, it's even better to proactively seek them out. This shows you are

taking the initiative to continue to get better. It puts people at ease knowing that you welcome and look forward to their feedback. By asking them, you let them know you give them the green light to be frank, you value their feedback and you want to build a good working relationship with them. Here are some of the best practices for you.

- **Listen**. If you initiate the conversation, let them know at the beginning of the meeting that you appreciate their time and you value their feedback. You especially look forward to receiving constructive and productive feedback to help you improve. Also be specific about what issue you are asking for feedback on. Is it about a recent presentation you delivered or an analysis you recently completed? Is it about your participation or interaction with the team members of the project? Is it about how you handled a recent conflict?

  Whether you asked for or agreed to receive feedback, the first and foremost important thing is to listen. Listen carefully to what they say. Try not to get defensive. Repeat their comment to make sure you understood. For example: "What I hear you say is that my presentation was good but was missing supporting data. Did I hear you correctly?" Or ask them to clarify if you are unclear about their comment: "I just want to make sure I understand what you said. Can you elaborate your comments for me?" Make a note of the feedback so you can reflect on it at a later time. This is especially useful for critical feedback because we may get defensive when we first hear the feedback and not consider it objectively.

  If you feel they are being personal and criticizing you, again, stay calm and try not to take it personally. Instead, ask them for specific examples. This will confirm if they are being constructive or just wanting to give you a hard time. For example: "How is what you just said related to what I did, can you help me understand?" or "Julie, I'm not sure I understood clearly. Could you give me a specific example of what I did?" If Julie is still vague and making general comments, suggest that she comes back with some examples: "Julie, it would help me if you could think of a specific example. We can get together later when you're ready." Now the ball is in her court.
- **What to do with the feedback you received**. First of all, with an open mind, reflect and consider the feedback. Was it constructive? Was it valid in your mind? Was it specific enough? Did you agree with it? Was it something you can act on? If there are other people involved and have knowledge of the situation, you can also validate

with them. You don't need to reveal the identity of the person giving you the feedback. You can mention that you recently received some feedback and wanted to validate with them. For example: "John, I received some feedback on my presentation in our meeting a couple of days ago and I would love to run it by you to get your thoughts. I want to make my presentation better and your feedback would be great. Would that be okay?" Then describe the feedback and listen for his response.

Next, decide what you would like to do with the feedback. Do you think it was valid and want to make corrections or implement their suggestions? Or do you decide to do nothing because the feedback did not have validity? If you decide to take actions based on their feedback, take an opportunity to get back to that person and let them know. They would appreciate your taking their feedback seriously.

- **Make it a habit to seek regular feedback as appropriate**. Your manager is an excellent person to give you feedback. Seek opportunities after a key project is completed, when a key milestone is achieved or after your presentation that your manager attended. If your report will be viewed by important stakeholders, ask your manager to review it first. If you seek feedback regularly and take positive actions, you increase your chance of getting a good performance review because you will be able to demonstrate your effectiveness and success in working with people. Moreover, you less likely will be caught blindsided during your performance review.

Chapter 16

How To Handle Conflicts And Difficult Situations

As a new engineering graduate who recently joined an aerospace company, I encountered a volatile situation at work during my very first project. Each of the software engineers on the team, which was tasked with delivering a test program for a fighter aircraft, owned a specific software module of the overall program. In order for the program to work properly, all the modules had to integrate seamlessly and work flawlessly together. When I and another senior programmer - Jim, who had been working at this company for several years, tried to integrate our respective modules, they failed to work. This was a bit of a disaster since other team members couldn't move forward without our successful integration. When this failure occurred, Jim's face started to get red and formed an angry expression and he began yelling at me, blaming the failure on me and saying my program was a piece of "crap" (he used a more colorful word). Throughout your career, you will face difficult situations –work conflicts, unexpected events or surprises that will test your ability to stay calm, keep poise under pressure and think on your feet. These situations could arise from any number of circumstances - dealings with co-workers, company management to external parties, including customers, partners and suppliers.

While it is impossible to anticipate and prepare for every situation, there is a basic approach you can apply to any situation. In this chapter, I'll discuss the general best practices and behavior we should utilize when facing a challenging situation. In addition, I'll cover some specific scenarios, their unique differences and the best ways to handle them.

Common Approach

Whether you face a conflict with a co-worker, your boss or a customer, there is a set of principle practices to follow:

- **Keep your professionalism**. Stay calm and resist the temptation to give in to your emotions. If someone is yelling at you or making demeaning remarks, it's easy to return the favor and lash out at them. If you do that, the two of you will appear to other people like unprofessional people behaving immaturely. In Eckhart Tolle's book "The Power of Now," he talked about handling your emotion and how to control your urge to lash out (Tolle, 1992). While it may make you feel good temporarily when you lash out and say something you may regret later, it may damage your chances in the long run to have good working relationships. The first step is to acknowledge the emotions you're feeling, such as anger. Just acknowledging your feelings will help you calm down and reduce your urge to strike back. Also keep in mind that when you let your emotions dictate your action, you are giving your "power" to the other person. Ask yourself if the other person is that powerful for you to lose your control and give him the power over your reaction. The answer is most likely no. When you feel increasingly upset, acknowledge your emotions and take a break. Avoid an unnecessary emotional confrontation by walking away, even for just a few minutes. Similarly, when you are in a tense situation and feeling a lot of pressure, don't deny it. You have heard of the expression "poise under pressure" – it's the ability to stay calm and think rationally. You can do this by acknowledging your feeling at the moment – tense, pressure, scared, etc. Then take deep breaths to calm yourself down and maintain your professionalism by not blaming others, looking for excuses or behaving immaturely. If you're not familiar with this kind of self-control practice, continue to patiently work on it, and over time you will gain more emotional discipline.
- **Focus on listening**. When faced with a conflict, we have a tendency to jump to conclusions and solutions right away without understanding first. Lack of communication or miscommunication often is the root of a conflict. When people are talking over each other instead of stepping back and listening to what the other person is saying, confusion and misunderstanding can happen as a result. Then as things escalate, they become more personal, emotional and before they know it, things have blown up into a real conflict. Sometimes what we thought we heard is not what the other person meant. To avoid this, ask: "what I hear you say is ABC…. did I hear correctly?" or "Can you give me an example…?" When you ask for clarification, you put the onus on that person to explain. Moreover, when people see that you're listening, they feel assured they're being

heard, and this helps create a good communication channel which encourages them to be open minded to your views.

- **Be prepared as best you can**. In any conflict or difficult situation, the more details we know about the situation, the better we are at keeping an open mind and being able to use our creativity to come up with the best solution possible. Some of the situational details include the nature of the conflict, possible causes, people involved, any impact on them and external factors that come into play. With the knowledge and information we have, we are in a better position to help get everyone on the same page and work to come up with the best solution. Spend time upfront to really understand the issue by talking and listening to the key stakeholders.

- **Use a logical problem solving approach**. The first step in solving any problem is to define clearly what the problem is. It's not uncommon to see some people on the team trying to solve a problem while others have a different understanding of what the problem is that they're trying to solve. It's important to make sure everyone have the same understanding. This misunderstanding happens often in business negotiations where one party is working on one issue while the other party is focusing on a different one. Secondly, once the problem is understood, find out possible causes of the problem. The third step is work with key stakeholders to brainstorm possible solutions and weigh the pros and cons of the different options. And finally, choose the best option among the ones considered.

How To Deal With Difficult Situations

Now, let's look at several different scenarios and discuss them in more detail using the suggested approach above.

1. **Difficult customer.** A customer is unhappy because your company didn't meet its commitment and may make life difficult for you when you meet them. It may be obvious but needs to be repeated that it's especially important to be professional and use your listening skills in this situation. Let the customer vent; listen and make sure you understand their issues. Moreover, when you interact with them, remember you're representing your company and not just the department you work in. Avoid blaming others in the company or being defensive that the customer is taking it out on you when it's not your fault. The customer doesn't care about your company problems and since you represent the company, you need to answer to the customer. Moreover, you need to be clear on the resolution or

the next steps before you leave the meeting and make sure you follow up accordingly.

Let me repeat a story I told in the "How to communicate and present to different audiences" chapter. I once took a customer visit trip with the purpose of getting their input on a future printer technology. Per my request, the account Sales Representative (SR) set up the meeting for me. When a co-worker and I arrived and met a couple of executives from the customer's company, they proceeded to lay into us about issues they had with their computer systems and their dissatisfaction with our company. We could sense their frustration and anger as the volume of their voices got louder. We were caught completely by surprise since we had no prior warnings from the SR. To make the situation worse, he wasn't there to handle these issues with the customer and since we were from the printer business unit, we were in the dark about their computer system issues. There was only one thing we could do - we sat down and listened patiently to the customer. We asked questions to make sure we captured their problems accurately. When the customers were done venting and giving us a list of items they wanted answers on, we calmly thanked them for their feedback. We told them that although we were not involved in these issues, we will make sure that the right people from the company work on their request and get back to them quickly.

After this resolution, the customers felt their concerns were heard and were satisfied with the next steps. They calmed down, listened and discussed our company printing technology and even spent an extra hour with us on this topic. I also learned a good lesson from this visit - I should have talked with the SR to understand more about the customers and any potential issues I needed to be aware and to address before I met them.

2. **Work conflict/difficult situation with co-workers**. One typical scenario here is you and other people are working on a project in which everyone's work is an important part of the overall project and if one person delivers subpar work, the whole project would be negatively impacted. You discover a co-worker's deliverables are not up to the team's standard. You want to let him know but you also know he has a big ego, is sensitive to criticism and does not have to answer to you. What do you do?

We'll apply the approach we discussed at beginning of this chapter to this scenario. In this situation, focus on the business issue at hand. The key here is trying to understand, giving constructive feedback and emphasizing his ownership of the team's goals.

Approach the person to confirm or clarify his understanding of the team's goals to make sure that you and he are on the same page. If he doesn't have the same understanding of the team goals, that could indicate the root cause of the problem. The team project's goals should be clearly written and communicated to everyone on the team. Go over these goals with him if you need to. Before discussing his specific work, ask for his feedback on the status of the team project and suggestions for improvement. Then tell him you have some constructive feedback and suggestions for his work. The key word here is "constructive" feedback, not negative criticism. Again, focus your feedback on his work and not him as a person. Give specific examples. For example: "the ROI analysis was missing key assumptions to validate the results" as opposed to "You completely missed the boat on the ROI analysis." Emphasize to him that everyone's work is critical to the overall project and if someone doesn't deliver their best work, the whole team suffers. Then offer your help and close the meeting with the timeline for him to review his work with the team again. If your message doesn't get through, suggest to him that the team may need to ask management for help to make sure they deliver the best results possible.

Let's take another real life example of a story I heard from a friend and former colleague. Henry worked as software (SW) Test Engineer on an engineering team. The team was on the hook to deliver and launch a new application on schedule. When going through the testing, Henry discovered the program was buggy and had logic errors. One of the SW programmers he needed cooperation from was very protective of his work and sensitive to criticism. Tom, a senior SW engineer, had been with the company for several years and believed there was nothing wrong with his work. He didn't want to cooperate and would get offended if the test team approached him about his software code. The test team thought it was possible the issue could be his code but not sure. How would you handle this situation? Would you take him to the woodshed and read him the riot act? Or do you escalate this to management immediately and force him to cooperate.

I asked Henry how he handled this situation. He said he approached this with an open mind without assuming that the issue was Tom's code. He dealt with this difficult situation professionally and focused only on the business issue. He approached Tom to explain that the overall program was not working and it was critical to find out the root causes so the problem could be fixed. Henry then asked him for his thoughts on the possible causes and how to go about diagnosing the software bugs. This assuaged Tom from getting defensive or feeling he was being blamed. At the same time, Henry put the onus on him to get involved. Tom's demeanor changed and he suggested a couple of good ideas to go about discovering the bugs, including comprehensive integration testing of everyone's code. Henry then confirmed with Tom that the testing would include his code as well. The lesson here is by focusing on the business problem and having Tom involved in helping find the solution, Henry was successful in addressing this sensitive issue with him.

Let's assume despite all the effort from Henry, Tom remained stubborn and uncooperative. I would suggest the next step is to escalate to management for help to resolve the issue. Henry should also let Tom know he would bring this situation to management. At least Tom would be in no position to complain since Henry is not going behind his back and he knows Henry had tried his best reaching out to him.

Regarding my situation where my co-worker Jim was blaming me and throwing me under the bus, it was just as easy for me to point fingers back at him and get into a pissing contest. However, I chose to maintain my cool and waited until he had yelled enough. Then I calmly told him that the yelling was unprofessional and wasn't going to solve the problem. I then told him we needed to find the root causes so we can fix them. And if it turned out it was my work, then I would be happy to acknowledge my error and fix it. He was taken somewhat aback that I didn't lash back at him and he seemed a bit embarrassed. After working together for the next couple of days, we were able to diagnose the problem, fix it and move the project forward. The next day, he apologized to me for his outburst. After that incident, Jim was more aware of his behavior and controlled his emotions better, at least with me. We continued to have a good professional working relationship. By not reacting badly back at him, I gave him an out and that enabled us to continue our working relationship. I was in control of the situation.

3. **Conflict or difficult situation with your boss**. A conflict arises when your boss assigns you additional work when you are completely swamped. You might feel upset that your boss doesn't appreciate you have too much work already. You may feel you're being taken advantage of and your boss doesn't care he's driving you too hard. You don't want to take on this new assignment. How would you handle this?

    Treat this as a negotiation session on how to say no. Refer to the "How to say no smartly" chapter for suggestions. The key again is to focus on the business issue and not get personal or emotional. Don't assume your boss knows how much work you have on your plate. Give him the benefit of the doubt. He is likely busy and not always able to keep tabs on your workload. The way to approach this is to give your boss visibility of your workload and have him prioritize for you. This gets him involved in solving this issue with you.

    First, explain all the tasks you have on your plate, the effort and time they require and be clear with him that it is not possible for you to take on more. However, you would be happy to take this work on if you can drop something else off your plate. Next, ask him to prioritize how important his request is relative to your current tasks. This forces him to evaluate carefully. If he prioritizes his request higher than your other assignments, then it would be reasonable to delay or drop the less important priorities. You need to be firm on this – if you take it on, something has to go. Or if he sees that his request isn't important enough, he can assign it to someone else who may not have as much going on. Either way, it is a win/win situation for you and your boss.

4. **Pressure situation with executives**. There will be times in meetings when management may grill you with tough questions or challenge your work. Normally, they're not doing this to be mean. Rather, they want to test if you have done your homework, thought things through and could back it up. How well you prepared for meetings like this will determine how you will perform. If you are prepared you will come to the meeting with confidence and that will carry you through. Refer to the "How to communicate and present to specific audiences" and "How to organize and develop presentation content" chapters to help you prepare and conduct yourself in the meeting.

To prepare answering questions from executives, put yourself in their shoes and ask what tough questions you would ask yourself. Since you know the content of your material, think about where you are vulnerable and where the potential holes or weaknesses are. Ask yourself tough questions about those areas and figure out how you would answer them. Executives tend to see the big picture and ask open ended questions such as: "Where do you see the risks of your project?", "What if things don't go as planned?"," What is your contingency plan?", "What are your key assumptions?", "What key stakeholders have you talked to?" and "What are the key requirements to achieve success?" Some executives are number centric and would focus on your analysis to test for discrepancies. While you can't anticipate every question, preparing yourself with these questions and answers will give you the confidence and the ability to think on your feet when you get a question you had not thought of.

If you get questions from the executives, don't appear ruffled, even if you feel tense and nervous. Remind yourself that you have done your best to prepare and to project confidence. Appearing timid or unsure about your recommendation will not instill confidence in the executives. Even if you're coming to the meeting not fully prepared and hoping the management team will give you a pass, you need to do your best to maintain your poise. Here are some ways to handle yourself professionally in this type of situation.

o If you get a question you don't know the answer off hand but can get the answer later, "Good question. I don't have the answer off the top of my head but I can find out and get back to you after this meeting" is a perfectly fine answer.

o If you are asked to give an opinion but you want to think about it before answering, you can buy some time. For example: "Great question. I'd like to give that some thought. Can I think about it a little bit and get back to you?" While the meeting is going on, you can think about that question in the back of your mind and get back to the questioner later in the meeting when ready. This is a good and professional way to handle this type of question.

o If an executive expresses doubt about your analysis or recommendation, don't get defensive. Focus on the business issue. Ask for clarification from the executive, such as: "Can you help me understand the specific area of your concern?" or "What I heard is that you're not sure about my conclusion on ABC because I didn't show enough data to support it, is that right?"

When you get the clarification, you will more likely be able to respond better. Don't get flustered when they push you. Sometimes they want to see how strong your conviction is on the recommendation. If you did not have enough data or analysis to support your argument, acknowledge their question and propose to come back with more analysis. For example: "Thank you for the question. Let me look into this further and get back to you with a more detailed analysis."

o   If an executive starts to drill down on your data and rat hole on the numbers, try not to get dragged down this path. It's a no win situation and distracts everyone from the meeting's objective. Instead of focusing on the results, focus on your assumptions. For example, you may say: "Since the outcomes of the analysis are the results of the assumptions, let me show you my assumptions to get your thoughts and we can debate on the validity of these assumptions." Then proceed with your assumptions. By definition, assumptions are your educated guesses on the future or on the unknown, so they are not right or wrong at the moment. Therefore, the assumptions are open for debate and you can modify your analysis if the assumptions change. By handling things this way, you're being mature, professional and show you are open to people's opinions. If some assumptions need to be modified, thank the executives and say you will look at the analysis again based on the new assumption changes. In this process, you have gotten the executives to get involved and take some ownership of your work.

5.   **How to handle surprises in real time**. Last minute surprises are toughest to handle. One of my former companies hosts an annual customer event in New York where the company invites a couple hundred customers - executives from Fortune 1000 companies to come for updates on the company's future plan and strategy. We usually offer simultaneous sessions for the guests to choose which ones to attend. At this event one year, our server business unit was allocated a big portion of the agenda to present to customers and we planned to have three speakers for this talk – two co-workers and me. On the morning of the presentation, the two co-workers were nowhere to be found. Moreover, the presentation materials the team worked on were on their laptops. We received no answer calling their hotel rooms or cell phones. Then we received a fifteen minute heads up and my manager was now in full panic mode. We asked

another business unit to present in our time slot but they weren't ready either.

Out of desperation, I told a Sales Account Manager I had worked with about our predicament and asked her if she had any idea. She thought for a couple of minutes and then suggested I could buy some time by opening the session and inviting the customers to give feedback on any topics they want. And it would be a great opportunity for the company top executives to hear their feedback directly. That was as good of an idea as any and I informed my boss of the plan. To my pleasant surprise, the feedback discussion went on for over an hour and was so successful I had a difficult time stopping the customer discussion so we could proceed with our presentation. The two missing speakers finally made it there after thirty minutes into the session. Afterward, many of the customers thanked my boss and even suggested that every future session should allocate time for customer feedback. We heaved a sigh of relief because of how close we cut it.

The lesson learned here is to think of possible unexpected events and to prepare for them as best you can. And if it does happen, stay calm and keep your poise in order to think creatively and engage the right people for help.

Chapter 17

How To Deal With Difficult Co-workers

While we all want a friendly and productive work environment, there are people of all types and personalities, and the difficult ones can make things uncomfortable and not fun for other workers. For the most part, we cannot control people or choose whom to work with. However, if we know how to handle these "difficult" workers, it reduces the frustration and more importantly, allows us to get our work done while keeping the work environment as friendly and enjoyable as possible. In this chapter, I'll cover effective ways to manage and deal with difficult co-workers.

1. **Party pooper**. This person is Mr. No. He presents an impediment to what you want to do. He doesn't like anything he sees and shoots down your work. He looks for what can go wrong with your plan and potential negative outcomes. While it can be useful to have a set of critical eyes examining your idea, he only sees failure, and does not offer constructive feedback or useful suggestions. His main message is that your plan has no chance to succeed. His comments can be condescending; for example: "You did not think this through."

   o   With this type of person, you need to stand up to him. However, stay calm and keep it professional by focusing on the issue. The best way to respond is to put the ball in his court and force him to respond to the topic at hand instead of just shooting down your plan. For example: "Give me specific examples of my plan that you don't think are good," and wait to hear from him. If he's being vague, repeat your question again with: "I can't improve on my plan unless I can get specific examples from you." If he gives you some useful examples, then thank him and follow up with: "Can you give me suggestions on how I can improve my proposal?" If he asks to get back to you later, be sure to follow up with him. If he was just shooting off his mouth, he looks foolish and loses credibility.

2. **Downer.** This person is not a happy person generally and lives by the motto "misery loves company." She is a glass half empty kind of person who looks at the negative side of things. For example, when company management is having an employee communication meeting, she tends to draw negative observations and cast suspicion on management's intention. Being around this person too much can bring you down and make the work environment less enjoyable. This type of person wants to draw you into their company and share their negative attitude.

   o Since people like to be listened to, try to listen for a little bit but don't get drawn into a conversation. You can say something like: "That's an interesting point and I didn't think of it like that, but I would rather talk about something else." Or if you feel the need to refute her, say: "I hear what you're saying, but I really didn't take it the same way." Or if you have more time, you can ask for specifics: "Give me an example of why you feel this way." Responses like these let the person know that while you want to listen and understand where they are coming from, you have a different view. Then ask to talk later since you need to get back to work.

3. **Bully**. This person uses strong arm tactics. Intimidation, thinly veiled threats, pressure and name droppings are some tactics he uses. He tells you if you don't do what he says, bad things will happen to you. Your job performance will take a hit, you will be perceived negatively by other managers or he will let important people in the company know it was your fault the work didn't get done. He tends to come across as having power, self-perceived power, over you and other people and that he's well connected in the company.

   o While it's easy to get angry and let this person get on your nerves, or worse, you feel intimidated or victimized, do your best to resist this. You may feel the urge to tell this person to "take a hike," but there are better ways to tell him to get lost. Similar to the above example, stay professional by addressing the issue at hand and nothing else. Remind yourself that he's not worth wasting your energy on. A good response technique is to pepper him with questions to force him to be explicitly clear on the what's and the why's. This way you let him know you're not intimidated and wouldn't just follow his instructions blindly. Ask him for the specifics of the task – why the need to do this, what problem he is trying to solve, what the goals are, and why this task is more important than other tasks that are being worked on. Force him to answer these tough questions. It's also important for you to understand how this request fits into the priorities that you and your manager have agreed on. Then with confidence, you can say no by explaining this doesn't fit into your priorities at the moment. However, if you think this is a big enough deal, be sure to let your manager know in case it comes back to him later. If the Bully pulls the "name dropping" card or uses threats, calmly tell him that you will be more than happy to discuss this with your manager and together will make the call on the priority. Then discuss this with your manager and let him know your thoughts.

4. **Bragger**. As the name implies, this person is a talker who is all about "me," who likes to brag about himself, puts himself in the center of attention, and has a tendency to embellish and exaggerate. He's also prone to name dropping to show his importance, but generally is harmless, although he can be quite annoying.
   o The trick here is to look beyond the braggadocio, focus on the substance and judge the value of the content yourself. Ask for facts and tangible results and don't take his words at face value. When it's not a topic related to you, just ignore him. There's no need to set him straight or make his head any bigger.

5. **Exploiter**. This person takes advantage of your generosity. Once you helped her, she'll keep coming back, knocking on your door with more requests for help. She can appear needy, making self-pity comments and is especially good at making you feel guilty if you turn her down – "If you don't help me with this, I'll get in big trouble with my boss." This person uses your generous nature against you to get you to do what she wants.
   o As much as we like to help and don't like to say no, there are times we need to say no because otherwise, we can't get our work done and it will negatively impact our own job performance. If we were able to help someone complete their task but got behind on our work or delivered less than stellar results, we only hurt ourselves and would get no credit for helping others. Remember, before we can help people, we need to take care of our job first. Refer to the "How to say no smartly" chapter on how to respond. I would suggest listening to the request, then telling her you are empathetic to her situation, but your plate is full with tight

125

deadlines and your manager wants you to focus on these priorities first. As a result, you cannot help but you may have more time later when you finish your work. Be firm with your answer.

6. **One upper**. This person has a need to be better than you, especially if you are in a similar job. No matter how good your work is, she needs to find weak spots to pick on. This trait is a little bit similar to the "Party Pooper," but this person is not just critiquing your idea but also wants to show that her work is better. You would hear comments such as: "I don't see clear benefits of your plan," "This plan is confusing," "This plan requires too much time to implement," or "It's not very useful."

Let me share with you an example. The pricing team at a previous company developed a tool that allowed the users - Product Managers (PMs), to easily and quickly run different pricing scenarios and compare the results. This tool was best for the "what if" analysis, a key part of a PM's role. Previously it would take days to run this kind of analysis, and now it would take minutes to see the results, thus saving a huge amount of time. However, it would require the PMs to invest some initial time to learn how to use the tool. When the pricing manager, Mark, explained the features of the tool to the product management team, one of the managers in the meeting, Jane, shot it down, saying: "This tool is really complex and difficult to use and is not foolproof and prone to people making mistakes." Jane then brought up her own tool she has been using and compared against the pricing team's tool. It turned out her tool was good for her own specific use but not for other PMs, whereas the pricing team's tool was designed for multiple uses by different people.

o The way to respond to this person is to seek clarity of their critique first. Avoid getting defensive. Instead, focus on the subject matter. If it turns out that their work is better or can improve yours, acknowledge and thank them. Otherwise, let others make the comparison and decide. From my example above, after asking Jane for more details, the pricing manager explained that his goal was to create a tool that meets different needs of the Product Managers, and they should use whichever tool is best for them. Then he opened up the discussion to get other people's feedback. A couple of managers thought the pricing tool was a good fit for their needs and they didn't think it was too complex. In addition, they also thought Jane's tool was too limited for their needs. They then suggested having their teams try both tools and then give an assessment after a few days. After the testing was finished, they chose the pricing team's tool. The key point here is to not be defensive in this situation and let objective stakeholders be the judge.

7. **Gossiper**. This person talks to you about other people and maybe to other people about you. He likes to start or spread rumors and engage in conspiracy theories. The gossips often are personal. He sometimes pits people against each other. Even on company issues, the Gossiper often engages in company rumors such as potential reorganizations, firings and promotions. Although the gossip can be about any number of things, most of them tend to be negative. This person doesn't seem to focus on the wok at hand but enjoys mingling with people. This not only makes you feel uncomfortable, but also distracts you from doing your work.

   o The way to deal with this person is to avoid engaging if you could. If you have no choice but to listen for a few minutes, just listen but don't participate. Don't give your opinion or ask for more details, especially when it is a personal matter about someone. Look for a break in the conversation and excuse yourself to go back to your work. If you really feel uncomfortable about the topic and don't want to hear the gossip, just be honest and say you prefer not to know because it makes you uncomfortable since you may need to work with the same people.

   If you find out from reliable sources that the Gossiper has been gossiping bad things about you to other people, one way to handle this is to confront him directly, but professionally. State that you heard from other people what he had said about you and you want to confirm if that was true. If he admits it, ask for clarifications. Regardless of the explanation or denial, you can be direct by saying that you absolutely prefer to talk directly with people who have things to say about you, that you welcome and want to hear feedback but not through second hand. Moreover, express that in the future if he has something to say to you, even negative things, you would like him to talk to you directly.

8. **Hidden dragon.** This person disappears, remains silent and doesn't get back to you on your question, message and inquiry. She does not keep you updated on her work progress that impacts you and she

doesn't share relevant information with you. For example, you send her an email message asking for a date on when she can give you the result of her work so you can do yours. One day, two days, three days go by and no answer. You resend the message and still no response. You see her in the hallway, ask her about it and she says she will get back to you. We can speculate why she is this way – maybe she is absent minded, unorganized, inconsiderate or irresponsible, but whatever the reason is, it's not important to you. The key is how to deal with this person.

o   The way to handle this person is make sure you have your question/message in writing. If she was assigned an action item that you depend on, make sure the deliverables and the due date are clear to her as well as to other people on the team. Send a confirmation message to her, copy other team members and her manager. The day before the due date, forward your previous message to her with a reminder of the action items and due date. She may find this annoying but will get the message. If she still doesn't deliver, you can escalate to her manager and you have evidence to support your escalation.

9. **Avoider**. Avoider is a master of delegating work to others, deflecting his responsibilities and not taking accountability. He's good at coming up with excuses to avoid taking on action items. He does the minimum to get by and is prone to point finger when something goes wrong.

o   Similar to the "Hidden Dragon," clear and written communication is key to dealing with this person. If you are the project lead or even just a team member, make sure that the work is assigned fairly and everyone has action items. The way to handle his attempt at avoiding work is to give him a choice: "We all have to share the work, so you can take on action item #1 or action item #2," and you move on only after this is decided. Then make sure the expected results and deadlines are clear. Summarize all the action items and send a summary message to him, copy team members and his manager.

THRIVING AT WORK

Part 4

Negotiating

Winning isn't everything, but wanting to win is.

Vince Lombardi

Chapter 18

How To Become A Good Negotiator

Negotiate, as defined in the dictionary, means to have a formal discussion with someone in order to reach an agreement. Even if we don't realize it, we negotiate frequently. We negotiate with people at work, our friends, family members and even strangers. We negotiate on all kinds of activities such as where to go eat, which movie to see, where to shop, what to buy, which work assignments to work on first, and how much salary is fair. Being good at negotiating is a valuable skill in any job and position in the company. The more responsibilities you have as you move to higher positions, the more critical your negotiation skills. Good negotiators get results, achieve win-win outcomes and build productive working relationships. You will find that successful employees and managers are very good negotiators.

What Do Negotiations Involve?
Money comes to mind when we think about negotiations, but there are many other items we negotiate over. I'll describe some common ones here.
- **Money.** This is a popular negotiation term. When we go shopping, we bargain over the price of an item. Buying a car is synonymous with negotiating. I remember being afraid of getting ripped off, and having to negotiate in order to not pay too much for my car at the dealership.
- **Terms and Conditions (T/C).** When we rent an apartment or buy a house, we need to come to an agreement with the other party over items in addition to money. One such item is called "Terms and Conditions" (T&C). If you are renting an apartment, the T&C to negotiate include the duration of the lease, number of people living in the apartment, early lease termination and alterations to the apartment. While some of these are held firm by the landlord, other items are open to negotiation.

- **Time.** I hire a general contractor to build an additional room to my house and I want the project to be completed in two months but the contractor has a much longer time frame in mind. A similar situation at work would be if you're starting on a project which your boss has a deadline in mind. As you're scoping out the project schedule, you realize you need more time. Or you would like to take vacation on a certain date and your boss is afraid that the project may not be completed. These are examples of negotiating over the time component.
- **Job assignments**. Job assignments are another item you may negotiate over. Your boss has a list of job assignments that he would like you to take on; however, you're already working on other projects and can't take on additional tasks. Or you're working on a project and the project leader is discussing with you about your deliverables. However, certain tasks on that list you don't find interesting and you would rather take on other more exciting tasks.
- **Other non-monetary items.** You can exchange one item for another, or exchange your service for something tangible or service of another person. For example, you propose to fix a friend's car and in exchange, he agrees to build you a storage cabinet. Or in negotiating a job offer, you may want to take less pay in exchange for more flexible work schedule. And if you represent a professional union, you may negotiate over health benefits.

As you can see, negotiating situations can occur in our professional life or personal life, at work or at home or practically anyplace, even online. However, for the purpose of this chapter, we'll focus on work situations. My objective here is to provide you a successful negotiation approach to any work situation.

Who Do You Negotiate With?

- **Inside the company**. This includes anyone employed by the company such as co-workers on your team, co-workers on other teams, your manager and the executives of the company. Keep in mind that if you work for a multinational company that has business offices in other countries outside the US, you need to be aware of cultural differences and language barriers when negotiating.
- **External party**. This includes customers, suppliers, service providers, competitors, industry partners, government agencies, etc.

What Is The Goal Of Negotiating? *The goal is to reach an agreement that is better for you than without an agreement!*

- **Strive for a win-win.** Contrary to what many people believe the purpose of negotiating, the goal here is not to get the best deal for you at the expense of the other party. You may wonder why this is not a good thing. After all, doesn't it demonstrate how shrewd you are in getting the most for you? And if the other person wasn't smart enough to look out for themselves, well, that's not your problem. While this may give your ego a boost, it's not a successful strategy in the long run, especially in the workplace. If the other party realizes they've been had or screwed over by you, they likely will carry a grudge and are much less likely to negotiate with you in good faith in the future. If they do, it would be under a cloud of suspicion and mistrust, which is not a good recipe for achieving a good, professional working relationship. The ideal outcome is a mutual agreement that both parties are satisfied with.

Analysis Approach for Successful Negotiations

As described in the book "Negotiating Rationally" by Max H. Bazerman and Margaret A Neale (Max H. Bazerman, 1992), here are the key steps I summarized to help you conduct your negotiation successfully.

1) **Understand the true issues and parameters of the negotiation.** While it might have been clear to all parties involved, people may get off track and forget what they were negotiating about as discussions drag on and nerves get fragile. When I was a project lead negotiating with an international company, BTP Inc., to produce a printing product for my company, I thought we were clear on the negotiation goal – to come to an agreement to design and manufacture a printing product for my company. The true negotiation issue was the price and the parameter was the volume of units. As the negotiation dragged on, got more intense and emotional, BTP's CEO went off on a tangent and accused my manager of being a bully, not interested in their proposal and just toying with him. This had nothing to do with the negotiation issues. Finally we had to take a break for both sides to cool down, and when we reconvened, we reminded both my boss and the CEO what we were there to negotiate on.

I have also seen situations where both parties started negotiating on one issue, then got sidetracked and began negotiating on something else. Labor union negotiations are perfect examples of this. Without a clear understanding of the main issue and its parameters set at the beginning of the negotiation, it would be difficult to get both parties to focus and the negotiation faces the risk of getting derailed.

2) **Assess where possible trade-offs exist**. While the parties may only talk about the factors they want to negotiate on, they may not realize there may be other variables they might want to consider trading off. In the example I cited above, the BTP's executive was focusing on the highest price he could get for the product, even though there were other possible tradeoffs that would be worthwhile to consider. For instance, by partnering with a bigger company and a well-known brand, his company could get much more marketing exposure than he could on his own. Moreover, my company could help them with their quality process to achieve higher production yields as well as connect them to a broader community of material suppliers who could provide his company the same components to build but at a lower cost. So don't get fixated on one variable in a negotiation and remember to consider all possible variables to trade off.

3) **Determine your desired outcome value AND the walkaway value**. This helps you stay disciplined and not be swayed by your emotions or the excitement of the negotiation. Of course, these values are not carved in stone, but it should take something significant for you to change them. Usually a negotiated agreement comes somewhere between your desired outcome and your walkaway value. You must be certain about your walkaway value and willing to end the negotiation with no regrets if you cannot at least achieve it. The useful question to ask yourself is: "What do I do if I don't reach an agreement?" or "Would I be better off not having an agreement if I don't achieve my walkway outcome?" If it's not better, then you need to rethink your expected outcomes. To determine your outcomes, especially the walkaway value, you need to understand your situation, your priorities and your tradeoffs. With our negotiation with BTP, the main variable was the price of the product and we had determined that our walkaway value was the break-even price where we would not lose money selling the product. Since we believed this product would help sell other products our company produced, we were willing to set the walkaway value at the breakeven price. At anything below this price, we would be better off walking away instead of having an agreement that would cause our company to lose money.

4) **Make your best estimate of the other side's walkaway value**. This can be difficult to predict and is an educated guess. If you have a good idea of the other side's walkaway value, you can try to validate your educated guess. If you find out that you are in the ball park, you are more likely to succeed in reaching a negotiated agreement. Keep in mind, however, that the other side's values may change during the negotiation, depending on what information they learn or what additional tradeoffs exist. After discussing the possible tradeoffs my company could offer to BTP, including more market visibility for their brand, better production yield and lower cost from suppliers, they seemed more flexible on their pricing stand. Sensing this, we tested their possible walkaway value and were able to make an educated guess on their price.

Strategy For Creating Mutually Beneficial Agreements

I'll discuss here how to put the Analysis Approach to practice and describe the best ways for achieving a win/win agreement.

1) **Build trust**. This is an important criterion for a win/win negotiation. When the other side trusts you, they are more willing to share information, more open to possible options and more willing to reach a mutually beneficial agreement. Spend lots of time to getting to know them. People in general love to talk about themselves and their world. Don't rush into negotiation right away. When you feel you have built a rapport, proceed with the negotiation. If you find them hesitant to talk, be patient. One good way to break the ice is to share with them some information about you. This usually enables them to be more comfortable and open up. Moreover, have these social talks outside of work where people tend to be more themselves in a more relaxed setting.

2) **Ask lots of questions**. The goal here is to find out as much as you can. Information is power. The more you know about the other side's business – their priorities, challenges, needs, weaknesses, flexibility, etc., the more you will be able to propose meaningful options for them to consider. While you probably won't get information directly from them, through the course of talking, you may be able to infer and draw insight. Through several conversations, we learned BTP Inc. was at risk of losing a major OEM (original equipment manufacturer) and that loss would cut significantly into their company's revenue stream. With this knowledge, we believed they

would be motivated to reach a deal with us and use our company as leverage with this OEM. Moreover, we learned their product profit margin had been declining due to their high component cost. All this information was valuable to us and helped us understand why they focused so much on the product price. In addition, it helped us think creatively about solutions that would help address their needs and enable our company to be profitable at the same time.

3) **Evaluate between expectations and risk preferences to create trade-offs**. All of us have different levels of tolerance for risks. If you tend to be more risk averse, you may want to take a more "sure thing" deal while compromising on other terms. On the other hand, if you're a risk taker, you may be willing to take a deal with less certainty of results but has potential for bigger returns. Knowing the other side's expectations and risk preferences will greatly help you formulate your strategy. Again, the way to formulate an educated guess of this is by talking to them and asking a lot of questions. With the BTP negotiation, we speculated that, given their company's vulnerable business situation at the time, they would be more likely to accept a "low risk" deal in exchange for a lower price and better terms for my company. Given this, we came up with a few options to offer.

4) **Make more than one offer at the same time**. This is a good practice to implement. If you offer only one option, the other side has limited options to response. They either accept or reject your offer, or they can propose another deal. By offering more than one option, you have control over the options, all of which should benefit your company and achieve a possible win-win outcome. If you offer only one option and they reject it, you have reached an impasse. If you come back with a better option, they know your interest level and they can negotiate for an even better deal. If they counter offer, they likely will counter with more favorable terms to them.

By offering multiple offers, the other side is under certain pressure to choose and less likely to reject all options and propose their own counter offer. You can even ask them to rank your options in order of preference which gives you more insight into their thinking. We offered BTP 3 options: 1) Guaranteed large number of units at a low fixed price, 2) Small initial unit volume with a higher price and then a lower price if we exceed certain volume levels, and 3) A higher fixed price with no guaranteed unit volume. Moreover, all these options included our company's additional benefits to them – more marketing exposure, better production yield and lower supply chain cost. As we suspected, they chose option #1 since it guaranteed them a revenue stream. At the same time, with a lower price, our company would be able to achieve profitability.

Common Mistakes In Negotiating

- Desire to win at any cost. Keep in mind that this is not a competition and you should keep an open mind and be flexible. I was involved in a bid against other competitors to acquire a company's product. Because this was an important product and I was competing with other competitors, I felt a strong sense to win the bidding war. As a result, the bidding price kept going higher, reaching a point of being unreasonable. In the end, one competitor apparently had an even stronger desire to win and ended up bidding a very high price to win the deal. This turned out to be an expensive purchase for their company. If my company had won the bid at that price, we would have lost money selling that product.
- Assuming your gain must come at the expense of the other party. This does not achieve a win-win agreement. In addition, it limits your creativity to find beneficial tradeoffs and explore all possible options. While it may be a short term win for you, it's not beneficial for future working relationships.
- Taking certain information at face value. Keep in mind that the information presented by the other side can be skewed. Treat the other side's information and initial offer with skepticism. Instead, take their information and do your homework to validate and verify its accuracy.
- Not thinking about the other party's perspective. A key requirement for being a good negotiator is to be able to seek information from the other side to help you better understand their situation and anticipate their offer or their response to your offer. Without having some idea of their perspective, you're operating in the dark and hoping for the best.
- Being cocky about attaining outcomes in your favor. This is a dangerous trap. Overconfidence induces complacency and inhibits thorough research and possibilities for creative solutions. Remember you are trying to get the best possible win-win outcome.

Additional Tips

- Maintain your professionalism. Don't get emotional or personal. Negotiation can get intense and contentious. There usually are a lot of egos and personal pride involved. You must be able to control your emotions, even when the other party is trying to provoke you through snarky remarks or put downs. You don't have to take it lying down but you should also try not to lash back at them. Instead, channel all your energy to the issue being discussed. Refuse to get personal and bring them back to the business issue at hand. If you are not successful getting the negotiation back on track, maybe it's time to have a time out so everyone can cool off and resume the discussion at a later time when ready.

- Understand and respect potential cultural and language differences of the other party if they are from a different country and ethnic background. Before engaging in the negotiation, take a little time to learn about their culture and how best to work with them. One of the common sense practices is to avoid using your language's jargon or slang since they may not understand and may even see that as a lack of respect.

- Document progress and status of negotiation in writing to avoid potential confusion or disagreements. At the beginning, document the negotiation issues and the parameters for both parties to make sure everyone has the same understanding. Document key milestones achieved or any changes to the negotiation issues. And if there are any disagreements, documenting them allows these to be brought up and resolved right away.

- Do your best to achieve a win/win agreement. This creates positive professional relationships and sets you up for productive future negotiations.

- Do not make promises you may not be able to keep. Don't agree to a deal if you need final approval from company management, even if you are very confident you have gotten a great deal. When I was a product manager in my early years of employment, I once agreed to purchase a large volume of a computer component for my company. I was very confident that my company would be able to sell and, better yet, it was at a great price from this supplier. I later informed my manager that I had agreed to this deal and just needed his signature on the contract the supplier would send over the next day. To my surprise, my manager was quite upset I had committed without clearing it with him. I then learned that this business division, as a business practice, does not commit to that kind of agreement since the risk can be high due to unforeseen factors the company may not have control over.

As a result, I had to go meet with the supplier's sales manager the next day and renege on my agreement. After some tense discussions and my sincere effort to explain, the sales manager reluctantly agreed to void our agreement. Technically, I wasn't legally bound to the agreement since the contract had not been signed, but my words were good enough for him. Needless to say, I was embarrassed and lost a lot of credibility with the supplier. It took a lot of effort to rebuild my credibility with the supplier again. It was a good lesson learned.

Chapter 19

How To Negotiate A Job Offer

A common question I get from graduating students is if they should negotiate when they get a job offer and if yes, how to do it. My answer is you should absolutely negotiate, especially if you have multiple offers. The best time to negotiate for the best compensation package, of which salary is a big component, is when you receive the job offer because that is when you have the most leverage. By making you an offer, the employer showed that they wanted you more than the other candidates. They would prefer to not lose you over the compensation package terms and they will more likely do what they can to get you to say yes.

While salary is the most significant variable, there are several other components to a job offer. A job offer includes salary as well as other incentives such as stock options and a sign on bonus. With respect to salary, each job position is associated with a job level and each job level has a predetermined range of salary from which the HR manager and hiring manager can decide on the salary amount to offer. The salary offered would likely be somewhere in the middle or in the lower half of the range. This leaves room for negotiation if necessary and for future salary increases for the employee. If they offer you a salary near the top end of the range, the manager has limited flexibility on how much salary raise he can give you in the future. The company also has guidelines on the flexibility of the other benefits, such as how much cash to offer for sign on bonus.

The HR manager would likely be the person you negotiate with since HR has the final approval on many of the offer terms. The HR manager consults with the hiring manager during the negotiation and makes counter offers based on the hiring manager's input. However, there may be other components that make sense for the hiring manager to negotiate with you directly. I will cover these later in this chapter.

Companies may differ on the degree of flexibility of the offer components. Some companies are firm on salary but flexible on stock options or sign on bonus. Do your best to find out where they are limited and where they have the flexibility. Here are some of the typical job offer components:

Monetary Components

The HR manager plays major role here in helping the hiring manager decide on the offer terms.

- Base salary.
- Stock options. These are shares given to you that you can exercise over a number of years at a given price. For example, 5,000 shares at $30 per share price vested over 4 years. If you sell all 5,000 shares after 4 years at $40 a share, you gain $50,000 pre-tax.
- Restricted Stock Units. These are shares given to you out right ($0 cost) vested over a number of years.
- Sign on bonus. This is a one-time cash bonus – typically 1-3 months of the base salary.
- Relocation expense. This covers your moving expenses if you have to relocate from another city or state.
- Temporary housing. This covers for a temporary period while you try to find permanent living arrangement.

Let me explain the importance of the starting salary. Typically, companies determine employee salary raises and bonuses as a percentage of the employee's base salary. For example, if your starting salary is $70,000 a year and you get a 5% raise and 10% bonus after one year, you receive a $3,500 raise and $7,000 cash bonus. On the other hand, if your starting salary is $80,000 and you get the same 5% raise and 10% bonus, you receive $4,000 raise and $8,000 cash bonus. Comparing the two scenarios, you receive $1,500 more with the higher starting salary. Assuming you stay in this job for 3 years and get the same 5% raise and 10% bonus every year, you will earn a total of $4,500 more. So if you were able to negotiate for a higher starting salary, you not only get paid more in your base salary but also more in salary raise and bonus.

One more point. Typical salary increase is small because it's based on the overall company's performance, projected budget and the entire employee population. Typically, an average salary increase is in the range of 2-5%, not very much. Because of this, negotiate for the best salary you can. With the example above, if you took the $70,000 offer when you could have negotiated for $80,000, it would take you almost three years to reach an $80,000 base salary.

Non-monetary Components

The hiring manager is likely the decision maker on these items and the person you would talk to directly.

- Work schedule flexibility. For example, how often you can work at home.
- Job responsibilities. In addition to your core job responsibilities, are there other exciting and interesting projects you can be a part of? Can you get assigned to a company-wide project where you get more exposure to other aspects of the company? Is it possible to work on a temporary project in another country, if that's what you like?
- Vacation benefits. If you move to this company after a long period of employment with another company, your vacation days may be quite a bit less compared to your vacation benefit in your last job. You can negotiate to get more vacation days than the company policy allows. However, this tends to be a "handshake" agreement between you and the hiring manager and not something that would be in writing. The downside is, if your manager leaves the company, you may lose this benefit. Also note that many companies now have the "unlimited vacation" policy. There is no set amount of vacation days for employees and approval for taking vacation is between the manager and the employees. Obviously, for these companies, vacation benefits are not a negotiating term.
- Travel flexibility and requirements. Do you want to travel more or less? If you prefer to travel less than what the job stipulates, you may be able to negotiate for less business travel or travel to business locations closer to home. Before you consider negotiating on this term, make sure you are clear on the importance of business travel in your job. If this is a critical part of the job, it may not be an option for you to negotiate.

Case Study Example: let's examine and negotiate a job offer scenario.

- You are a new college graduate and recently received an employment offer as a Business Analyst from an HR manager of Stay InTouch Inc. – a social networking company.
- The manager expressed in the offer letter that the company is very excited to have you join its family. The company's offer includes

$70,000 a year in base salary and 2,000 shares of company stock option.
- You will need to relocate to another state to join this company.
- The offer seems low to you.
- The job market is good for new college graduates this year based on credible market information. However, you don't know for sure but guess that the company has other candidates as backup in case you turn down the offer.
- You currently don't have other offers, but you had excellent interviews with two other companies and received positive feedback.
- You want to negotiate a better job offer.

How I Would Negotiate This Offer

Let's review the Analysis Approach as described in the "How to be a good negotiator" chapter
1) Understand the true issues and parameters of the negotiation.
2) Assess where possible tradeoffs exist.
3) Determine your desired outcome AND the walkaway value.
4) Make your best estimate of the other side's walkaway value.

I'll use these steps to help me with my approach:
1) Understand the true issues/parameters of the negotiation. I am negotiating the job offer as a package, not just the salary although it is a big factor. While only salary and stock options were listed in the offer, I want to think about other components that are important to me. I am currently tight on money; I would need it for my move and to find temporary living arrangement when I start my job. In addition, I'm interested in international experience and I want to explore the possibility of working overseas on an interesting project.

2) Assess where possible tradeoffs exist. From my thinking in #1, the variables I want to negotiate on are, in order of importance: salary, relocation expense/sign on bonus, stock options and opportunity to work on a temporary assignment overseas. Therefore, I want to negotiate for a higher salary and relocation expenses/sign-on bonus in exchange for receiving less number of stock options. Working overseas is a bonus and I can ask for it if I cannot get an agreement on other components.

3) Determine your desired outcome AND the walkaway value. Before I do this, I need to find out as much information as I can from the

company and research thoroughly about the job market. Specifically, I need to talk to the HR manager to find out how flexible they are on the offer terms and whether they are open to other items not mentioned in the offer letter. To do this, I need to ask a lot of questions:

- o "I'm very interested in joining Stay InTouch and I'm doing my due diligence to gather as much information as I can to help me with my decision, and given my understanding of the job market, the salary offered seems low. Do you have any flexibility on the salary figure?"
- o "Can you let me know where the company is more flexible and where it's not?"
- o "Are there other items not included in the offer the company would be open to discuss?" Be prepared to give your own suggestions if asked.
- o If the manager does not bring up the items you have in mind, ask: "Does the company have the flexibility to provide relocation expenses and a sign on bonus?"

I generally find employers are willing to share information with you because they want you to join them and would try to make it work for you. I would also talk to the hiring manager and ask about the flexibility on the work items that I wanted. Let's assume that I found out the company has a little bit of room to increase the salary, no flexibility on the stock options, and is willing to offer relocation expense and sign on bonus. Typically, the hiring manager owns the budget for some of these expenses for his department and he has to decide how much he can afford to spend on me. In talking to the hiring manager, I also found out that he's open to a temporary overseas assignment in the second year, depending on my job performance.

With my knowledge about of the company's flexibility and my own assessment that I may get at least one more offer from another company, I come up with my desired and walkaway value. My walkway value is: 5% above the offered salary, 2,000 stock shares and $5,000 relocation expense. My high value is: 20% above offered salary, 2,000 stock shares, $5,000 relocation bonus and 2 months of salary for sign on bonus. I want to shoot for achieving the final agreement somewhere in this range. However, because I like the company a lot, I would accept an offer closer to my walkaway value if that's the best I can get. I also understand that I'm willing to turn down the offer if I don't achieve at least the walkaway value because I feel confident I can get a better offer from another company.

4) Make your best estimate of the other side's walkaway value. Based on the information I have, my best guess for the company's lowest acceptable value is somewhat higher than my lowest acceptable value, but since I'm not absolutely certain, I am comfortable keeping my current walkaway value.

The final step is to make a couple of counter offers that are attractive to me. By offering multiple offers, I encourage the HR manager to consider which one of the counter offers is better for the company. This is better than offering only one counter offer which the HR manager has to either accept or rejecting or come up with another offer that may not be ideal to me.

Additional Tips
- Don't be arrogant or give the impression of arrogance. Coming across as a hotshot and having an "I don't need this company" attitude is a real turnoff. Even if you ended up joining the company, you're not starting off with the best impression.
- Don't give ultimatum. "Take it or leave it" or strong arming tactics usually don't work. There is no need to do this, especially since you don't know for sure where the company is flexible or firm. If your "take it or leave it" offer doesn't work for the company, the negotiation is over. Keep in mind no one is irreplaceable in the company, not even the CEO, and you're not a must hire. Companies almost always have other candidates to choose from. If you do decide to use this tactic, be sure you're ready to walk away. But my recommendation is to stay away from this tactic.
- Don't be confrontational or adversarial. Keep in mind this is one of the companies you want to join and they also want you since they have made you an offer. It's prudent to maintain your professionalism and cordial discussions in your negotiation. Don't push them into a corner, use "unprofessional" language or accusatory tone if you don't like the offer terms or feel the company is not accommodating. Even if the company plays hardball, stay calm and don't let your emotions get in the way. After all, this is a business negotiation.
- Don't lie. Don't make up stories or offers you don't have in order to give yourself leverage. The business community can be a small world where people know each other, and if you're caught lying, the

company may rescind the offer and you have a black mark on your reputation.

- Don't push past the limit and try to go for every last dime you can get. If you have an offer that's in the range of your high and lowest acceptable value, consider taking it and not pushing it further. You need to use your judgment here. If you and the company have gone back and forth a few times and it feels like they're running out of patience, it may be a good idea to accept. Keep in mind the adage "penny wise and pound foolish." It's more important to start off on the right foot with a good impression than to get a little more money and leave a bad perception.

- Be professional in your communications with the company. When in doubt or not clear, ask for clarification. Maintain a positive attitude and show the company representatives that you very much are interested in joining the company. Even if things do not work out or you decide to take another offer, explain to them honestly and professionally. If you have conducted your negotiation in good faith, the company representatives would understand if you have a better offer they could not match. Keep in mind to never burn bridges because you never know if you will cross paths again with these people.

- There are good websites offering useful information about specific companies. For example, on glassdoor.com, you can get information on a specific company's annual salaries by job titles, reviews of company benefits, feedback on the management team, etc. These sites are good resources to research and prepare for your negotiation.

Chapter 20

How To Ask For A Raise

Before we discuss the question of how to ask for a raise, it's important to understand the salary structure and the impact performance review has on salary increase. In this chapter, we will cover how performance evaluation impacts salary review as well as examining possible reasons that may merit a raise and an approach you can use when you meet with your manager.

In a typical salary structure of a company, each job is associated with a job level that is tied to a salary range where the salary of all employees with that job level falls in that range. Different job levels have different salary ranges and the higher the job level, the higher the salary range. When you're hired, your salary is likely to be in your job level's salary range. As long as you remain in the same job level, your salary increase cannot push your total base salary above the upper limit. If you're at or near the upper limit, in order to increase your pay significantly, you need to be promoted to the next job level.

Understanding How Performance Review Impacts Salary Increase
Formal job performance and salary review is usually done once a year and changes in salary are based on how the employee is evaluated. Many companies still use the forced distribution ranking system, and employees are ranked relative to their peers. Other companies evaluate employees individually instead of relative to their peers. Regardless of evaluation method, you are evaluated on two dimensions: 1) the results you produced versus expectations and 2) your effectiveness in delivering the results. The outcome of your performance review plays a key role in how much salary increase you'll get.

Human Resources (HR) provides guidance for managers to manage the salary increase they give to their employees based on their evaluation. The salary increase guidance can be changed year to year, depending on a number of factors, including company business results, market condition and competitive environment. Another thing to be aware of is that your manager has a fixed budget to administer the salary for all his employees. He has to decide how to allocate salary increases so as not to exceed his budget limit. While this is not your concern, it's good to be aware of the constraint your manager faces.

The amount of your salary increase is determined by two factors - the outcome of your performance review and where your current salary is in your job level's salary range. I think employees put too much emphasis on salary increase. Generally, the salary increase is not significant. If you are ranked in the middle of the pack or you delivered results that met expectations, you may get 2-3% raise, nothing to write home about. If you are ranked in the top 25% or you delivered results that significantly exceeded expectations, you may get ~5% raise, a little more but not a huge increase by any means. For example, if your salary is $80,000, a 5% raise comes out to $333 more per month pre-tax and deductions. It's an okay raise but nothing to be too excited about. The way to significantly increase your salary is to get promoted to the next job level so you salary can be moved into a higher salary range. It's not uncommon to see a 10% salary increase after a promotion to the next job level.

Possible Reasons To Justify A Raise

Before you sit down and request your manager for a raise, you need to be self-aware and objective about the reasons to justify a raise. "I am not able to keep up with my bills so I need to get paid more," "My friends are getting paid more than I" and "I haven't gotten a raise in a while" are not relevant reasons to justify a salary raise. Achieving a high ranking or an excellent performance review is the best way to get a raise. Do your best to maximize your chance of getting an excellent review. Before you approach your manager, examine closely the possible rationale to support your request for a raise or to determine whether you are in a position to ask for one. Here are the possible reasons:

- You are underpaid for your job level in the company. One way to determine if your salary is within the salary range of your job level is to ask your HR representative or your manager for this information. The company should have a salary table showing the salary range for each job level by job function in the company. Although it's not common, I have seen cases where an employee's salary was below the minimum range of their salary level. If this is the case, it needs to be rectified.

- Your pay is not competitive. Comparing to your peers in other companies in the same industry shows that you are paid less than they. You need to do your homework to obtain the information and industry salary data to back your claim. Online resources such as indeed.com or glassdoor.com provide useful information on salary compensation and benefits of different companies. However, this is a difficult sell because it's not a straight forward comparison. The HR manager would want to compare the total compensation package and not just the base salary. This includes, among other things, bonus, vacation days, stock incentives, 401K matching and health benefits. Because it's difficult to get accurate data from other companies to support your claim, this would be a tough hill to climb.

  However unfair it may seem, companies usually are not inclined to change your salary in this case for a couple of reasons. One, your company already has a salary structure and as long as your job level's salary is within the designated range, there is no problem to be corrected. Secondly, if the company adjusts your salary for this reason, it may open up a can of worms for other employees in the company. As a result, it's unlikely your company will accommodate your request. The one situation your company might be more open to re-examine your salary is when you receive a better job offer from another company. That may be your best chance to negotiate a better salary for you. Refer to the "How to negotiate your job offer" chapter for more details. Due to the need to hire strong performing employees, companies need to be competitive in their offer. This can create an undesirable situation where current employees are paid less than new employees in the same job level. Unfortunately, this is a fact of life. There may come a point where the only option you have to increase your salary significantly, outside of getting a promotion, is to look for a job with another company. When you receive a better offer from another company, you can decide whether to accept or use it to negotiate a better salary with your current company.

- You are paid lower than your peers in the same job level. An example of this is when a new employee joins the company with a base salary higher than yours even though that employee has the same job level as you. Unlike you, this employee has not contributed to the company; so it seems grossly unfair that you get paid less. Another example: a co-worker is doing a similar job and has the same performance ranking as you but received more pay raise than you. One likely reason for this is that his starting salary was higher than yours when he joined the company and the salary increase is a percentage of the base salary. While both cases have a reasonable argument, you're unlikely be able to convince the company to make the changes. As I discussed earlier, employers compete for workers in the market place and at times they have to pay a high salary to get the candidates they want.

- Your salary increase was negatively affected because you were "unfairly" evaluated. It's best to prepare your manager to represent you fairly before he goes into the evaluation meeting with other managers. Or if the company evaluates employees individually, prepare your manager thoroughly before he sits down to review your performance. It's much more difficult to change the review outcome once the review results are completed. The one recourse you have is to convince your manager you deserve a better performance review outcome and to negotiate with him to make an exception and give you more of a salary increase than your review result allows. However, if you feel strongly about this and you're not getting satisfactory answers from your manager, you may want to escalate to a higher management level. You odds are long here, but I have seen a few cases that worked out in the employee's favor.

How To Approach Asking For A Raise

You have done your homework and determined you have a strong case and wanted to move ahead. You should consider asking for a raise if you have confidence that your manager values your work and wants to keep you on his team. Think of this as a negotiation and make sure you read the "How to be a good negotiator" chapter to help you develop an effective game plan. Here is the approach to use in negotiating:

1. Understand the true issues and parameters of the negotiation.
2. Assess where possible tradeoffs exist.
3. Determine your desired outcome AND the walkaway value.
4. Make your best estimate of the other side's lowest value.

Let's apply this approach.

1) **Understanding the issues and parameters**. The issue here is clear. You want to negotiate for a salary raise and are equipped with information, rationale and data to support your case.

2) **Assess where possible tradeoffs exist**. From your perspective, think about possible tradeoffs you can make. Be creative. Instead of a

raise, would you settle for stock options, a cash bonus or other non-monetary items such as extra vacation days, opportunities to attend popular industry conferences you have wanted to go or a new project that will give you more visibility? From your understanding of the manager and his flexibility, think about the possible areas he may be willing to compromise. You may not have a lot of insight here, so when you sit down to talk with your manager, ask questions to find out as much information as possible. This will help you think of potential options you can propose.

3) **Determine your desired outcome AND the walkaway value.** This is an important step. Based on all the information you have so far, think about these two values. The walkaway value is especially important to consider since you are willing to walk away if you get less than this outcome. To help you determine the walkaway value, think about the lowest outcome you would accept before you would be willing to look for another job. Let's assume that you are generally satisfied and like your job, the company and the people, and even if you didn't get what you wanted, you would be willing to stay put. In this case your walkaway value is status quo - no change to your current situation. Or you are willing to search for another job and join another company if you don't get some compensation above what you are currently getting. Give serious consideration to what your walkaway value is.

4) **Make your best estimate of the other side's lowest value**. If you don't really know, ask yourself questions that may give you some clue. Questions such as: "How much does your manager value you and your work?" and "How willing is he to lose you, and how hard would it be to replace you if you leave?" may give you some clue about his flexibility. If you believe that he doesn't value your work enough to try to keep you if you leave, then you may not want to go through with the meeting. On the other hand, if life would be really difficult for him if you leave, you have leverage here to negotiate since he's more likely to accommodate.

When it's time to sit down and have this discussion with your manager, follow these steps:

- Explain to him that you have been putting your best effort into your job and contributing to the company as much as you could. You have been given this a lot of thought and believe your salary is low and would like to request a raise. Here is an example of what to say: "I have been with the company for a while now and I have always given my best effort to contribute to the company. I have been giving my salary situation a lot of thought and I believe my salary is not competitive with the market and I would like to request a raise. Let me tell you why." Then give the manager the reasons, data, and any information from your research to support your case.

- Ask him for his thoughts. Listening to his comments will give you some ideas of where he stands. If he's open to your request and asks what you have in mind, be prepared to give him a percentage raise and explain why. If he says he has no flexibility, ask him to explain and then probe for areas where he may have more flexibility. Ask: "If it's not possible to give me a raise, which areas do you have flexibility?" and listen to what he comes up with. If you don't hear anything meaningful, ask: "Is giving stock incentives an option? Do you have any flexibility on that?" or "What about a cash bonus?" If he is open to these ideas and says he will check with HR, let him know you appreciate the effort and ask for a follow up time. In general, if your manager values your work and wants to keep you, he will look for some ways to appease you, even if he cannot give you a raise or much else. If he is a good manager, he should ask you for any other ideas you have besides the salary increase. If he does, take advantage of this and give him your ideas, something like: "I would really like a raise, but if that's not possible, I would prefer to get company stocks or a cash bonus."

- Your objective of the meeting is to get closure or the next actionable step. The outcome of the meeting should be: 1) yes, your manager agrees and supports your request and will ask for approval, 2) no, there is nothing he can do or seems willing to do for you, which tells you where you stand, 3) he's open to consider your request but needs to look into it, or 4) he cannot give you a raise but is open to other ideas. Don't end the meeting until you are clear on the next step. Ask and clarify the next step if you're not sure, and confirm when he will follow up with you. And if you haven't heard from him past that date, follow up with him. Your ultimate goal is to get closure on your request, one way or the other, so you're clear where you stand and can figure out your next step.

While some of the above examples are difficult to achieve your goal of getting a raise, it may still be worthwhile to discuss with your manager. Even if you don't get your wish, your manager is likely to keep your request in mind, especially if your case has merit. At the next salary review time, he may be more flexible in giving a higher raise than he would normally, assuming that you get at least a decent performance review.

Additional Tips

- There are good websites offering useful information about specific companies' salary compensations and benefits. For example, on glassdoor.com, you can get information on a company's annual salaries by job titles as well as reviews of the company benefits. These sites are good resources to research and prepare for your meeting.
- Don't use personal hardship or financial difficulties as justifications for your request. Reasons such as "I cannot afford to make ends meet or pay my bills," "My husband is unemployed and I need to make more" and "My kid's school raised the tuition" are not the company's problem. Companies focus on business issues so you should focus on the business justifications. You earn respect by staying on the business side of the argument.
- Don't be arrogant or give the impression that your case is so obvious, you should not even have to ask for a raise, or come across as "I am entitled to a raise." It's a real turn off.
- Don't give an ultimatum or threat. It doesn't serve any purpose other than push your manager into a corner. If you do decide to use this tactic, be sure that you're ready to walk away. However, my recommendation is to stay away from it.
- Don't be confrontational or adversarial. It's prudent to be professional and cordial in your negotiation. Don't push your manager into a corner or use "unprofessional" language if you don't like what you hear or feel the company is not open to your request. Even if your manager is inflexible, stay professional and don't let your emotions get in the way. Treat this as a business negotiation.
- Don't lie. Don't make up stories or data you don't have in order to give yourself leverage. If you're caught with a lie, you will lose credibility and trust from your manager and it can hurt your case in the future. He will be less likely to give you the benefit of the doubt.
- Don't push past the limit and try to go for every dime you can get. If you can get something between your desired and walkaway value, consider taking it and not pushing it further. You need to use your judgment here. Keep in mind the adage "penny wise and pound foolish."

Chapter 21

How To Say No Smartly

M ost of us have good intentions. We want to help and please people. We want to say yes to their requests and hate to say no because we don't want to disappoint them, even sometimes at our expense. We want to be a good team player. However, in work environments, requests and demands of your time have no boundaries. Many people are not aware of or sensitive to the constraint of your time, even though they work with you and see firsthand how busy you are. While they should be sensitive to your time and be selective in their requests of you, they may not be. They want to satisfy a need they have and they assume you would let them know if you cannot accommodate.

Having co-workers value you and respect you is important and is a key factor in your success at work. As I talked about in the "How to stand out and promote yourself" chapter, showing ability to work well with people and being a good team player who provides value to the company is a big plus for you at performance reviews. Even more importantly, when promotional opportunities open up, you would be in a select group of people considered. After all, who doesn't like someone who goes out of their way to work with them and help them succeed?

However, the trick is to balance between getting your work done and helping other people. First and foremost, you must get your work done on time and do an excellent job before you can help others. If you fail at doing your job or are perceived as ignoring your work, your boss is not going to be happy. The ability to prioritize and balance between getting your work done and helping other people is important to your success. Be clear at all times about your job priorities, deliverables and deadlines. When you get an unexpected request, you are in a position to assess objectively your availability.

The ability to say no while expressing a sincere desire to help is a good skill to have. In this chapter, I'll offer ways and suggestions on how to say no smartly.

How To Say No To Your Manager

Throughout your job and career, you should expect "unplanned" requests from your manager to take on certain projects or short-term tasks. If you can accommodate and the request is important to your boss and gives you good visibility, by all means say yes. However, before you agree to take it on, make sure you understand clearly the task's objectives, expected deliverables and timeline. If you're unclear, make sure you ask for clarification. If you don't feel confident about the timeline or ability to deliver some of the expected results, this is your opportunity to negotiate. You can negotiate to extend the deadline, reduce some of the deliverables, or ask your manager for additional resources in order to complete the task. Make sure that taking on this request will benefit you as well in some ways – whether you will get visibility with upper management, credit from your manager, or get a chance to learn other skills you don't have. This is not being selfish, but achieving a win-win situation for both of you.

Sometimes, however, your manager may get a request from her boss or other executives and may ask you to take it on for her. In these instances, even if the task is trivial and doesn't offer much benefit to you, you may want to take it because she's doing her boss a favor and you want to make her look good.

If you're already swamped with work and feel you can't accommodate her request without jeopardizing your own work, you should say no. You don't like to disappoint our manager. But when you need to say no, there are ways to say no and still come across as a team player. Here's how:

- Ask for details of the requests, including goals, expectations and deadlines. By listening first, you show that you care and want to know as much as you can before considering. So if you end up saying no, at least you have considered and not dismiss her request out of hand.
- Be clear that you want to help, but given all the work on your plate, you cannot do so without making changes to your priorities.
- Put the ball back in your manager's court by having her help you prioritize how important her request is relative to the tasks you currently have on your plate. Don't assume that she knows all the things you're working on. Chances are she doesn't know the full

picture. Explain by giving her a full run down of what you're working on, how much time/effort they require and how much longer they will take. Then ask your manager to prioritize her request against your tasks. If she prioritizes her request higher than some of your tasks, you can agree to take it on, but only after making it clear to your manager and gain her agreement to drop or delay the other less important work. If she deems that her request is not as important as your work, then she has answered her own question and, as a result, will take back the request or consider some other ways to get it done.

One word of advice: be firm on the prioritization. Be clear that it is a zero sum game – meaning that if something gets on your plate, something else must come off. Don't give in. If your manager is still pushing, push back by saying: "You know I'm swamped already and if I take one more thing on, I will squeeze everything in and end up doing a half-baked job and delivering poor quality work which is bad for me, for my team and a bad reflection on you and I don't think we want that to happen."

- Offer alternative ideas if possible. For example, do you know someone on the team or outside the team who is capable and may be available to help your manager? Or is this something that your boss can hire outside help, such as contractors you may know who can do the job.
- Strive for a win-win solution. The idea is to involve your manager in the decision making and not feel you have to make the decision on your own. This way, once a decision is reached, she will have taken some ownership in the decision. And even if the decision is no, you still are perceived as a team player and you don't have to feel bad or disappointed that you let your boss down.

After the decision is reached, write a short email message to your manager confirming the decision. This is to make sure that both of you are on the same page and to avoid any miscommunication later on. It eliminates the "I thought we decided that you would do it." If that happens, you can clarify by referring back to you email message. Managers are often busy and can be forgetful.

Let's take an example: your manager asks you to take on a project. You learn that will take 25% of your time for three weeks. You ask for the details, expectations and timeline. You realize you can't take this on as you plate is full. The question here is how to say no. Let's apply the steps described above.

"I would love to help taking this on, but I am not able to, given all the things I have on my plate. Here are the major projects I'm working on currently: task 1, task 2, task 3, etc." Describe each project briefly, focusing on expected deliverables, timeline and amount of time required. Summarize by saying: "These projects are taking 100% of my time at least for the next four weeks."

"Can you help prioritize your project with the projects I have on my plate? Is it more important than some of the projects I'm working on?" This puts the ball in your manager's court to prioritize for you. If she confirms that this is more important, then you can suggest: "How about I take this project on and delay project xyz which has lower priority until I finish this new project?" Or after understanding all your projects and the manager decides that her request is not as important, she will withdraw her project and you have your answer. Then you could offer some alternatives, such as: "I know a couple of people who would do a good job for you and they may be available. Would you like me ask them?" Or "Maybe this is something we can outsource to some of the contractors we have used in the past."

With the information your manager has, she can choose to have you work on her new request and delay one or more of your other projects. Or she can take her request back and have you continue with your work. If the manager chooses this path, she has some alternatives to consider – other people at work or contractors. Whatever she decides, it's an acceptable outcome and you come away looking good since you presented yourself as a team player.

Sometimes you're available to take on a last minute request, but the deadline is unrealistic. Don't assume your boss knows how long it takes to complete. She knows when she wants the results, but not necessarily what is needed to get the job done. You need to set the right expectation. It's not good if you commit but cannot deliver. If you think it will take longer but not certain, tell your boss that you will scope it out, see what is required and come back to her with a timeline. If you learn that it actually will take longer than she would like, explain why and support your assessment with data and solid reasons.

My boss came to me one afternoon and asked me to do a "professional services" analysis to see if there could be an opportunity for the company to generate more revenue by offering "value-add" services to customers. When

I asked her for the deadline, she said her boss would like to receive it by the end of the next day. While I wasn't certain how long it would take to get the data, I had a feeling that it would take longer. I told my manager I would do a quick assessment to see what is required. I then went to an IT expert in the company to get an idea. I learned it would take about three days to get the data manually because the company did not have an automated system to extract the data. I explained this to my boss and clarified that it would take five days to complete a thorough analysis with a full written report. Although it wasn't the answer my manager wanted, she understood and was able to explain to her boss. It's better to set an expectation and beat it than over commit and miss the deadline.

How To Say No To Co-workers

Showing ability to work well with people and to be a good team player who provides value to the company is a big plus at your performance review and when a promotional or better job opportunity becomes available. If you could help out without compromising your work, you would earn good will, credibility and visibility with your colleagues and their managers. You also have chips you can cash in when you need them in the future. However, if you can't accommodate the request without compromising your own work, you need to say no. Here's how to say no smartly in this situation:

- Listen to their request and ask for details and timeline to determine if you can help. Before you say no, it's important to have a good understanding of the request to help you decide. This also helps the other person know that you listened and considered their request.
- Be clear that you want to help, but can't. If you don't have the expertise to help them, let them know. They would appreciate your honesty. If you can't because you don't have time, explain that you have so much on your plate at the moment.
- Offer alternative ideas. For example, can they wait until you finish some of your tasks so you will have more time? Do you know someone else who is capable and maybe available to help? While you're saying no, you are giving your co-worker options to consider. Even though you turn them down, you come across as a team player willing to help.

Word of caution: think carefully about accommodating other people if there are risks of compromising your work. You will not get extra credit from assisting other people if you don't do a good job with your own work. We may have a tendency to think that we can take our work home and do it later; so we say yes to our co-worker. Doing this over and over a long period of time can add more stress to you and add to the risk of getting burned out.

161

How To Say No To External Parties

If your job involves working with suppliers or partners, you probably have developed professional relationships with them over time. After many hours working together and getting to know each other, you may develop a personal connection and trust with your suppliers and partners. This sometimes can put pressure on you to say yes because you don't want to disappoint them. Here are some suggestions to keep in mind:

- Listen to their request and ask for details and determine whether you can help. If you turn them down, at least they know you have listened and considered their request.
- Focus on the business reasons for saying no. It should be why it doesn't make business sense or it's not a win/win for both of you.
- Offer alternative ideas and solutions.

THRIVING AT WORK

Part 5

Taking Care Of Yourself

I think the truth of the matter is, people who end up as 'first' don't actually set out to be first. They set out to do something they love and it just so happens that they are the first to do it.

Condoleezza Rice

Chapter 22

How To Stand Out And Promote Yourself

Not surprisingly, this is one of the most popular topics people requested me to write about. Many of us, whether because of our culture, the way we were raised by our parents or influenced by important people in our lives, believe that if we work hard, stay humble, don't complain and let our work results speak for themselves, we will be rewarded accordingly. Well, most of us eventually learn that we aren't going to get very far in our career with that belief. I was one of those people. From day one in my new career, I was all heads down doing my job. I was a good worker, never complained, created trouble or bragged about my work. I also wasn't too excited about public speaking and I stayed away from speaking opportunities, especially with customers. Instead, I was happy to have my co-workers presented to the company executives and customers about our project which I had been a key part of. And of course, my team members ended up looking good and getting the credit, at least in the executives' minds since they didn't have any visibility of me and didn't really know me.

I remember, to this day, about a meeting I had with my manager and her peers. When I was finished and started walking back to my office, I heard one of the managers commenting: "Michael just does his job, does what we ask him and never complains." I think they meant that as a compliment, but looking back, that didn't do justice to my career. Since they figured I was low maintenance and not one to complain, they didn't know about my aspirations and felt little motivation to promote me when they already had people banging on their door for promotional opportunities.

Another example: after having been in the job for three years after graduating, I sat down for my annual performance review expecting a really good ranking. To my dismay and disappointment, my manager, Cindy, told me I was ranked in the middle of the pack, a mediocre ranking even though I delivered excellent results. According to her, other managers said they weren't aware of my work and the results I produced. Basically I was invisible to them and they would not agree to give me a higher ranking. It was a humbling and a painful lesson for me. It taught me that I needed to take charge of my career and to make sure my work is known, valued and appreciated by not only my peers, but my manager, her peers and other executives. Over the years I got better at this as I observed and learned how other successful people conducted themselves.

In this chapter, we'll discuss how you can go about promoting your accomplishments, making yourself standout in the workplace while still maintaining the respect and healthy working relationship with your colleagues.

- **Nail the basics**. Before you can be considered a standout performer and a star in the workplace, you must establish a strong work foundation with your peers, your manager and other executives. This strong foundation means you establish a track record of being reliable, delivering on your commitments and doing what you say you will. This must be your work ethic and not something you do once and forget. You must continue to deliver on your commitments. Continue to build on the trust and credibility with the people you work with. Once you have established and maintained your strong work ethic reputation, people will take you seriously when you want to promote yourself and management will be willing to give you more important and "high profile" projects which give you more opportunities to stand out and shine.

- **Be a great team player**. Go above and beyond to help your team complete the job, deliver results and meet their commitments. Go out of your way to help your co-workers when they really need it, as long as you don't compromise your work. By doing this, you establish yourself as an important team player who puts the focus on the team and in turn, creates a positive impression in people's minds. In addition, take the time to give credit and praise to your team members when they achieved a key milestone or did something well. A simple thank you or acknowledgement message to their managers would be greatly appreciated.

- **Become a persuasive communicator and presenter**. This is a must. I have highlighted this skillset throughout this book and I cannot emphasize this enough. In order for you to promote yourself, you must be visible. How you communicate, speak and present to various audiences determines to a great extent the impression people will have of you. If you are articulate and a good presenter, people will be impressed and form a positive image of you. I have seen numerous instances where company executives were effusive in their praise about someone who delivered an outstanding presentation for the first time in front of them. This positive impression will likely be a positive factor in that employee's next performance evaluation. If you believe communication is a weakness for you, make it a priority to work on improving. Without this ability, you will face a steep uphill battle to get notice. If you demonstrate this skill, it will go a long way to help you achieve a successful career.

- **Look for opportunities to show your work**. If your work affects other teams or provides value to them, look for opportunities to share it with them. Request time in their manager's staff meeting for you to come in to discuss and present. Although one of your objectives is to gain visibility, keep in mind that what you present or discuss must be of some interest to the audience. The topic should have a positive impact on the audience. Another idea is to use the time in the meeting to seek their input on something you and your team are working on. If some people in the audience have also been working with you, use the opportunity to give them credit and visibility in front of their manager. In the process, you are also making yourself stand out because you're the one presenting. Make a point of doing this with different teams periodically.

- **Get face time with executives**. When you're working on team projects, inevitably you and your team will be asked to review your project or give updates to company executives. When you have these opportunities, jump on them, prepare and deliver the best presentation you can. These are your chances to shine. Of course, it is a high risk and high reward situation. However, if you hit it out of the park, you will earn great stripes and valuable credit. If you perform poorly, it can have the opposite effect. It is a risk, but if you don't take advantage of it, you will never be noticed. So embrace the opportunity, make sure you are prepared and give your best effort. Continue to look for opportunities to get in front of the executives to discuss specific ideas you have or are working on.

During my time as a Marketing Operations Director, I had a new manager after the previous manager took another position in the company. During the one year with the previous manager, I didn't meet or present to company executives at all. A month into her new job and after I reviewed my work with her, Bridgette set up a meeting for me to meet with a high level executive team – a Senior VP, several VPs and Senior Directors, and to share with them the detailed worldwide business analysis I developed. That gave me a golden opportunity to highlight my work and get great visibility. At the same time, my new manager knew my work would be of interest to these executives who had wanted a simple way to regularly assess the company business worldwide, but had not been able to. I knew the subject matter well and I prepared thoroughly for my presentation, and as a result, my boss and I had a great meeting. The Senior VP commented that he didn't even know the company had some of the data I presented and asked to be updated on a quarterly basis. I had a manager who not only highlighted my work to her management team, but in the process, also impressed her boss and other executives.

If you don't have a manager with a keen eye for when to highlight the team, proactively work with your boss to identify opportunities to get in front of company executives. You can achieve this by showing your manager how your work is addressing a business need and would be valued by the executives.

- **Seek more face time with executives and other management teams**. Another way to get face time with executives is to ask your manager to take you to certain meetings he has with the executive team. You're not looking to present, but to be there to support your manager, to be his right hand person. Whenever I have meetings with company executives to review progress of my team's project or to update them on an initiative, I would take one or more of my employees with me. I would introduce them to the executives, let them know that my team is doing the work and they are there to back me up. Inevitably in the meeting, there would be times I needed them to provide answers to the management team. It was a win/win for my team and me. If your manager is not intuitively looking at these opportunities, take the initiative to encourage him to do so.

- **Get face time with customers**. If your job allows opportunities to meet, present and discuss company plans or other topics with customers, take advantage of it. Customer opinion carries a lot of weight with key company stakeholders, including sales people, their management team and executives. When you meet and present to customers, the Account Sales team is usually present and frequently, company executives would be there as well. You're seen as a subject matter expert and if you come across as knowledgeable and skillful in managing customer interaction and you delivered a strong presentation, you will be sought after. Sales people aren't shy about giving feedback and if you can help them with your ability to interact and communicate with customers, they will let your manager and the company executives know. A good reputation with the sales force is one of the best ways to help you stand out. The sales teams will make sure you get the recognition you deserve. Moreover, they will seek you out for more customer engagements. While this is a good thing, you need make sure this doesn't take away the time or distract you from your core work responsibility.

When I was a product management manager, my new manager was not keen on having me travel to meet with customers. She was focused on cutting expenses and had not seen me present in front of customers to have confidence in my ability. On a customer event, we met with CIOs and IT managers to update them on the company plan and future technologies. In my presentation session, the Sales Executive team was present as well as my manager and her manager's boss – Executive VP of Enterprise Group. A short time after I wrapped up my presentation, my manager walked up to me and told me the Sales Managers were impressed with my talk and wanted to request me to come out to meet with their important customers individually. After that, she couldn't stop encouraging me to fly out to meet with more customers. Better still, the sales team's feedback was reflected positively in my next performance review.

- **Volunteer to lead an important cross-functional project**. This will enable you to demonstrate your ability to lead a team to deliver results. This may be a high risk, high reward opportunity and you need to have confidence in your skills and ability to successfully lead this project. Find out all you can and assess the feasibility of the project as well as your own workload before volunteering. If you want to take this project on and your plate is full, negotiate with your manager to remove some of the less important tasks from your plate.

One other idea to make a name for you is to look for an opportunity to work directly with one of the executives on a project they need help on. For example, when I was a manager in the Product Operations group, I found out that the Senior Vice President of the Product Operations business unit needed someone to be a part-time chief of staff to help him manage his organization. I learned that it would take ten to twenty percent of my time for six months. After discussing with my manager who agreed to reduce some of my work load, I took it on and did it for a year until the Senior VP was able to hire a full-time Chief of Staff. The insight I gained on how a high level executive worked with his team and other executives, about the decision making process as well as how he dealt with the organizational challenges and company politics was invaluable. In addition, I had great exposure and developed good relationships with people across organizations that paid dividends later on.

- **Be an expert in a high demand area**. Many respected people who stand out in their company are also recognized for their expertise in a particular area. They could be recognized as an expert in a new and emerging technology, a master presenter or as a business analyst guru while someone else could be recognized as a creative marketing expert. These are the "go to" people who other people reach out for assistance. These are the people company executives assign important work. When I was in Product Operations, we had a person who was responsible for Business Analytics and Metrics. She was the person our manager and other executives went to when they needed a quick turnaround business report, a deep dive analysis on a business problem, or analyses to prepare them for upcoming meetings with industry analysts. Everyone knew her as the go to person in the business analytics area.

Typically in your department, organization or company, there are "gaps" in one or more areas due to lack of people with the right skills, expertise or people with already too much work on their plate. By talking to your and other managers to find out what important areas are not being covered or, if they had the means, where they would invest the resources is an excellent way to identify areas where you can take the initiative. Managers frequently are forced to focus on short-term goals which leave them with little time for longer term priorities, such as what the company needs in the future in order to continue to compete successfully.

In addition, in your research, you may discover an innovative idea that will help improve your company business. If you do, develop a proposal and discuss it with management. If they find it compelling and believe it would contribute significantly to the company business, they may agree to fund the initiative and appoint you to lead it. One of the customer support engineers on my team came up with an idea to increase customer experience by reducing the time required to set up a networking system. Kent discussed it with me and I set up a meeting for him to pitch the plan to our Senior VP. The pitch went well and Kent got the approval and funding to implement a pilot plan. After the plan was proven to be successful, he was put in charge to implement the plan throughout the company.

- **Public recognition and reward**. Most companies on a regular basis choose employees to recognize for their outstanding work, such as excellent customer service, going above and beyond, innovations, teamwork, etc. Employees are nominated by their peers or their managers. This is an effective and public way to receive recognition and a potent way to promote yourself by letting others promote you. When you have one-on-one meetings with your manager, find out what you can do to be considered for this kind of recognition. And if you have done something worthy of the recognition, discuss whether it merits consideration.

Additional Tips

- You may have heard of the saying "an emperor with no clothes," meaning someone who has style but no substance; someone who talks the talk but doesn't walk the walk. It's important and only meaningful if you have tangible, positive work results to show. Otherwise, you come across as an empty suit. I admit, I had seen people who got by with self-promoting without having meaningful accomplishments because they were excellent talkers who could get away with their smooth talking. However, this tends to catch up to them eventually when they are exposed for who they really are.
- Don't take credit for other people's work. There is no faster way to lose credibility and people's trust. A person may get away with it once, but good luck getting other people to work or collaborate with in the future. It's reasonable and legitimate to get credit as part of the team. If you're the team leader, a good way to earn credibility and respect with your team is to give credit for the entire team and then recognize key team members for their unique contributions.
- As part of a team, learn to say "we" instead of "I" as much as appropriate. Say: "We got creative and found ways to finish our project ahead of schedule" instead of "I was the one with the creative idea…" I learned this lesson early on in my career when in one presentation to update the executive staff on a team project, I apparently used "I" too many times without realizing it. A manager from another department approached me after the meeting and told me that it was a team effort and I should try to remember to say "we" and give the team credit as appropriate in the future. I realized I was being selfish without doing it intentionally. I apologized to him and explained that it was not my intention and I would learn from it going forward.

Chapter 23

How To Manage Time And Prioritize Effectively

To many working professionals I know, achieving a work life balance goal remains elusive and seems more like wishful thinking than a realistic goal. They never seem to have enough time to get work done even though they spend many hours at work and even take it home. With the availability of high tech devices, they seem to be on call 24/7. As a result, they have less personal time and feel more stressed. They wonder how they can spend less time working and still get their work done in order to have more personal time. In this chapter, I will look at non-productive and time wasting activities we do at work, possible ideas to reduce these activities and a strategy to prioritize so we can focus on getting work done more effectively and efficiently.

Time Wasters

According to a Harris Poll and CareerBuilder survey report (Economy, 2015), the top 10 time wasters were:
1. Cell phone/texting (50 percent)
2. Gossip (42 percent)
3. The internet (39 percent)
4. Social media (38 percent)
5. Snack or smoke breaks (27 percent)
6. Noisy co-workers (24 percent)
7. Meetings (23 percent)
8. Email (23 percent)
9. Co-workers dropping by (23 percent)
10. Co-workers putting calls on speaker phone (10 percent)

I modified the above list from my observations and ranked them as follows:
1. Cell phone/texting/social media.

2. Gossip/socializing. This includes hallway mingles and long lunches.
3. Internet browsing on non-work activities.
4. Excessive number of meetings, including team meetings, projecting meetings, company/organization meetings, one-on-one meetings, emergency meetings, etc.
5. Email (reading and responding). This includes personal and work email.
6. Taking extra coffee/smoke breaks throughout the day.
7. Interruptions. This includes people coming by and interrupting you at your desk.
8. Commute time. This depends on where you live and how far you are from work. In many locations where traffic is terrible with no convenient public transportation, this can impact your time significantly.

In addition to the above time wasters, unexpected events, which may be out of your control, can consume a significant amount of your time. For example, your manager comes to you with an urgent request or you get called into another meeting to clear up the confusion from a previous. Furthermore, when you get sick and have to take time out of work, your work is not getting done and the longer you're out, the further behind you get.

According to The Telegraph, half of all workers waste up to two hours a day (Huth, 2015). I would say that's a low estimate. But even two hours is a huge amount of time that could have been used to get more work done. Imagine if you could cut that time in half and use that time to get your work done and be able to leave earlier, how much more productive your life would be.

How To Reduce Unproductive Activities And Manage Time More Efficiently

It's unrealistic to eliminate all "non-work" activities. Moreover, it can be beneficial to our well-being and productivity to spend some time on those "time wasting" activities. Taking a coffee break or a short walk helps us clear our mind. We cannot go through the whole day without touching base with our friends or responding to our family. Hallway chats are a good way to build relationships with our co-workers. The idea here is to not spend excessive amount of time on these activities but to keep them in moderation.

Here are the best practices to help you reduce time wasters and be more productive:

- Reserve two continuous hours every workday to work on your highest priorities. If possible, choose the time when you do your best work, early morning for example. Block this time on your work calendar to prevent people from schedule meetings with you for that time. Otherwise, your calendar is an invitation for people to schedule you. Of course, there are times when you won't be able to keep this time for yourself, but be disciplined and try to stick to this practice as best you can.
- When you get an unexpected request from your manager, determine if you are the best person for this request. It tends to be by default that managers automatically come to the person they trust and depend on to get the job done. Refer to the "How to say no smartly" chapter to help you with this situation. One benefit of the two-hour block is that you have "extra" time to work on your manager's request in case you didn't have to use all of that time.
- Apply discipline to determine which meetings you need to attend versus the optional ones. Usually, we have many more meetings at work than necessary. Whenever there is an issue, someone will call a meeting instead of trying to see if it can be addressed offline by a few key people associated with the issue. And if there are meetings where you and a team member are invited and the purpose of the meeting is information sharing, determine if you and your colleague can take turns attending. To help you decide whether you need to attend a meeting, ask yourself what the impact to you would be if you skipped it. Moreover, many meetings are run inefficiently - running longer than scheduled or worse, multiple meetings are held to go over the same topic. While this sometimes is necessary, it's frequently a result of poor meeting management.
- If you and your team are preparing for an important presentation to company executives, you probably need to review your work with your manager and others before meeting the executives; this exercise can be time consuming. While it's a good idea to have your manager's support before you present, there are ways for you to manage this task more efficiently. Refer to the "How to organize and develop presentation content" chapter for tips on developing effective presentation slides.
- Unless you need to work at your desk, find a guest workstation or an empty conference room where you can "hide" and do your work. Since a majority of interruptions are not important, this reduces the potential disruptions from people coming to your desk unexpectedly. If an urgent matter comes up and you're not at your desk, people will either email you, call you on your cell phone or text you.

- Taking coffee breaks or walks is a good way to clear your mind, but be disciplined about the number of times a day you do this. Sometimes people come by your desk and invite you to take a coffee break; you can factor this into your daily number of breaks. Also limit the amount of time you spend on coffee breaks and be disciplined about it. However, we're not robots so we will need to be somewhat flexible with the times when we want to take more or longer breaks with our colleagues, but they should not be frequent occurrences.

- Moreover, resist spending time on the Internet for personal use. If you need to, by all means. But before you start, ask yourself if you need to do it right now and what would be the impact if you did it later in your personal time. The risk of Internet browsing is that once you start, you can move from one site to another or from one topic to another and lose track of time. Similarly with social media, unless you cannot wait, make a habit of using it during your break or lunch hour. Again, ask yourself the same question - what would happen if you waited to do it later in your personal time. In terms of texting, we do use it as a regular form of communication since it is quick and we can do it pretty much at anytime and anywhere. For non-work related texting, limit yourself to when you take coffee breaks or your lunch hour. Let your friends or family members know you may delay in replying to them.

- Emails are a notorious time waster and they come in all kinds of forms – junk email, information only email, personal email, work email that you need to reply to, etc. There could be hundreds of email arriving at your inbox daily. Use filter tools to filter out as many spam emails as possible. If you're unorganized with email, it can cost you a lot of time when you need to find a specific email urgently but have no idea where it is. One way to combat this is to organize your email folders in ways that work for you and help you locate email quickly. You can organize your email by main topics and have sub folders for topics within the main topic folder. For example, you may have different "job" folders (folders containing materials you need for your work), one for each functional area you work with, and folders for external company partners you interact with. You may want to have a dedicated folder for email messages between your boss and you. This will help you quickly find a particular message and a good way to indirectly organize your boss.

Moreover, prioritize your email by working on important/urgent emails first and leave non-urgent or unimportant ones for later.

Lastly, make a habit of cleaning up your email on a regular basis. Having hundreds or thousands of emails in your inbox is a recipe for trouble when you need to find a specific email.

- Similar to email, organizing your computer folders will help you reduce time trying to look for forgotten files. I have seen unorganized employees who put all their working files on the desktop screen regardless of the document type, and later on spent precious time trying to locate a file among a forest of files. This laziness wastes valuable time. A few minutes of setting up a folder structure would have saved them a great deal of time later on.

- Getting sick is something we don't really have control over. Unfortunately, when we get sick, we're out of commission and may quickly fall behind work. Our work doesn't go away when we're sick and will pile up waiting for us when we come back. However, what we can do is to keep ourselves healthy and fit as much as we can. When we're unfit and stressed out, we are more vulnerable to getting sick. Fitness experts and doctors agree that a thirty minute workout done three times a week is good for our body and mind and helps us be more productive. If you're away from work and falling behind due to illness, you may want to ask your boss for an extension or to assign your work to someone else if the deadline is important. Refer to the "How to exercise when you have no time" chapter for suggestions to keep yourself in shape.

- Working at home from time to time helps reduce the commute time significantly, especially if you live far from your workplace. Even working at home during morning rush hours can save you a lot of time. Many companies allow work flexibility such as working at home some of the time. Check with your company and your manager to see if this option is available to you. At one point, I lived an hour away from work with no convenient public transportation and it took at least two hours of commute time each day. That was a huge amount of mostly unproductive time. However, I was able to work at home two days a week which reduced my unproductive commute hours significantly. Keep in mind that there is a current trend where some companies require their employees to be in the office at all times; so this option would not be available to you if your company has this policy.

How To Prioritize
We are inundated with many work activities and projects, from small to big tasks, from unimportant to urgent and important. We can get overwhelmed

trying to figure out how to prioritize our work and deciding which things to tackle first. While there are many complex tools, high tech applications and devices to help us prioritize, I believe simple tools and methods are often more effective. Below are a few practical methods to consider in prioritizing your work.

1. Important vs Urgent Task Box Method - popularly known as the Eisenhower Box (Brandall, 2016). Important tasks are defined as:
   o People or projects are affected if the task is not completed.
   o Other tasks depend on completion of this task.
   o The task contributes significant value.

   Urgent tasks are defined as:
   o The task required to be completed is overdue or soon to be.
   o The task demands immediate response and action.
   o The consequences of not doing the task will be felt quickly.

   You put your tasks in one of these boxes. If you have multiple tasks in the box, you prioritize the tasks within that box based on business needs (for example, does your manager's request have higher priority than your own task?)

1) Urgent and Important **Do It Now**	2) Important and Not Urgent **Decide When to Do It**
3) Urgent and Not Important **Delegate It**	4) Not important and Not Urgent **Skip It**

2. A similar technique is the 4 category boxes:

1) Things you want to do and need to do **Do It Now**	2) Things you want to do but do not need to do **Decide When to Do It**
3) Things you don't want to do and need to do	4) Things you do not want to do and do not need to do

Delegate It	Skip It

3. A variation of the first method that I use is as follows. I carry a work notebook where I take notes from meetings and write down information or things I learn throughout the day. I reserve a number of pages near the end of the notebook for me to list all the "To Do" tasks. Then I write the priority code and deadline for each task . For example:
    o   The task: complete business metric report for Quarter 3
    o   Priority level: 2 (Important but not urgent)
    o   Due date: July 10 (3 week from today's date)

    On the note book page, I write: "#2. Complete business metric report for Q3. July 10." I cross off each item from the list when I complete it or if I don't need to do it anymore. The advantage of this is I can keep a running list and add or cross off tasks as appropriate. It also allows me to keep a history of all the tasks and it gives me a sense of satisfaction when I cross a task off the list when completed. While there are a multitude of e-planners or calendars on phones or computers to keep track of this information digitally, I find that writing things down also helps me remember them. Instead of using your note book, you can also do the same thing using an Xcel spreadsheet which allows you to sort on the priority code or timeline as you want.

I'm confident that if you follow the suggestions in this chapter, you will be able to get more done at work and reduce the work you need to take home and, as a result, have more personal time to do what you like.

Chapter 24

How To Exercise When You Have No Time

It's easy to ignore or delay taking care of our bodies because there are no hard deadlines to meet, no immediate consequences, no bad reviews by our manager, and no getting called out onto the carpet to explain missing deadlines. Given the deadlines we have at work, it's easy to put exercising on the back burner and think that we can start later. However, later keeps getting later and we never seem to be able to start. This delay can last weeks, months or even years.

At one point in my career, I focused solely on my job; I devoted all my time to work and paid little attention to my health and diet. I ignored the long-term benefits of staying in shape and the worst part was, given all the pressure that was building up, I didn't have an outlet to release my stress. As the stress accumulated over the years, I finally burned myself out - a big wake up call for me. I had to bite the bullet and take a leave of absence to get my life back on track. It's widely agreed by medical experts that stress is a big factor in causing health issues, and while there are many ways to deal with and reduce stress, exercising is an important way to keep ourselves in decent physical condition and to release our daily stress. Studies have shown that as little as exercising thirty minutes a day eases your stress and increases productivity by giving you more energy and helping you keep your focus.

Given all the personal and professional demands of our time, many of us don't think that we can afford to carve out even half an hour to exercise. As a result, we don't, even though we understand the benefits of exercising a little bit every day. The trick here is figuring out how to fit some physical activities into our schedule that do not require a dedicated time from us. If you are able to find the time, make every effort to carve out thirty minutes to exercise every other day. But if you don't have the time, I will show you some physical activities to fit into your daily schedule without taking more time from your day.

- **Walking the stairs**. Studies have shown that walking the stairs can burn up to fifty percent more calories than walking and builds muscles in your lower body (Style, 2015). Instead of taking the elevator to a meeting, take the stairs instead, even if your meeting is on one of the upper floors. If you're afraid of being late to the meeting, try leaving for the meeting a few minutes earlier. You will frequently find that it takes the same amount of time or less by taking the stairs instead of waiting at the elevator. So try to make an effort to take the stairs every chance you get.

- **Standing more and sitting less**. Research has linked long periods of sitting to slowing down the metabolism rate and causing obesity, increased blood pressure, high blood sugar and abnormal cholesterol levels (Strutner, 2016). We sit most of the time while at work – in meetings, working at our desk, eating lunch, etc. We would be in better physical shape and have healthier life if we stand as much as we can. For example, stand against the wall during a meeting or while listening to a presentation. If your company allows, request a standing workstation where you can stand and do your work instead of sitting on a chair at your desk.

- **Taking a few short breaks**. Throughout the day take a couple of ten minute breaks and go for a walk. If you have a one-on-one meeting with a co-worker or with your boss, suggest having the meeting while walking. This was a routine between my previous manager and me when we had our one-on-one or impromptu meetings. We would walk around the building discussing our topics while my boss enjoyed his smoke and I got my walks in (while trying not to breathe in the smoke!).

- **Do simple exercises**. There are several easy stretching and muscle toning exercises that require no weights, just using your body as a resistant force. These exercises can help you tone up your muscles, loosen up your back and limbs, and can be done in a small space such as your cubicle. A simple search on Google will show you several exercises you can do.

- **Using a fitness application to track your activities**. There are fitness watches with programs that track and count the number of steps you walk throughout the day. You can set your goal and by keeping track of the number of steps, you will be more aware of your fitness and motivated to make an extra effort to reach your daily goal.

- **Do you bike?** If you like to bike to work, this is a great way to commute while staying in shape. Since many companies have a facility that allows employees to wash up and change, people are able to take advantage of this amenity.
- **Take advantage of your company's facilities**. If your company has a fitness facility onsite, this is a convenient way to exercise without a lot of time needed. Instead of taking one hour to eat lunch, exercise for the first thirty minutes and then have a shorter lunch.

These steps are by no means comprehensive and do not replace the expertise of a professional fitness trainer. If you can afford the time and the expense, a personal fitness trainer can design a comprehensive exercise program tailored specifically for you.

Chapter 25

How To Manage Stress And Burnout

Many factors contribute to professionals getting burned out at work - stress, long work hours, deadline pressure, urgent crises, dealing with difficult boss and co-workers, etc. I'm not including the personal stress and challenges we also face on a daily basis. For people working in a fast paced industry like high tech, there is no such thing as a 40-hour work week. With the availability of electronic communication devices, work is 24/7 for many people. We can get ourselves into a trap of bringing work home and working late into the night. If we're working with co-workers in overseas locations, we also participate in early morning or late night phone conferences. Moreover, the constant working in crisis mode also drains much of our energy, physically and mentally. If these factors continue over an extended period of time to the point beyond physical and mental exhaustion, we risk burning ourselves out. To maintain a healthy body and mind, we must do what we can to prevent getting burned out.

For the majority of my working life, I was a workaholic. Work came first, second and third. At first, it was exciting, traveling all over the world and broadening my horizons. I didn't care how many hours I put in at work. I was single and willing to work days, nights and weekends. Eventually, stress caught up with me and I ran myself into the ground without realizing it. After trying my best to hang on, I finally faced the music and realized I couldn't continue. I requested and was granted a non-pay leave of absence. Looking back, I am grateful for the leave; it changed my life. In this chapter, I'll share with you what I learned, how to recognize the symptoms, how to prevent getting burned out and how to deal with it if it happens to you.

How To Recognize Burnout Signs
Getting burned out is defined as "exhaustion as a result of long time stress and overwork." Symptoms include exhaustion, fatigue and apathetic attitude.

Getting burned out is a lose-lose situation for both the company and the employee. It causes work delays, mistakes, reduces productivity and hurts company business. More importantly, it hurts you, personally and professionally. As logical as it may seem for companies to take proactive measures to help their employees balance between work life and personal life (work-life balance), I have not seen much of this. The fact of the matter is the pressure to get to the market first and stay ahead of competition has always outweighed the concern for the well-being of employees. We need to take it upon ourselves to recognize the burnout signs early in order to take appropriate steps right away. Some common signs include:

- Physical and mental fatigue over an extended period of time.
- Lack of caring about job responsibilities and even job performance.
- Lack of motivation. Getting up to go to work is a real struggle.
- Lack of attention to your work and activities in the workplace.

When I experienced burnout earlier in my career and ended up taking a one-year leave, I didn't even realize at the time I was getting burned out. I went through months feeling tired, mentally and physically, not caring about work, and losing my attention in meetings; I was going through the motions. Sunday night was the worst, because Monday morning would come all too soon, and I absolutely dreaded getting out of bed in the morning to go to work. I have always been a bit of a perfectionist who never knew when my work was good enough because there was always something that could be done better, some little thing that could be tweaked just a little more. But now I didn't really care about my work quality. At the same time, I felt guilty doing just enough to get by and not giving my all to my work and my team.

Then one day after taking a shower, I glanced at myself in the mirror and I was horrified at what I saw. I played soccer and tennis for my high school team. During college I played in the university's intramural basketball league and was a bit of a gym rat. I was in great shape. Now, through the mirror, I could not recognize this person with a bulging belly and a body with no muscles. Yet I gained almost twenty pounds over what I weighed in college while looking ragged and exhausted with dark circles under my eyes. That was my rude awakening and I decided to take action. During my one year of leave, I realized the terrible mental and physical shape I let myself get into, and I wish I had recognized the symptoms and taken action earlier.

How To Prevent Burnout

A common phrase we hear in the workplace is "work-life balance" as we seek to maintain a balance between our work life and personal life. In many companies, it's little more than lip service. Work pressure forces us to spend much more time on our work than on our family, friends and ourselves. We must take control of our lives and do our best to make sure we have some balance. Following are ideas and suggestions to help you achieve some of the balance and reduce the risk of getting burned out. Since the pace of our work and schedules often limit our flexibility, it may not be possible to implement all these ideas all the time. However, it's absolutely possible to squeeze these steps into your work day to give yourself a little break from work stress and to recharge your battery.

- Carve out "me" time and stick to it. For example, if you are off limit from 6-9pm and after 11pm, let people you regularly work with know, including your boss. Resist the temptation to check email and reply to messages. If people see you replying to their messages, they will continue to send you email messages at any time.

- Take a couple of small breaks at work throughout the day to walk and get some fresh air, even for just ten minutes.

- Take the time at lunch to eat a healthy meal with friends and co-workers. Avoid working and eating lunch at your desk. Or take 30 minutes out of your lunch to exercise first. These are good ways to unwind and clear your mind for a little while.

- Be judicious about time management. Refer to the "How to manage time and prioritize effectively" chapter for details. Figure out which meetings to attend and which ones you can skip. Filter out junk emails and reduce time reading "FYI" email. It's amazing to see how much time is wasted from unnecessary meetings and activities. Block off your work calendar for a couple of hours each day when you are most productive getting your important work done.

- Invest time in yourself to exercise regularly to release stress. I realize time is precious and there doesn't seem to be enough time for other important things as is. I devoted a chapter on simple and easy to do activities you can squeeze in during your work day. Refer to the "How to exercise when you have no time" chapter for suggestions.

- Learn to handle stress better. In Stephen Covey's book "The 7 Habits of Highly Effective People" (Covey, 1989), he talked about identifying your circle of control and influence – who and what you have control over, who and what you can influence and act accordingly. Most people worry and waste their energy on things they can't control, as opposed to what they can control and influence, and as a result, they get stressed out and frustrated. I highly recommend this book.

- Learn how to say no. We like to help people, sometimes at our expense. We're doing ourselves more harm than good if, by helping others, we miss our own deadline or did not meet expectations. Refer to the "How to say no smartly" chapter for details.

- Get regular sleep. Don't compromise on this. I was as guilty as anyone; I treated sleep like a luxury and not a necessity. As a result, when I needed more time for work, which was frequent, I took it out of my sleeping hours. Although I knew I needed seven hours of sleep to function well, I regularly got less than six. Many medical professionals had published work on the importance of getting good and sufficient sleep to be able to function well. Of course, there are times when we have to burn the midnight oil to meet a deadline, but it should be an exception rather than the norm. If you fail to keep discipline in other areas, do your best to not bend on this one.

How To Deal With Burnout If It Happens

While the goal is to avoid getting burned out, we may get so immersed with our work and our desire to meet tight deadlines that we ignore the warning signs and run ourselves into the ground. If you unfortunately reach this stage, here are some ideas to help you deal with burnout.

- Recognize burnout symptoms. Don't deny them. Ask your family and friends to look for the signals. Tell yourself you need to do something about it sooner rather than later.
- Discuss with your boss about your situation. Your boss should be sympathetic and understanding. Chances are he has faced a similar situation in his career. And if he doesn't empathize with your situation, that's his problem. You are taking control of your life because you cannot help others until you help yourself.
- Take time off from work – a few days to get away from work to refresh your body and mind. You may be thinking you can't afford to stay away from work. Remind yourself that you're not much good in this state anyway so you might as well take a little time to recover.
- Let your family or close friends know what you're going through and ask them to give you some space and help reduce things that give you stress.
- Focus on yourself, do things that you like to do and make you feel good, such as getting a massage, going for a run, a walk or a hike, exercising, seeing a movie, or reading a book you have wanted to read. Whatever you want to do to relax is good for you. Don't worry about how work is going to get done without you; it will always be there. The important thing here is to not work, not checking email, voicemail, not logging into the company network to check on work status. Nothing!

- If your burnout situation is serious and you have to take a longer break from work, one suggestion I have is to use some of the time off here to think about planning your future. Think about other less stressful work options at your company you may want to pursue or ideas you may want to pursue with your manager to modify your work responsibilities. This may involve sacrificing some income you currently earn but may be worth the tradeoff. Consider other ideas that you may be interested in doing that would generate income and give you more flexibility. I find that having choices and not feeling stuck in a particular job gives me confidence and hope with a future to look forward to.

Shortly after I started my leave, a friend suggested real estate as a new business idea. I started to read about real estate investing and the more I researched it, the more I became interested. I wasn't aware that I had an interest in real estate and I found it to be a very diverse and interesting field. Moreover, during this break, I started to seriously work on my "financial independence" plan, and I decided that real estate investment will be my next step after the high tech career. I was blessed and enjoyed my high tech profession, but I paid a steep price for it because high tech professions are a rat race that can demand all our time and energy. I knew I wanted to leave earlier than later and do something exciting and rewarding in the next phase of my life. So I studied and passed the real estate license exam, got my license and started practicing it in my spare time in the weekends. Looking back, taking a leave of absence was a blessing. Going through this process and discovering ideas I could pursue gave me the confidence and optimism I needed to go back to work feeling energized and motivated.

I also did some volunteer teaching and learned I like mentoring and teaching people. And with a friend's help, I got a part-time teaching position at a university and started teaching voluntarily as well. Each of us is different and may have different interests we want to pursue. While the frantic work pace doesn't give us the time to reflect, it's worthwhile to invest time figuring the next steps in your career.

In this chapter, I shared with you my experience, observations and suggestions to help prevent getting burned out and dealing with it if it happens to you. Moreover, by staying alert and recognizing burnout signs in your co-workers, you can help them recognize their own situation and take measures to manage it. Many companies offer services to help employees deal with stress and burnout, including professional counseling assistance. If your company offers these services, take advantage of them. What I shared here was information I learned and researched for myself. There are many available sources and professionals who are trained and have the expertise to assist you in dealing with burnout situations.

Chapter 26

How To Handle Layoffs

In today's world, it's rare for people to stay with the same company their entire career and, whether by choice or not, most of us will have worked with a few different companies by the time we're done. It's best for us to have control over our career and we should always explore and plan for the next step in our career. Job security with the company, unfortunately, is not in our control and we can get caught by surprise when we get laid off. Loyalty is different now than in the "old" days and it's up to us to take control of our career.

By and large, business performance greatly influences how a company manages the size of their workforce, whether to add or reduce head count. We should have loyalty to ourselves and not so much to the companies we work for. While we should always do our best to contribute to the company business, we must keep in mind to plan our job and our future based on what is best for us, not the company we work for. Layoffs do happen, and more frequently than we like. One of my friends worked for a Fortune 500 company that laid off employees every year for the past five years. One of my former companies laid off employees each year for the last 4 years, and twice in one year. In this chapter, I will describe an approach to manage your layoff if you unfortunately get the pink slip.

- **Lay off process**. Once the executive team decides on a layoff, this process is usually kept very quiet as they work out the layoff details which include impacted employees, severance package, communication inside and outside the company, programs for laid off employees and legal clearance. If you're an individual contributor, your manager may not be involved in the planning until later in the process, sometimes just a few days before the announcement. Senior managers have a series of meetings where they will decide, among other things, which employees to let go.

Human Resources (HR) typically takes the lead role in planning and managing this process. HR will give the managers training on how to communicate with their laid off employees as well as employees who remain. As much as the company is trying to keep a tight lid, rumors have a way of getting out and chances are employees will hear or see indications of an upcoming layoff. If you hear rumors, recognize that you have little or no control over it, and all you can do is to prepare as best you can.

- **What to do before the layoff**. When you hear about the rumors and believe the rumors are credible but not sure about your fate, prepare as if you're at risk. Below is a list of what you should do. Don't wait until you receive the pink slip because you usually don't have much time to pack and leave the premise after getting the news. Sometimes companies even have a security person watching you pack.
  o Create a list of contacts from your company that you want to stay in touch. Also include a list of key company contact phone numbers for you to contact if you have questions in case the company doesn't provide this list.
  o Make a copy of relevant materials, including files from your work computer that you want to keep, including personal possessions you received from the company such as stock certificates. One note to keep in mind: you need to comply with company confidential policy.
- **Keep things in perspective**. Getting the pink slip is an unpleasant and upsetting experience. We may feel disappointed, embarrassed and even ashamed. We may feel a loss of self-confidence because we weren't good enough to be employed by the company. However, do your best to keep things in perspective. Companies make layoff decisions based on business factors and can be arbitrary in deciding whom to let go. The layoff decision could be based on cutting a business unit, certain projects, or reducing certain functions such as marketing. If a business unit is eliminated, people associated with that business unit are typically let go. I have seen strong performers get laid off. It may not be an indictment on you, so don't need to take it personally. Rather, treat it as a business decision.

For many people, when they look back at this experience, they're glad it happened because it gave them a chance to consider a new start. Many of us get complacent in our jobs and over time, we lose motivation, interest or become jaded. We're miserable in our job but we don't consider leaving because we have become too comfortable.

- **Layoff day**. Managers will inform affected employees they are laid off. The HR representative may also be present in the meeting. In many of these situations, employees typically need to clear out their desk and leave by the end of the day. Managers have been trained to go over the layoff details, including the severance package which may include medical benefits and pay, training programs, forms to sign, equipment to turn in, and any restrictions to adhere to. Managers are instructed to state the company's official communication message, something like: "The company has made a business decision to downsize and decided to let you go." They are not allowed to add their own commentary.

Regarding the layoff package, make sure you understand the details thoroughly. Take your time to listen and read through the information given to you by your manager. Make sure you have all your questions answered. If you haven't done the list of things mentioned above, you will have a short time to pack so use this time to complete the important items.

- **What to do after the lay-off**
  - Read through the layoff package again and make note of the important dates and deadlines. For example, if the company offers temporary medical benefits, make sure you read and understand what you need to do when the deadline comes. You may have the option of continuing to have the same medical coverage but at your own expense. You need to figure this out before the medical benefit expires.
  - Apply for unemployment benefits. You should have the information in your layoff package and be able to apply online.
  - Take a little time to recharge and assess. You may feel anxious to start your job search right away, but it may be beneficial to take a little bit of time off, even for just a couple of days. Use this time to unwind and refresh from this emotional experience as well as to assess your career and think about your next steps.
  - Attend employment counseling and training services if your company provides it. Many companies hire third-party consulting companies with expertise in this area to provide assistance to impacted employees. These companies help you objectively assess your professional skills, interests, goals and plan for next steps.
  - Review your financial situation and budget. Regardless of your severance package, plan to be more conservative in your spending to make sure you can get through this period without

being constrained financially. Financial planners recommend having enough money for at least six months (from your emergency fund plus unemployment benefit payments and severance pay off).

○ Update your resume and start your job research. I have included chapters in this book to help you create your resume, build your network, search for job openings and prepare for interviews. Although this process can take a lot of time and test your patience, keep in mind this is your chance to assess your skills, interests and seek the best job you can or the best path forward for you. Just because you got laid off doesn't mean you should settle for any job. As part of this process, it's a chance for you to connect with your friends, former colleagues and your network of contacts that may be a great source of employment information.

- **Do not burn bridges**. Getting laid off can be an upsetting and emotional experience. It's completely understandable if you have these emotions and feel the urge to lash out. In your layoff conversation with your manager and HR manager, stay as professional as you can. Stay calm. Take a break to cool off if you need. Keep in mind these people might not have had any influence over the layoff decisions. They're just the messengers, so while it's legitimate to feel upset and express your disappointment, it would be unfair to shoot the messenger. In addition, you never know if you will cross paths with these people in the future. It happens more often than not, so it would be wise to leave on civil terms and earn their respect for your professionalism.

  Moreover, avoid having too much contact with people at work right after your layoff meeting to avoid the risk of unintentionally telling them things you may regret in the future. Wait until you're less emotional and contact them later. I have seen many laid off employees come back as consultants or get rehired. Burning bridges may give you some short-term satisfaction but it may hurt you in the long run. Keep in mind it's a small world, people move to different companies and you never know who you will run into while looking for jobs or who you need to give you references and recommendations.

Since it's uncertain when a layoff will impact us, we need to be prepared to handle and manage through the layoff process. Don't wait until it happens to try to figure out what you need to do. No one knows when an earthquake will happen but people who are prepared to handle it are in a much better shape if and when it happens. While it's not the most enjoyable activity, don't put off the preparation. The good news is the activities you should be proactively preparing for the next great job opportunity will also be very useful to you if you get laid off. The preparation includes building, maintaining and growing your network, creating and updating your resume and preparing for interviews. If a layoff happens, you won't feel overwhelmed, anxious or scared. Instead you will feel confident and ready to tackle the next phase in your career.

Chapter 27

How To Achieve Financial Independence

The best advice I can give you is have a plan to achieve financial independence sooner rather than later. Financial independence is generally described as having sufficient personal wealth to live and to be able to do what we like without having to work actively for basic necessities. I believe in having the freedom and flexibility to do what we like to do. This is not "retirement" in a sense that we play golf and be a couch potato all day long. Rather, it means having the freedom to pursue your dreams, your hobbies and do what you like to do, without the burden of working to pay the bills.

A 2017 Gallup study discovered that two-thirds of American workers are disengaged at work – they don't feel any real connection to their jobs and even resent them (Gallup, 2017). If you're one of the fortunate people who get to do what you want to do and make a good living from it, good for you; count your lucky stars. However, for the vast majority of people, given that they spend at least half of their waking hours working, this is a miserable way to live. It's understandable many of us have limited choices available to us and we have to put up with the job we don't like for a while because we have to pay our bills. The key words here are "for a while," not the rest of our professional career. I've learned to appreciate the motto: "we work to live, not live to work." Imagine how satisfactory life could be if we were able to do what we like without the pressure and struggle of making ends meet.

People talk about being able to retire, but I think the real goal should be to reach financial independence as soon as you can. Reaching financial independence gives us choices and the power to choose how we want to live. That's a wonderful feeling to have. If you reach your financial independence goal and want to continue with your job, by all means, continue. Isn't it a great feeling to make the decision to continue with your job because you want to, not because you have to? The key to financial independence is savings and investing. If you cannot figure out how to save money and invest wisely, short of winning the lottery, you will be unlikely to reach financial independence before your Social Security retirement age. Moreover, you should not count on Social Security as your sole source of income in your retirement years. While you don't know what your Social Security check will be, you can be fairly certain it will not be enough to live comfortably and enjoy the lifestyle you want.

To achieve financial independence, you must take it upon yourself to make it happen. Although I started my plan late, I was thirty five years old and wish I had started earlier, I am grateful for a conversation I had with a colleague at work. One day during our conversation about life, Steve shared with me his ten year plan to reach financial independence. After that conversation, I started thinking seriously and working on my own ten year plan. Although it took fifteen years to achieve my goal, I'm extremely glad I started working on my plan, even at the age of thirty five. So while it is always better to start as early as possible, it's never too late.

One disclaimer: I'm not a financial planner. In this chapter, I want to share with you what I learned personally and what I learned from other people who were successful in achieving financial independence. My goal is to give you a general framework for a plan and ideas to consider. If you want to pursue this goal but don't feel confident to develop a plan yourself, I recommend selecting a trusted financial advisor to work with you.

How To Plan For Financial Independence

When should you start? The most frequent advice we hear is as soon as possible, regardless of how long you have been working. If you are a college graduate starting your first job, you can start on day 1 of your job. The key is to develop an ambitious but achievable plan. Your plan should include the following considerations:

- If you don't have a budget, do an assessment of your current living expenses and then create a budget. See Table 1 for example. This will help you determine what your expenses are and what they should be. Having a budget will help you understand if you're spending more or less than your income and figure out where you can improve on your expenses so you can have savings to invest. If you're spending more than what you take in, you need to examine your expenses closely and take actions to reduce them, especially the unnecessary expenses. This example table assumes you don't have family expenses such as children's education and other expenses. If you do have family expenses, you need to factor these in on your budget plan.

As your personal situation changes such as having a family, you need to examine and adjust your expenses and budget accordingly. Getting married may enable you to save and invest more if you have a two-person income, but you probably will have less money when you have children. You need to take these life changes into account as you plan your budget.

Table 1. Budget Table	Own a House		Rent	
	Month	**Year**	**Month**	**Year**
Expense				
Mortgage or rent	$2,000	$24,000	$2,000	$24,000
HOA	$200	$2,400		
Property tax	$500	$6,000		
Hazard insurance	$60	$720		
House maintenance/repair reserves	$100	$1,200		
Car payment	$300	$3,600	$300	$3,600
Car insurance	$100	$1,200	$100	$1,200
Car repair reserves	$100	$1,200	$100	$1,200
Car gas expense	$50	$600	$50	$600
Other loan payment Front yard and backyard maintenance	$80	$960		
Medical expense reserves (incl dental)	$200	$2,400	$200	$2,400
Food	$800	$9,600	$800	$9,600
Clothing reserves	$100	$1,200	$100	$1,200
Household items	$100	$1,200	$100	$1,200
Entertainment (movies, electronics, etc.)	$200	$2,400	$200	$2,400
Utilities (gas + electricity)	$100	$1,200	$100	$1,200
Garbage/recycle	$50	$600		
Water:	$50	$600	$50	$600
Other expenses (student loan, etc.)				
Vacation reserves	$500	$6,000	$500	$6,000
Emergency reserves	$500	$6,000	$500	$6,000
Total expenses	**$6,090**	**$73,080**	**$5,100**	**$61,200**
Income				
Take home pay (after taxes, after 401K)	$6,000	$72,000	$6,000	$72,000

Other income	$500	$6,000	$500	$6,000
Total income	**$6,500**	**$78,000**	**$6,500**	**$78,000**
Savings (Income less Expense)	$410	$4,920	$1,400	$16,800
Est. tax refund from mortgage + prop tax		$5,000		$0
Total Savings	**$410**	**$9,920**	**$1,400**	**$16,800**

- Have an emergency fund reserve to account for unexpected events such getting laid off and looking for work. Financial experts recommend at least six months' worth of reserve.
- Determine how much money a year you will need to have the lifestyle you want when you reach financial independence. From your budget, you can project how much money you will need for your "retirement" years, factoring in expenses that you will spend less on such as dining out, transportation and taxes as well as other expenses that you may pay more for, including health care and vacations. Looking at the above example and assume the average yearly income you need when you "retire" is $60,000 with inflation factored in, your gross income needs to be $75,000 (assuming 20% federal and state tax). Obviously, the more money you need for your lifestyle, the more income you will need to have. For the purpose of this example, I did not include any Social Security income since it doesn't become fully vested until the age of sixty seven at the time of this writing.
- What net worth do you need to have in order to achieve financial independence? Continuing with the above example of $75,000 gross income a year. Assume you anticipate living forty years from the time you reach your financial independence goal (at fifty years of age for example) and 5% return rate per year, your goal is $1.35 million net worth (your assets minus debt). Your net worth assets should include items that can be converted to cash fairly quickly, such as stocks but not your house. For this purpose of discussion, exclude your house from the net worth calculation. This is your goal to reach financial independence. The earlier you want to reach financial freedom, the more "retirement" years you need to factor in your calculation, and as a result, the higher net worth amount you need to have.
- How much money do you need to save and invest each year to reach your financial independence target of $1.35M? Assuming starting with $0 net worth , and 8% average annual compounded return rate, this is the estimated amount of money you need to invest each year:

- Reach $1.35M net worth in 15 years: $45,000 invest each year ($3,750/month).
- Reach $1.35M net worth in 20 years: $28,000 invest each year ($2,300/month).
- Reach $1.35M net worth in 25 years: $18,000 invest each year ($1,500/month).

If we assume a 10% compounded annual return rate:
- Reach $1.35M net worth in 15 years: $40,000 invest each year ($3,330/month).
- Reach $1.35M net worth in 20 years: $22,000 invest each year ($1,830/month).
- Reach $1.35M net worth in 25 years: $13,000 invest each year ($1,080/month).

A few key points from these results:
- The power of compounded rate of return is significant. The longer you invest, the more your money multiplies.
- While the yearly investment amount may seem steep, if you max out your 401K contributions (the IRS allows $17,500 per year as of 2017) plus your company's matching, if available, you should have at least $20,000 to invest yearly. If your plan is to achieve your goal of $1.35M in 20 years, you need to come up with an additional ~$700 a month to invest.
- The calculations above do not assume any additional monetary amount from potential stock incentives, employee stock purchase program or bonus your company offers.
- The yearly income in your "retirement" comes solely from your net worth and does not include any Social Security payment or additional income you may earn during these years. This is a conservative calculation. If you include the Social Security payment and any additional income during your "retirement" years, you can either increase your lifestyle or increase the number of years in your retirement.
- The earlier you start your plan, the better shape you'll be. If you start when you are twenty five years old and invest for twenty five years at $18,000 a year, you'll reach your goal of $1.35M by the time you are fifty years old. You won't even need to max out your 401K contribution to reach this goal.
- The above calculations are for discussion purpose only and used to illustrate the important point of starting as early as possible.

Note: visit my website www.careeratwork.com for additional information and practical tools for budgeting and planning.

- How you should invest with your savings. I'll discuss the easy options as well as more aggressive options in this section.
  - Low hanging fruit
    - o If your company offers a 401K program, max out your 401K contributions. 401K is a tax deferred program where you can allocate a certain amount of your income to invest for your retirement before you pay taxes. Many companies also offer to match your contributions, some as much as half of your contributions. Since the company's matching is free money for you, definitely take advantage of it. You can start drawing from your 401K at fifty nine and a half years old. Because of the stiff penalty and income tax if you withdraw before this age, it is critical to treat your 401K money as untouchable. Your company offers a range of investment choices, from bonds to mutual funds, for you to invest your 401K money.

      Note: with certain restrictions, you also can start drawing when you reach 55 years of age without incurring the penalty.
    - o Employee Stock Purchase Plan (ESPP). Many companies allow their employees to purchase company stock at a discounted price, typically 15% less than market price. If you purchase these stocks and turn around and sell them right away, you gain a cool 15% profit. You should definitely take advantage of this employee benefit. This program is after tax, so you need to determine how much of your pay, after paying taxes, you can use to purchase ESPP. Many companies allow employees to use up to 10% of their salary.
    - o Many companies give employees stock options or stock shares outright (Restricted Stock Unit) when they begin their employment and throughout their time with the company. These are rewards for good job performance as well as incentives to keep you with the company. With the stock options, you will pay tax on the profit when you sell them. With the RSU, you pay income tax upfront when you were given the shares and then pay tax on any additional gain when you exercise the stocks. Treat these

stocks as your investments, so when you exercise them, put them into your savings or better yet, into other investments you have. Be disciplined and do not view the proceeds as a license to spend.

o For public sector employees, most employers (federal, state and local agencies) offer each employee pension upon their retirement. Agencies may implement their pension plan differently, but they typically offer a percentage of the employee's yearly salary for each year of service. When the employee retires and meets the eligibility requirements, they will be able to collect their pension payment on a yearly basis. Eligibility requirements include number of service years, employee's age, etc. An additional great benefit offered to retirees is medical coverage. Overall, a pension benefit package is an attractive factor in people's career decisions.

▪ In addition to the above ideas, build into your budget a "pay yourself first" amount as savings for you to invest toward your financial independence goal. Before you pay any bills, automatically allocate a certain amount from each paycheck into your saving or investment account. Even if this amount is small, it creates a good habit of saving money. Treat this like you would with your 401K – forget about it. This may seem difficult if you have a lot of bills to pay, but with a little discipline it'll become easier.

▪ Other investment options. You can invest your "personal savings" in several ways:

o A mix of stock, mutual fund and bond investments. A number of brokerage firms and banks offer extensive research resources to help you research and determine what, where and how to put your money. If you're not comfortable doing this yourself, these brokerages offer investment and consultation services to help you. They may require a minimum amount of money in order for you to take advantage of their service. They may also charge service fees.

o Real estate investing. It has been proven that over the long term, this is a good investment option. You can invest in a REIT (Real Estate Investment Trust), invest by yourself or form a partnership. A REIT is typically a corporation that owns and operates income-producing real estate. They are similar to a mutual fund where investors combine their capital to buy shares of commercial real estate and then earn income from their shares. Brokerage services have plenty of information on this and you can also find it online.

You can purchase real estate properties on your own and lease them out to tenants. One downside of investing in real estate yourself is you need to have a lot of capital. You may need to have money for 20% down payment to get a residential property loan or 35% for a commercial property to be able to obtain a mortgage loan. Since many people don't have this kind of capital, one way to make this more practical is to form a partnership (LLP) or LLC (Limited Liability Company). By pooling the partners' capital together, the partnership has more capital to invest in real estate properties. There are many types of real estate properties for you to consider, from single residential properties to commercial real estate properties such as offices, professional service buildings, neighborhood shopping centers, etc.

o   There are many business investments you can consider, either on your own or through partnerships or LLC's. These include retail shops, restaurants and services businesses. There are also franchising businesses spanning from food - Burger King and Applebee's, to service business like FedEx and cleaning services. There is a plethora of resources to research in this area. For any business you may consider, I strongly suggest that you write a business plan for it. A business plan serves as a guide and roadmap to help you assess your business viability, risks, investment and actions required to start and operate the business. Throughout my career, I have started businesses on my own as well as formed LLCs in real estate, and I find that having a business plan is a critical step before jumping into it. Having a business plan doesn't guarantee success, but it does force you to do your homework and develop an action plan. I have seen many businesses started without business plans and unfortunately, the failed ones inevitably didn't invest the time to develop one.

- Other ways to generate additional income
  - Learn a secondary skill for a part-time job. Through a suggestion of a friend, I studied and obtained my real estate sales license. While maintaining my full-time job, I practiced in my spare time to earn some good extra income. Practicing this also helped me learn a lot about real estate and provided an added benefit of helping me with my own real estate investments. There are other real estate professions such as notary, loan servicing and appraisal that you may want to pursue. I have known people who started their business part time and eventually left their primary job to run their business full time. This is also one of the best ways to transition into your new career. The real estate field is just one that I know quite a bit about. However, there are numerous hobbies/interests you can pursue and also be able to earn extra income. As always, research thoroughly before deciding on any endeavor.
  - Well, many people have achieved financial independence through hitting it big with the companies they joined. Many people have joined startup companies and made out superbly when their companies went IPO. A son of my close friend decided to join a startup company after graduating from college, and in a span of eight years, he worked for three companies, two of which had a successful IPO. He took the risk and it worked out very well for him. On the other hand, I have known friends and colleagues who have gone through many startups without having financial success. The probability of financial success is quite low, and if the company doesn't make it, you will need to search for another job. On the other hand, you can gain more experience in many different aspects of the company business than if you worked at a big, established company. If you have a high risk tolerance and have a desirable skillset, trying start-ups might be a worthwhile path to take.

As I have mentioned in this chapter, my intent here is to give you a twenty thousand foot view of a framework to achieve financial independence. I recommend doing thorough research with assistance from knowledgeable experts before starting. Life is too short to get stuck in a job you don't enjoy because you feel you have no other option. I am glad I listened to Steve and started my path toward financial independence, even if it was a little later than I would've liked. If you have not started your planning yet and decided to begin after reading this chapter, you've made my day and my effort in writing this chapter worthwhile.

THRIVING AT WORK

Part 6

Managing Your Manager

An overburdened, overstretched executive is the best executive, because he or she doesn't have the time to meddle, to deal in trivia, to bother people.

Jack Welch

I wouldn't ask anyone to do anything I wouldn't do myself.

Indra Nooyi

Chapter 28

How To Manage Up

S ome people view "manage up" with disdain, equate it to butt kissing and playing politics. They hold low opinions of people who manage up well because, in their mind, these people don't really produce results and brown nosing is the only way to climb the corporate ladder. If you hold this negative view, I want to persuade you to see manage up in a more positive light, as an effective method to get work done successfully and help make yourself stand out at work at the same time.

What does "manage up" mean? One common definition is "to build a successful working relationship with a superior or manager." I would describe managing up as working to help your management be successful and for them to help you do your job effectively. Most people confine manage up to only their manager, but I think this is too narrow. Manage up includes having a good working relationship with other managers as well as executives. In order to be promoted, you need to show you already know how to work with management, how to communicate with them and how to handle yourself in their company. It's another skillset to learn and have in your bag of professional tricks.

Moreover, it's a skill you can apply throughout your career as you interact with executives from different companies, or in the future if you decide to go out on your own, to interact with "high-power" clients. It's a skill you can learn, practice and continue to improve on. In this chapter, I will discuss effective and practical ways to manage up from any position you hold in the company. In addition to reading this chapter, I encourage you to read the "How to stand out and promote yourself" and "How to work effectively with managers and deal with difficult ones" chapter as they contain complementary information to what we will be discussing here.

Follow these best practices to manage up:

- **Help your manager work effectively and efficiently**. By understanding your manager's management style, you can help her be effective and successful by adapting to her management style. Managers seem to not have enough time, and they would appreciate your proactive effort to work with them. In your initial meetings with your manager, discuss how she prefers to work with you – getting updates, her hot buttons, one-on-one and team meeting structure, annual plans, etc. By proactively doing this early on, you create an environment for your manager and you to work efficiently together and reduce unnecessary and wasted time by eliminating guesswork and miscommunication.
- **Complement your manager's weaknesses**. Like all of us, every manager has weaknesses. For example, some managers are unorganized, some don't have good analytical skills, and some aren't good at creating compelling presentation slides while others are not good with details. If you can discover your manager's weakness and have the skills to complement it, you will become valuable to her.

  Let me demonstrate a couple of examples. I had a manager who wasn't great at and didn't want to deal with the detailed, nitty gritty part of managing the department budget. I was good with numbers and ended up taking over this responsibility for him. It relieved him of a burden he didn't enjoy doing, and at the same time, I earned his trust and confidence by having the skills to handle the budget for him. Being unorganized was another manager's weakness. She wasn't good at organizing, following up on meeting details, and had a hard time keeping tabs of her action items. Recognizing this, one of my colleagues, who had great organization skills, volunteered to help her. Kim helped the manager come up with meeting agendas, arranged all the logistics for our department meetings, kept track of the action items from our staff meetings, her manager's meetings, and organized employee ranking sessions. This relieved her manager from having to do something she was not suited for, and Kim became her right hand.
- **Make your manager look good**. One of the best ways for a person to stand out is to let others sing their praises for them. Look for opportunities to do this for your boss, but make sure you do it when warranted and not just shamelessly kissing up to her. During one meeting with the US and international Marketing regions to discuss the upcoming product launch, I presented the marketing plan to several Vice Presidents of Sales and Marketing. I pointed out to the

audience that my manager was instrumental in helping to create a successful plan and working extremely hard with the CEO executive staff to secure a significant amount of funding for each international region. The international VPs were immensely impressed with the plan and effusive in their praise and appreciation. The Senior VP of marketing was at the meeting and heard directly from these sales VPs. My boss looked good to a very high level executive and to other executives who would be influential when it came time for her promotional consideration. She earned the praise she received and in turn appreciated my effort to give her the credit she deserved. At the same time, I also gained her confidence and loyalty.

- **Invite your manager to important meetings**. Invite your manager to meetings you believe she would receive useful information and be able to use it to help her with a key project she has been working on. At the same time, you may be able to gain her support for what you're working on. You may think managers have visibility and know about all the important meetings to attend; however, keep in mind that your manager can't possibly know about all the meetings you and the team have, not to mention which ones to attend. When I was working on a proposal to get money to build a number of product prototypes to promote and train our resellers, I realized that it might be an uphill battle since we had a tight budget and the company was looking for ways to cut expenses. I invited my manager to a meeting with the reseller representatives to discuss their needs for a successful channel program. In this meeting, she heard directly from these representatives why they needed the prototypes and how the program would help them sell the product successfully. In addition, they provided her with insight on other important business aspects which she could incorporate into an overall channel business strategy she had been working on for the company. Walking out of the meeting, she thanked me for inviting her and appreciated the insight she received from the group. It was a win for me as well since it helped me get the funding I needed.

- **Get a mentor who can be your champion**. Getting a mentor is a fantastic way for your career development. This should be a must requirement on your career checklist. A mentor who is a member of the management team can provide you honest advice on how to manage up, interact with other executives, respond to different situations as well as give you visibility to a broader group of company executives. When I first met with my mentor, a Vice President in another function my boss suggested to me, I told him that I didn't really know what managing up meant or how to do it.

Through talking with him regularly, observing his interactions with people and practicing what he suggested, I came to understand managing up better and more importantly, how to do it effectively.

- **Become a needed expert**. One of the great ways to manage up is to become an expert in an area that would add value to the company and will help other people do their job better. This will put you in a high demand position and provide you with valuable opportunities to interact with the management team. When you're able to offer help to the executives, they're more likely to become advocates for your ideas and have your back when you need it.

But how do you become a valuable resource if the executives don't know you? The answer is to find opportunities to show your work and demonstrate how it can help them. When I started my new job as a Pricing Strategist, I developed a regular business dashboard for the product management teams to use. The dashboard showed company business results, trends and potential challenges. I explained to my boss how this dashboard would enable her and other managers to make better informed business decisions by providing real time analytics and insight. She bought into it and invited me to present at her manager's staff meeting. The management team loved it and they wanted the dashboard to become the standard reporting tool.

After that I was known as a Business Metrics expert. Over time, several executives came and asked me for help with their business problems and as a result, I gained a lot experience working with them and earning their support. I remember succinctly a meeting when a colleague and I were to present a new initiative to a group of managers. I was nervous walking into the room because I knew several high level managers would be in attendance and I only knew one of them, Richard - a Senior VP of Customer Solutions whom I had worked with on a business issue a year ago. At the start of the meeting, each of us introduced ourselves, and when my turn came up, Richard piped up and told everyone in the room that I was an expert at analyzing business problems and that I was the go to person for anyone with a business challenge. Needless to say, the rest of the meeting went very well and we had full support for our proposal. Although I felt we had a strong proposal, having Richard's support helped grease the skid greatly.

- **Act professionally**. In your interaction with your manager and other executives, respect their status and give them the reverence their position deserves. At the same time, don't feel that you're in a subservient position where you need to do everything they ask or agree with everything they say. You need to have the confidence to push back, to advocate your views or ideas in a polite and respectful way. Be professional and never get personal. In a meeting with a group of managers, maintain your poise and don't get rattled when they question you. Refer to the "How to communicate and present to specific audiences" chapter for suggestions on how to handle meeting situations with executives. Much of the impressions people form of you is optics – how you come across in your expression, your behavior and what you say. For example, if you disagree with a manager's conclusion in the meeting, push back with something like: "I understand and appreciate your point. However, based on the information I have, I have a different view on it. Could I share my view?" Then go ahead and explain. Remember to back up your response with facts and solid data, as appropriate.

- **Seek personal facetime with key executives**. When you have one-on-one time with your manager or other managers, they can be more themselves, and more comfortable revealing the side that you may not have seen before and may have a better understanding of them as people. These kinds of insight are helpful as you learn how to work with them effectively. It's difficult to get this kind of interaction but seek out opportunities. As a young Product Manager, I sometimes met with the General Manager and his staff to present recommendations on business issues such as the forecast for our products. During one meeting, the GM felt the forecast was too high and should be reduced. After I explained my rationale to him, he still was not quite sure about my forecast. I then jokingly suggested a bet – the one who lost would buy the other dinner. To my surprise, he accepted. Well, I was lucky enough to end up winning the bet. He took me out to dinner and I had two hours of his time to myself. I learned a few important and interesting nuggets about how his mind worked, how he worked with his staff and managed up to his superiors. At the risk of over extending my welcome, I suggested to have dinner periodically if he was available. To my surprise, he agreed to do it and we had dinner two to three times a year for a couple of years.

Seek out a couple of key executive that you like to have a one-on-one lunch with and send them a request. It makes it a bit easier if you have a little bit of a rapport with them through meetings that you attended or presented. They may surprise you by accepting your invitation. After all, some executives want to keep their finger on the pulse of the company and would welcome opportunities to hear from the employees. Other executives, from time to time, have open invitations where you can sign up to have lunch and discuss company business.

- **Managing up to a promotion**. Hopefully, our managing up effort to earn the management team's support will pay dividends for us in the future. By demonstrating our contributions to the company, helping the management team succeed and making ourselves standout in a professional way, we put ourselves in a position to be considered seriously for promotions when the opportunities arise.

Chapter 29

How To Work With Different Types of Manager

In my twenty five years of professional career, I have had twelve managers, the shortest stint being three months and the longest four years – they all had different managing styles and personalities. This averages about one manager for every two years. There were a multitude of reasons for having gone through this many managers: changes in my job, my manager's job or the company organization. Some management changes were my choice while others were not. In talking to other professionals, I found my career situation was quite similar to theirs, and I suspect yours will not be too different. It's not unusual to have many different managers in your career. While your career may not have the same frequency of management turnovers, don't be surprised if you have a new one every couple of years.

You seldom get to pick your manager. Of the twelve managers I had, there were only two that I knew and wanted to work for. Accept the fact that throughout your career, you likely will work for many managers with different management styles; therefore, to be successful in your career, you need to know how to earn their trust and work with them effectively.

In this chapter, I'll share the best practices to work with managers in general, regardless of their specific management style. Then I'll cover specific types of managers and how best to work with them.

The Best Practices To Work Successfully With Your Manager
- **Adapt to your manager's management style**. Many problems occur between employees and managers as a result of miscommunication or misunderstanding. Your initial meetings with your manager are good opportunities to figure out how to work effectively with him. Ask your manager about his managing style,

"hot buttons," expectations and how he likes to work with his employees. Find out if he prefers to communicate via email or face to face, how frequently he likes to have one-on-one meetings with you, how often he wants to be updated on your work, what kind of information he cares about and how other successful employees have worked with him. Having this meeting to hear straight from the horse's mouth will save you headaches and frustration later on. Once you have a good idea of his management style, write down what you have learned somewhere you can easily refer to for reminders.

- **Low maintenance**. Because managers need to do their own individual work as well as managing a team of employees, they're quite busy. Just attending all the required meetings as part of their management responsibilities consumes a significant amount of time. As a result, managers love low maintenance employees – employees who don't require a lot of time from their manager, are not frequent complainers and don't need a lot of hand holding to do their job. This, however, doesn't necessarily mean that a high maintenance employee is a low performer or a low maintenance employee is a high performer. I have had employees who delivered good results but were frequent complainers and needed a lot of TLC (tender loving care). These employees can drain a manager mentally and soak up his energy. If you are self-motivated, can stay focused regardless of distractions, work independently when given direction, guidance and support from your manager, he would appreciate you immensely. Remember to keep him in the loop and seek his guidance and approval as needed.

- **No surprises**. This is one of the biggest pet peeves managers have. They don't like to be caught off guard, especially with bad news. If your manager's boss asks him about some bad news that he wasn't aware of, he comes off as "not being on top of things" and looks bad. This is not going to make your manager happy; so when in doubt about whether you should give your manager bad news, don't hide it. Tell him. If your project is running into a major problem, risking delays and you're unsure of what to do next, let your manager know and ask for help sooner rather than later. Resist the urge of trying to solve it yourself. You may feel you are failing if you can't find a way to solve it on your own; however, that is what a manager is for. Chances are he has been through these experiences and can help you. It's better to escalate to him now than for him to find out through his peers or worse, his manager. In addition, keep your manager in the loop on important matters. If you're asked to meet with his boss or with other executives and you're not sure if he was also invited, let him know about the meeting, unless you were asked to keep it confidential.

- **Make your manager look good**. Making yourself successful and stand out at work also helps your manager look good. A manager, to a great extent, is a reflection of his team. If the team is doing well and getting the recognition from other managers and executives, the manager looks good and gets the credit as well. If you and your team receive recognition for a job well done and your manager played a role in helping you, thank him. Show your appreciation for his support and make sure his boss is aware of it. Moreover, avoid undermining your manager or throwing him under the bus. When you and your manager are in a meeting with other managers and executives, try not to contradict him directly. Before the meeting, you and your manager should spend a few minutes to make sure both of you know the purpose of the meeting and are in agreement on potential issues. If you hear your manager make inaccurate statements, determine if you can wait to correct him after the meeting to avoid making him look bad in front of people. However, if you believe you must correct him, do it diplomatically. Don't say: "You are wrong. That information is not correct." Instead, try something like: "I'm not sure if you have the most updated information, let me double check on that for you." This gives the manager a way out by deflecting the incorrect information off of him. He would appreciate the "I got your back" gesture and it would go a long way to earning his trust.

- **Don't come to your manager with just the problem**. While there can be exceptions, don't come to your manager with just the problem, but come with possible solutions as well. Or at least be prepared to discuss potential options. When you have a business problem you need to bounce off your manager, you can help make the meeting more productive by discussing the problem and then presenting potential solutions you have in mind. This gives your manager options to think through and give his opinions. Furthermore, it shows your proactive effort in addressing the problem and trying to come up with solutions. Good managers know to not give their employees answers but help them get to the answer on their own. If you're about to discuss with your manager a business proposal but you're not sure about your recommendation, share with him the potential ideas you're considering and ask for feedback to help you form a solid recommendation.

- **Make your manager's work life easier**. Managers have a lot of things going on and would appreciate your effort to use their time wisely. There are ways you can help them. For example, when you have a one-on-one meeting, optimize the time with him by being prepared. Before the meeting, send him an email asking for anything specific he would like to cover in the meeting as well as prepare a list of topics you want to discuss. If there are any decisions or follow up actions, send him a short summary message afterward to ensure that both of you are on the same page. When it comes to performance review, do your homework to prepare him as best as possible to give you a fair review.

If he is a "picture" kind of person and understands better with graphs instead of numbers, send or show him your analysis in graphics form. If there are meetings you can attend without needing him there, let him know and then give him an update afterward. Your manager would appreciate the extra time to do his work. For meetings you need him to attend with you, make sure you spend a little time with him prior to the meeting to brief him on the topic, objectives and any requests you have for him. This will help prevent confusion or miscommunication between you and your manager during the meeting. If he doesn't have time prior to the meeting, see if you can walk with him to the meeting and use that time to brief him. My manager and I used this practice quite a bit in my previous job and it worked out well for both of us.

- **Complement your manager's weaknesses**. All of us have weaknesses and managers are no different. Some managers are not well organized, some are not analytical, some are not skillful at creating compelling presentation slides, some are not good at handling details, some are good at managing up but not their employees, etc. If you can discover your manager's weaknesses and even better, if you have skills to complement them, you will become valuable to your manager. For example, if you sense your manager is not good at organizing and managing the details of his department meeting, offer to help with organizing the meeting, creating agenda, taking notes and keeping track of action items discussed in the meeting. A tactful question such as "I notice you have a lot of things going on, would you like me to organize our staff meetings and manage the meeting agenda going forward?" offers him a solution to consider without admitting his weakness. One of my former managers, a Vice President, was a straight shooter. He spoke to company executives the same way he did to his employees, without trying to be diplomatic. In a work environment, this sometimes created ill will and hurt feelings even though it was not his intention.

One of my roles was to be a sounding board for him in these situations.

How To Work With Difficult Managers

My focus here is to describe the different behaviors of managers and offer suggestions on how to work with them. It's not my attempt to try to understand or explain their behavior.

- **Hands-on/Micromanager**. This is one of the more common management types. Throughout your career, you either have experienced or will have the unfortunate experience of working for a micromanager. This manager is a control freak who looks over your shoulder and wants to know everything you're doing, who needs to review your detailed work and often tells you how to do your job. This manager seems to have difficulty figuring out what he needs to know or focus on, so instead, he tries to know everything. First time managers managing a team of employees who were their peers often exhibit this type of behavior. As they gain more experience and grow into their management role, they may change or moderate their management style; at least we hope so for the sake of their employees. This type of manager may seem to contradict my contention that managers are busy and don't have time to delve into their employee's detailed work. However, this type of manager cannot seem to help it, even if they're overwhelmed.

   Although it's easy to feel frustrated and not empowered, the way to work with a hands-on manager is not to fight him since it will create a lot of tension for both of you. Instead, take a proactive approach. In your initial meetings with your manager, discuss the best way to work with him. Here you may learn more about his "hot buttons" and come to an agreement on working together. He may not reveal his micromanagement style, but at least you are encouraging him to communicate how he would like to work together. At least he knows you're being proactive and that you want to work with him and not against him. In the initial period, update him on your work regularly, daily if you need to via email or face to face, whichever works best. Instead of resisting him, ask him for his opinion and be open to his comments. Once he feels comfortable that you are open and proactively working with him instead of keeping things close to the vest, he will start trusting you more, easing up and giving you more space. Also by overwhelming him with updates and information, he will likely reach a point where he needs to back off, physically and mentally.

Due to an organization change, I once moved to a team with a hands-on manager. Neither of us knew each other much. Initially, she was critical of my work, didn't seem to trust me and wanted me to provide her with every single detail. I had always wanted to work independently and felt that I did my best work without the pressure of someone constantly looking over my shoulder. Following the advice of a co-worker who had successfully dealt with this manager before, I made a conscious effort to meet with my new manager frequently, several times a week, to explain my work, my logic and ask her for her feedback. This routine went on for a few weeks and as she started to feel more comfortable and gained more trust in me, she eased up. Although she was never fully hands off, we eventually achieved a balance in our working relationship.

- **Clueless manager**. This manager is all talk and little action, all style and little substance. He talks a good game and speaks management talk, but there is no real substance in his words. He doesn't seem to have the skills to run the business and doesn't possess the judgement required to make good decisions. This kind of hiring could be a result of a manager getting promoted into a new function even though he had little knowledge of the new organization. Or he was brought in from another company without much knowledge or experience in the new company or industry. I have seen this happen multiple times in my career. Sometimes an executive wanted to bring in his buddy to run a department, regardless of the person's background or experience. When I was a member of the product marketing team, the General Manager of our business unit brought in an engineering manager to run our team when our previous manager left the company, even though she had no marketing skills or experience.

Moreover, there are different types of clueless managers. One type is a "Clueless but Harmless" manager who knows he lacks the business experience; so he leans on a few strong people on his staff to help him run the organization. The other type is the "Clueless and Dangerous" manager who does not seem to be aware of his lack of business skills and experience, and often makes decisions on the fly, sometimes depending on who he heard from last.

At one company I worked in previously, I was chief-of-staff for a Senior VP in the Product Group. He was initially hired to run the engineering department and when his boss suddenly left the company, he was named the acting head. Three months later, his boss appointed him to be the permanent head of Product Group. Coming from another company in a different industry, his background was in engineering and manufacturing and he had little industry knowledge or business experience. Yet, from day one, he expressed a lot of arbitrary opinions about the business and made rash and ill-informed decisions. He came across as forceful and people were too timid to push back. He disregarded recommendations from people who had extensive knowledge of the business and, instead, reacted and made decisions based on the crisis of the moment. Because of the lack of experience and judgment, he changed his mind frequently when things did not turn out right but he continued to make bad calls that cost the company millions of dollars. On top of that, he also had selective memory and was good at deflecting blame onto others. I witnessed this first hand for almost a year. Whether he realized it or not, he was in over his head and made bad and costly decisions for the company. After three years when the company reorganized, he was finally reassigned to do "special projects." To me, it was three years too late.

How should you handle this type of manager? Since he craves public attention and has a big ego, try to work with him behind the scene and persuade him to change his mind and adopt your well-thought out ideas as his own. Don't contradict or undermine him in public and do your best to not get on his bad side. With the example above, I made the mistake of correcting the Senior VP a couple of times in his meetings and that didn't sit well with him. In my career, I unfortunately have seen some of these managers stick around for years because they were very good at playing the game of politics. My advice is to be patient and find better opportunities outside of his control. But remember to leave amicably and to not burn any bridges.

- **Absent manager**. This is the opposite of the micromanager. For many different reasons, this manager is not very engaged with you or the team and does not seem interested in your job details or the team's. As long as things are going smoothly and there is no major crisis, he's happy not getting involved in your job. You don't have much interaction with him, other than the infrequent one-one-one meetings or when a crisis occurs. I have observed some managers who fit this category over the course of my career – some became jaded in their job, some reached a dead end in their career and were lost, some were too busy to be involved or, worst of all, some used their position's status to pursue other self-interest goals.

I remember one specific example where a manager moved from another function to manage the team I was on. She had no marketing knowledge, experience running a product management team, and from the beginning, she did not seem interested in learning how to. It didn't take long for the team members to see that she was only interested in "looking out for #1" – to manage up and make herself look as good and as visible to the General Manager as possible. She latched onto and took the lead on a PR (Public Relations) initiative aimed at promoting the company's leadership position in the industry, and by extension, making the company executives look good as well as getting her name out. She hired a PR consulting firm and focused her time exclusively working with them, the GM and his staff. It was crystal clear she was only using this PR campaign as a stepping stone for her career. Her team operated mainly on its own as she spent very little time with them. Fortunately, we were senior product marketing people with a lot of experience and didn't need much help from her. If we were a less experienced team, we would've been in a real tough situation.

However, the danger for you with these managers is that they won't care much about promoting their teams or providing support to remove obstacles for their employees. In addition, they may not have much influence over their peers, which obviously can affect your success and standing in the company, especially when it comes time for employee reviews or promotions. The downside for me and the team was that she didn't represent us well in the performance ranking meetings because she knew very little about our work, and as a result, we felt we didn't get ranked fairly.

If you have this manager, look for a better situation to move to because this manager will most likely be of no help to you. Meanwhile, you should take control of your own career and do your best to stand out and promote yourself as appropriate. You can't rely on this kind of manager to look out for you. If you are new in your career and need your manager's support or guidance, my suggestion is to seek out a highly regarded mentor with knowledge of your job functions and lean on this person for guidance and support.

Meanwhile, make sure your work is visible to your manager and her boss by updating them regularly on the progress and results of your work. Look for opportunities to meet and present to your manager's boss.

- **"Go where the wind blows" manager**. This type of manager goes with the crowd and has no strong ideas or convictions on how to make decisions or how he wants to operate his organization. He is easily influenced by "key" people outside of his organization and often acts according to whom he last spoke to or who was in his ears the loudest. This manager does not appear to be very self-confident and comes across as paranoid, even emotional at times. The difference between this manager and "Clueless and Dangerous" manager is this type of manager realizes what he doesn't know and is reluctant to make decisions whereas the latter has no qualms about making decisions, even though they often are ill informed.

When I was in the marketing organization, I had a manager who fits this type to a tee. She would question what I did, get emotionally upset at me and accuse me of hurting the organization. When I was putting together a budget, I requested two million dollars for a product promotion program in important international countries. When I met with her to go over the budget, she got upset without waiting for me to explain the rationale, and accused me of wasting company money. She then flatly rejected my budget proposal without further discussion. I was perplexed since this was the normal budgetary practice and was disappointed she didn't give me a chance to explain. Since I had had extensive discussion with the countries' managers to get their ideas for my promotional program, I sent her a voicemail message suggesting for her to touch base with the country marketing managers who wanted to know why they weren't getting the funding they needed. A couple of days later, she approved my budget and told me to go ahead with the marketing program. It turned out she spoke with the country managers and heard their opinions loud and clear.

A good practice in handling this kind of manager is first of all, to remain calm in the heat of the moment and act professionally. Resist the urge to get personal or emotional. Secondly, this manager tends to be highly influenced by other stakeholders in the company. If some of these stakeholders are involved in your project, get them to be your advocates by soliciting their input and support for your program. When you go over your work with your manager, make

sure to describe your involvement with the key stakeholders and ask
your manager to touch base with them.

- **"I'm the smartest person in the room" manager**. This manager
tends to be strong minded, not easily persuaded and can appear
intimidating, especially if he truly is smart. However, this style does
not promote individual creativity and limits employee empowerment
since they will just default to do whatever this manager thinks is
best. I have seen instances where a Senior VP got into a deep
discussion on data details with someone in the meeting in order to
show he knew more than the employee, even though the analysis was
a small and not a significant part of the meeting agenda. His behavior
made the employee feel undermined and belittled, and did nothing to
help the progress of the meeting. I don't think the SVP was
intentionally mean, but his personality and ego came across as
bullying.

  If you face a manager like this, you need to realize there is no benefit
  to getting into an argument to prove who was right and wrong. It can
  only create ill will for you if you make him look bad; it's a no win
  situation for you. Again, act professionally and let him have his way
  in the meeting. Take the high road. You don't have to agree with
  him, just acknowledge his assessment and move on. You can try
  something like: "Thank you for your comments. I'll check my
  analysis and get back with you later." Then verify your work and
  meet with him later to clarify. It could be that you might have missed
  something also. If you have a chance to go over your work with him
  before the meeting, take advantage of it because it's much better to
  resolve issues one-on-one than in a public setting. Make sure your
  work is solid so that he would have a difficult time poking holes in it.
  Moreover, avoid getting into a discussion about details. Rather, focus
  on your assumptions where you and other people can have a more
  productive and meaningful discussion. Another good practice is to
  persuade your manager to adopt your idea as his, which will make
  him look good while knowing you deserve the credit.

- **Unorganized manager**. This manager is not detailed oriented and
not very organized in his own work, not to mention being organized
with your work or his team's work. This manager tends to be
forgetful, lose things or have a hard time locating important
materials. Don't assume that he has the information you gave him or
remembers what you two had discussed and decided previously. This
is not helpful to you or your team, for example, when he has to meet

with his boss, peers or other executives to discuss his team's work progress.

The way to manage this situation is to pretend that you are your own manager and you organize and maintain the records, documents and materials in a way that you can easily forward to him when he needs them. Take the employee ranking review for example. To help your manager prepare, gather all the pertinent information and materials. Then write a one page summary of the key results, accomplishments, and people's feedback and any other pertinent information. Put them all in one electronic folder. When you sit down with your manager prior to the performance review meeting he'll have with other managers, use this folder to review with him, starting with the summary page.

When you meet with him in your one-on-one meetings, find out what major meetings or reviews he has coming up and what he needs to prepare for. Then offer to help him organize the information and materials he needs for these meetings. Unorganized managers tend to realize this is a weakness and would appreciate your help.

How To Deal With Bully Managers

You believe you have been doing your best, delivering results and meeting goals expected of you but feel you are treated very unfairly by your manager. This manager seems to want to make your life miserable, get rid of you or make you into a "whipping boy" for whatever reasons. You don't have to put up with it. I fortunately have never experienced this in my career but have had several colleagues who came to me with this situation. They were miserable, their self-confidence was shot and morale was very low. It's an unproductive situation for both the company and the employee. A good manager should not mistreat his employees and should not get into this kind of situation. Whatever the core of the problem is, it should be addressed and resolved professionally. I don't attempt to know why managers exhibit such behavior. However, I can suggest ways and ideas for you to deal with your manager, if you ever get into this situation.

One day I received a phone call from a former colleague Kim. I knew her well as a professional and as a person. She sounded distraught when she told me how miserable she was in her new job of six months. When she interviewed for the position, the hiring manager told Kim she created this new position with a specific set of responsibilities. She received the job offer and transferred from her current department to the new organization within the same company. Then shortly after starting her new job, Kim was told by her manager to stop performing those responsibilities and instead, to take on a new set of responsibilities which she didn't interview for, didn't have experience and hadn't been trained to do. When her manager told her about the new responsibilities, she did not provide Kim a new plan with clear goals, expectations and timelines. Kim asked for training but didn't get it. Then her manager began to demean her, criticize her work harshly in front of her peers and exclude her from the team and other company meetings, even the ones she was asked to attend by people who set up those meetings.

Up until then, she had received excellent reviews and compliments for her work from internal company partners - sales people and international field partners. She had been a high performer; during her years at her previous organization in the company, she was a highly regarded employee who received a top employee ranking.

Then one day, Kim's manager called her into her office and told Kim she would place her on the Performance Improvement Plan (PIP). When a manager puts someone on PIP, it's usually a step before removing that employee from the company. Imagine the shock Kim must have felt. Here is someone who had been an excellent performer in the company and was now told she's on PIP and if she does not show expected improvement in thirty days, she would be fired. I knew Kim as a high energy, driven, self-confident person but at that moment on the phone, she was a different person - low self-esteem, depressed, hurt and confused. She didn't know why her manager was treating her this way.

Before I describe how to go about handling this situation, I want to emphasize one point. Before you conclude that your manager has been treating you unfairly and harshly, you must be completely honest and objective with yourself. You need to ask yourself questions such as: Have I been performing my job according to expectations and goals set out in my annual plan? Have I received at least satisfactory performance evaluation? If there were changes to my responsibilities, were they documented and updated clearly in my plan and did I agree and understand them? Have I received negative feedback since my last review about any issues regarding my job performance? and Have I received warnings from my manager about my job performance and behavior? The answers to these questions will help you make an objective assessment. If you have received good performance reviews and no indication or warning about performance issues from your manager, then you have a strong case.

Let's talk about how to handle this kind of unfair treatment from your manager. Let me tell you a secret about managers. They don't want to deal with employee headaches. More specifically, you can make your manager's life as miserable as they make yours. Managers are typically busy and stressed in their own work life with pressure from their boss, company executives, their colleagues and their employees. They don't want to spend all their time on paperwork and dealing with personnel issues. As an employee, there are ways to make your manager's life miserable. This is not revenge or pay back, but a way to keep them honest and force them to do their job properly. However, when you get into this situation, try your best to reach a satisfactory resolution in the end.

- **Keep it professional, not personal**. Even if your manager is petty, condescending and behaves unprofessionally, you should maintain your professionalism. As difficult as it may seem, treat this as a business issue. After all, why waste your effort on someone who treats you like this. They are not worth spending an ounce of your valuable energy on. Last but not least, don't burn any bridges with anyone, including Human Resources personnel, co-workers or even your manager. This is a small world and you never know who you will cross paths with in the future. I also view it as a generous gesture on your part to give the manager the benefit of the doubt that they will eventually recognize their mistake and change for the better.

- **Document and keep a paper trail record of everything**. You need to keep all the evidence and have everything in writing so you don't get into a "she said, he said" situation which is extremely hard to prove. This includes email messages. When you meet and discuss with your manager, write down the minutes, what was decided or not and next steps. Also keep record of all materials, especially ones that support your performance and put you in a good light, such as thank you notes, complimentary messages from people you work with as well as the accomplishments you achieved – high employee ranking, employee award, recognition and performance review.

- **Start with your annual plan.** Managers are required to have an annual performance plan for each of their employees. The plan describes clear responsibilities, expected results, metrics and timeline for each of the key responsibilities. However, many managers do a cursory job of this just to have it on file with HR and to check off a box on the management list. If the plan is unclear with no specific deliverables and timelines, you can hold their feet to the fire and have great leverage. After all, managers would be hard pressed to justify their actions toward you when they were unclear to you about your job and their expectations of you.

- **Know how to utilize Human Resources (HR)**. Keep in mind that in a dispute between an employee and the company/manager, HR works to protect the company and is not there to help you build a case against your manager or the company. They are there to see if they can make the situation go away quietly. However, they are bound by law and company policies with regard to employment practices. Therefore, keep in mind what I mentioned earlier about the annual plan and having everything documented. In a conflict or dispute, HR's role is to work with the manager to resolve the situation. Moreover, companies typically want to avoid lawsuits which are costly and can generate negative publicity. You should use HR as a third party "witness," as someone who has visibility to all the communications between you and your manager, and as someone you can negotiate a solution to resolve the issue.

- **Copy HR and your manger's boss in your correspondence**. Managers don't want headaches from their employees. Your manager's boss definitely would not want to get involved with this headache either. Similarly, your manager would not want to look bad or have to explain to his boss about the "messy" situation. In addition to copying your manager's boss in correspondences between you and your manager, be sure to copy your HR representative as well as a high level HR manager - Senior Director or VP level. This is for your protection since you don't know what your manager is communicating to HR about your situation. By copying your correspondences and showing proofs of your job performance, you give HR visibility to your side. HR is required to keep all records of the dispute.

Regarding Kim's situation, I suggested to her to follow the above steps. Kim told me her manager did not reply to the messages she had sent previously. She then decided to follow my advice to copy her manager's boss. Once Kim sent her manager a message describing the lack of a clear plan with no training provided and copied HR and her manager's boss, she received a reply from her manager within one hour. Her manager responded with a much more professional tone. After that, she copied them on everything. Her manager finally got the message that Kim was no push over and she can make her life miserable as well. Her manager did a change about face and was more cooperative in working to resolve the situation.

- **Negotiate a best deal for you**. Refer to the "How to be a good negotiator" chapter for details. By and large, HR wants your manager to resolve the situation with you amicably, and if you are in the right and have leverage, you should negotiate a deal that is best for you but try to achieve a win/win agreement. If you decide you want to leave the company, negotiate a severance package that will also allow you time to look for another job while still being employed by the company. The terms of package should include payment for a number of months (1-3), length of time to exercise your stock if you have them and medical benefits. Each company has different policies on severance package and you need to get as much information as you can so you can negotiate effectively. If you want to stay in your current job or move to another job in the company, think about the type of job and responsibilities that fit your skills and interest. If you want to stay on the current team, consider carefully about your working relationship with the manager and whether it can be repaired.

Kim's story had a happy ending. Kim decided to leave the company while working through the resolution with HR and her manager. They gave her time to search for her next job which she used to get a great job with a successful up and coming company. As a bonus, she was also able to obtain a severance package. Most importantly, she got her confidence, self-esteem and self-worth back.

Chapter 30

How To Prepare For And Respond
To Performance Review

E mployee performance reviews play an important role in our career. How we are evaluated determines to a great extent, our salary increase and our chances of promotion. Beside tangible rewards, getting an excellent job review is a major boost to our confidence and standing among our peers, although I would argue that we shouldn't let our self-confidence be affected by external factors we don't have complete control. In this chapter, I will describe a couple of employee evaluation methods being used, how you can help prepare your manager to evaluate you fairly and how to respond to your manager when you receive your performance review.

Performance Ranking And Evaluation Process

Companies may differ somewhat on the method they use to rank or evaluate their employees. Typically, formal job performance evaluation is done once a year. Regardless of the methodology companies use, employees are evaluated on two dimensions – what results they achieved and how they were achieved (the "what's" and the "how's"). The former are tangible, measurable results while the latter is based on the employee's effectiveness in working with other people to produce results. The feedback from their peers, partners and other managers play a key role in how the employees will be ranked or evaluated. I'll describe two employee performance evaluation methods many companies employ – forced ranking and individual performance review method.

- **Forced ranking**. Employees are ranked on their job performance for the past year relative to other employees in similar job junctions. These companies adhere to a predetermined ranking distribution known as the Bell curve. Employees in similar job functions within a department or organization are rated relative to each other. Each department or organization is required to adhere to the Bell curve distribution policy.

Take one of my former companies for example. This company ranks employees on a scale from 1 to 5 –with 1 being the highest rank and 5 the lowest. Approximately up to 25% of employees can be ranked with 1 and 2 ranking, 50% with 3 ranking and 25% with 4 and 5 ranking. Employees with high rankings receive bigger salary raises and other financial incentives, including stock shares. Lowest ranked employees would be put on performance improvement probation and likely receive no raise or any other financial rewards.

- **Individual performance evaluation**. Unlike forced ranking, each employee is evaluated individually and there is no ranking scale. Each employee is evaluated based on their performance compared to expected results described in the employee annual plan and based on feedback from the key people they worked with in the past year. Each employee's results are compared to their annual plan to determine whether they met, exceeded or did not meet expectations. The managers also have more flexibility to apply salary increase based on their evaluation of the employee.

How Managers Conduct Employee Rankings And Evaluations

- **Forced Ranking**. Prior to the department ranking meeting, the manager should gather all relevant information on each employee on his team so he will be prepared to represent his team fairly in the ranking meeting. He compiles the results for each employee relative to the goals outlined in the employee's annual plan. In addition, he gathers feedback from people whom the employees worked closely with in the past year, including team members, co-workers, partners and managers from other functions. While all managers should follow this preparation practice, not all do. Some are more prepared than others. Needless to say, managers who are better prepared stand a much better chance to get a fair ranking for their employees.

I'll describe one ranking scenario in an organization I worked in. At the beginning of the meeting, all managers give their ranking recommendation for each of their employees. Once this is done, each manager explains his ranking recommendation by summarizing the employee's results, the manager's own assessment and other people's feedback on the employee. A discussion follows among the managers in the room on whether they agree with the manager's recommendation. Based on this discussion, the employee's ranking may get moved up, down or stay unchanged. Other managers' impression of you can have a big impact on your ranking. For managers who did not have frequent interaction with you, their limited opinion may skew their overall assessment of you. While this may seem unfair, it's the reality and I have seen examples of it.

When all the managers are done with the discussions, the revised rankings are compared against the Bell curve policy and if the rankings are off, adjustments will need to be made. The variance normally happens at the top ranking band and at the bottom ranking band. This is where tradeoffs and compromises are made. A manager may have to give up one of the high rankings to save an employee from being included in the lowest rank band unfairly. Employees, who are not known or who are perceived negatively by other managers, stand the greatest chance to be moved to a lower ranking band. I think this can be a painful and unfair part of the forced ranking distribution policy.

Once the rankings are finalized, each manager administers their employees' salary increase and other financial rewards based on their ranking and the company's guidelines. Finally, the manager completes a performance review report and reviews with each of their employees. This report also includes next year's plan. I want to emphasize a point here regarding other managers' opinion of you. If their assessment of you is not fair or inaccurate, the way for your manager to counter this is to be thoroughly prepared with facts and feedback from others. This is where you can help your manager.

- **Individual performance review**. This process is much simpler and less controversial. Your manager is the only person evaluating you. He compares your results to the objectives described in your annual plan; this is the "what" part of the review. He also assesses how effectively you worked with other people to achieve the results; this is the "how" part of the review. He reviews the feedback on you from people you worked with over the past year. In assessing both the "what's" and the "how's" of your performance, your manager determines if you have exceeded, met or did not meet expectations. Your manager uses this evaluation to determine your salary raises and other financial rewards.

How Your Salary Increase Is Determined

Several factors go into salary increase consideration. First is the company's business performance. If the company is doing well, employees may get better raises. If not, employees may not get any raises at all. Second factor is the result of your performance evaluation – if the result is good, you'll typically get a bigger raise. Third factor is where your base salary is within the salary range of your job level. Per company's salary structure, each job level has a salary range and salary for employees with this job level must stay within this range. If you are near the top of the salary range, you may not get much of a raise even if you received a good performance review or ranking. If this applies to you, the best way to get a significant raise is to get promoted to the next job level.

How To Help Prepare Your Manager For Your Evaluation

While we all want to have an excellent review or a high ranking, that should not be your goal. Your goal is to get as fair a ranking or performance review as possible. One more important point: you must take ownership of helping and preparing your manager and not assume he has what he needs. I learned this the hard way. As a product manager for a computer system company early in my career, I thought that if I put my head down and focused on giving the best effort, my manager would take care of me and reward me appropriately. I was managing a several hundred million dollar server business, responsible for several aspects of the business, including working with engineering to enhance the products, providing forecast for manufacturing, setting pricing and solving customer business issues. The product line business was successful and generating better than expected sales and margin. I was certain I would receive a high ranking.

I looked forward excitedly to the day of my annual performance review. When I sat down with my manager, Mary, she was very complimentary on my work and results. I was feeling good. However, my excitement came crashing down when she told me I was ranked a 3 (an average ranking on a scale of 1-5). In my dismay and anger, I asked her to explain. She told me she had wanted to give me a higher ranking, but other managers in the meeting told her they didn't have visibility of my work and my contributions to the company. She also told me she tried to fight for me but didn't have enough evidence to support her argument. In my anger, I thought about leaving the company. After all, I had busted my butt, worked days, nights and weekends to help my company be successful and my reward was a lousy 3 ranking – a ranking attributed to an average performer.

I took a few days off from work. The break gave me time to think, and after I calmed down, I realized I had no one to blame but myself. I had completely and blindly relied on my manager to know what I was doing and as importantly, to let other managers know my results and contributions. Although she didn't ask me, I did nothing to prepare her. I learned a hard lesson – I had to take ownership of my career and not rely on anyone else. Even though I didn't have direct control over my job performance ranking, I had to make sure to help my manager be as prepared as possible and not assumed she had it under control. In addition, I needed to make sure that other managers and key stakeholders have visibility of my work and my results. Refer to the "How to stand out and promote yourself" chapter for details.

Steps to help prepare your manager to evaluate your performance:
- Keep an ongoing track record of your results and feedback as the year progresses. Don't wait until the last minute. This is too important to wait until just before the evaluation time to start writing down your accomplishments and other people's feedback. And in the rush, you may forget to include some key milestones as well as gathering feedback from all appropriate people.
- Review regularly your results relative to your employee plan's objectives. If and when your plan is revised due to changes at work, make sure you and your manager are on the same page, especially regarding the expected results. Be proactive and review this plan and your progress with your manager at least once a quarter. This is also an opportunity to capture and revise any changes in your plan if necessary. In addition, if you have been doing a good job on an important assignment that was not part of your plan, make sure you capture this accomplishment as "exceeding or going above and beyond your responsibilities" when you review your plan.
- Whenever you receive a positive message from one of your colleagues, managers, partners or customers regarding a job well done, let your manager know and keep a record. In addition, make a habit to seek out your peers and other managers for feedback on key projects you are working with them on. If they do want to give you feedback, they will appreciate your being proactive. Moreover, you get real time feedback from them on things you can work to improve instead of hearing about it from your manager at your performance review meeting. And when it comes time for them to give feedback to your manager, they will more likely to give positive feedback on you.

- At least a month before your ranking or evaluation meeting, give your manager a list of names of the people you want your manager to obtain feedback from. He may ask you for this list, but will appreciate if you took the initiative to provide him the list. These are people who can give your manager constructive feedback with specific examples from their time spent working with you. They include peers who have worked closely with you on different projects and other managers who have seen your work and observed your teamwork skills.
- Provide your manager a list of your accomplishments since the last ranking or evaluation session or since you joined the company if you're new. Make sure to highlight the results compared to your annual plan – how the results impacted company business, whether the results met or exceeded the goals and/or timeline. In addition, if you took on additional important projects that were not originally in your plan, be sure to highlight this as "going beyond the call of duty" accomplishments. Among the criteria for getting a high ranking or excellent review is that you not only meet your job expectations, but exceed them. When you provide your manager the list, sit down and go over this list in person with him to make sure there is no confusion. Don't assume he will understand or remember. By going over with him in person, you eliminate the risk of your manager reviewing your list at the last minute and having no opportunity to clarify any detail with you first.
- Take advantage of opportunities to get visibility with other executives. How other managers and executives perceive you has a significant impact on your review outcome. Look for opportunities to present in front of them and when you do, be prepared to give your best effort and make the most positive impression you can. I had one employee, Mike, who was very good at this. He would seek out opportunities to go into an executive's staff meeting to present his work or a team project important to the company. He not only gained visibility but developed a reputation as an excellent presenter and a team leader. When I met with my boss to review Mike's performance later in the year, my boss not only agreed with my proposed high ranking for him but also wanted to give him even more raise and stock options than I had recommended.

How To Discuss Your Performance Review With Your Manager

You have done your best and given your manager all the ammunition he needs for your performance evaluation. Now the day comes for you to have your performance review with him. Once the ranking or evaluation result is final, it's very difficult to change. In my twenty five year career, I have seen only very rare cases where a ranking was changed as a result of employee escalation. Here are suggestions on how to handle different evaluation outcomes in your review meeting.

- You received a lower evaluation result than you deserved.
    - Maintain your professionalism. If you didn't get a fair ranking you anticipated, it's certainly understandable to feel disappointed and express it to your manager. While it may be difficult, be as professional as you can and resist throwing a tantrum or making comments you may regret later. But clearly express your disappointment. Take a break if you need to help you calm down.
    - Focus on the two evaluation dimensions I discussed at the beginning of this chapter (the "what's" and the "how's"). Ask him to compare your results versus expectations in your annual plan. You want him to explain and give specific examples to clarify your evaluation results. You want to probe to understand 1) if your manager prepared himself adequately with the details you provided, 2) specific reasons where you fell short in not earning a higher evaluation result, and 3) what you could have done differently to achieve a better outcome.
    - To find out if he was prepared, ask questions such as: "Give me suggestions on how I could have helped you better prepare for your management evaluation meeting" and "Of the materials I provided you, what was most helpful and what else did you need that I didn't provide?" To probe for more specific details, ask: "I would like examples in my job performance that held me back in my evaluation," 'Please give me examples of what, if I had done differently, would have enabled me to get a better outcome" or "Give me an example of where someone was able to get a better review than I was." If he makes comments regarding not working well with others, say: "Please give me specific examples where I wasn't effective working with people to get things done" or "Give me examples where other managers had a negative impression of me." Conclude this discussion with a question on what else you need to improve going forward in order to achieve a better evaluation outcome next time.
- If you received a very low ranking or very negative review, your manager probably has begun working work with HR to develop a "Performance Improvement Plan" for you. This plan spells out specific tasks with expected results and deadlines you must meet.

And if you don't meet them in a given period, you manager will proceed to terminate your employment. Ask your manager to provide an objective assessment of your results versus expectations in your annual plan. Focus on the two evaluation dimensions I discussed above (the "what's" and the "how's). If you have been taking the steps to monitor your own performance and how others perceive you, you should not be surprised with the evaluation outcome. You can avoid getting into this predicament by paying attention to your manager's feedback in one-on-one meetings and proactively seeking other people's feedback. You then can take actions to improve your situation or consider other job options. By the time you hear this in your performance review, it may be too late.

Note: if you feel strongly and objectively your evaluation result was unfair and unjust, you can escalate your dispute to HR and your manager's boss. Ask for a meeting where you can objectively lay out the facts to justify a better evaluation result. As I said earlier, you would face a very steep hurdle to have this changed, especially if the company uses the "Forced Ranking" process. My advice on handling this dispute is to be professional and use all the facts you have to make your case. Refer to the chapter "How to work with Human Resources" and "How to ask for a raise" chapter for more suggestions.

- If you received the outcome you anticipated or even better than you had hoped, use this opportunity to find out what you did right in your manager's views and where you can continue to improve. Ask questions such as: "Can you give me examples where you and other people see as my strongest areas?" and "Where can I continue to improve going forward?" You may also want to have a discussion on promotional opportunities. Ask questions on what the next steps are and what you need to do in order to merit promotional considerations. Look for concrete examples and suggestions.
- The next step in this meeting is for the manager to review with you your next year's plan. The plan should include goals, deadlines and expected results from your responsibilities and projects you will be working on. Ask for clarification on anything you aren't clear on and assess how achievable the plan is. What parts of the plan are within the scope of your job and what parts are "going above and beyond," where if you accomplish them, they would be a plus for your next performance evaluation. Most of all, once you have your questions answered and are clear on expectations, don't commit right away, ask for time to think about it. Even just for a day or so. You have a chance to step back, clear your head and assess more objectively.

Ask yourself if this plan is realistic to complete as required. Keep in mind the importance of meeting your commitments. Not meeting your commitment will affect your review negatively. If the plan is not realistic, negotiate to reduce the plan's expectations, or change some parts of the plan to "Want" from "Must" deliverables.

- Some companies' annual employee plan also includes employee development plan. This plan is intended to help employees continue to develop skills and grow in their career. Think about what you would like the next step in your career to be and draft a plan to support that. It may include trainings or classes you would like to take. It may be assignments to participate in a company-wide initiative which would give you additional skills and knowledge. Or it could be to identify a mentor who can coach and help you in your career path.

One word of advice: many managers tend to pay lip service to the development plan and don't put in a lot of effort. Managers are not really evaluated or measured on this responsibility. In my career I was never evaluated for my employee development plan. I had one manager who told me directly that it was my responsibility to come up with a plan for myself. It's up to you to take an active role in drafting your development plan. I had an employee who aspired to be a manager and wanted to know how she can prepare herself for this position in the future. She and I looked at the typical responsibilities of a manager and we came up with a list of activities to give her exposure to what managers do and help her develop some of the skills needed. The list of activities included getting a respected manager to be her mentor, shadowing me in my meetings, taking management training courses for employees who aspire to be managers and assisting me on some of my management responsibilities. Keep in mind that the development plan is for your benefits and following through is your responsibility. It's usually not a part of your job performance evaluation.

Chapter 31

How To Work With Human Resources

Human Resources (HR) organization plays an important role in the company. HR advices the company management team how to strategically manage people as assets and resources. Among key HR functions are design and managing recruiting/hiring, training/development, salary administration, mediating employee conflicts, etc. In addition, from my management experience, HR also has an objective to protect the company and management team. If there is a dispute between an employee and the manager, don't depend on HR to play a neutral role or be on the employee's side. In these situations, HR is there to keep the company and manager from taking the wrong or potentially illegal actions, not to help the employee win their case. Realizing this helps you know how to work with HR and not get frustrated from unrealistic expectations of your HR personnel. In this chapter, I will describe the roles of HR and how you can utilize their services.

HR's roles. Here's a sample list:
- Manages the recruiting and hiring process. HR plays an important role in helping managers hire employees by recruiting, screening, advising manager on hiring decisions, putting together offer packages and negotiating employment offers with potential employees.
- Recommends, designs and implements employee benefit programs.
- Recommends, designs and implements salary and compensation structures for company employees.
- Recommends, designs and implements training and development programs for employees.
- Implements and manages company organizational changes such as layoffs and acquisitions.

- Mediates employee conflicts.
- Facilitates employee performance reviews.
- Provides support and tools to managers and employees to help them do their job effectively.
- Provides career counseling to employees.
- Serves company business interest. HR's loyalty is to the company, not to the employees. HR is not there to be an employee advocate. They will do what is in the best interest of the company.
- Serves a supporting and advisory role to the management team.

When To Engage HR

In general, HR is a great place to go to for information and clarifications of company policies and programs – questions such as how do I get information for this or that, what options are available for me from company policies or programs, or I need clarification on this particular company policy, etc. This kind of information or clarification is clear and unambiguous. You probably can find most of the information on the company website. If you can't find it, contact HR for answers. Below are some specific items you can go to HR for:

- When you need information regarding your employment or your job, such as your job scope, available training classes and personal leave policy.
- You are a manager and you need to hire to fill a job opening, understand the performance review process or training programs for managers.
- If you face harassment or abuse at work.
- If you have medical related issues and want to know what treatment and programs are available to you.
- When you want career counseling and advice.
- When you want to negotiate the job offer you receive from the company.
- When you have a dispute or conflict at work.
- When you face an ethical issue and want clarification regarding company policy.

What Not To Expect From HR

In general, you should not rely on HR on matters requiring HR to give judgment, make decisions or take sides. You should not expect HR to be your advocate when it comes to dispute between you and the company. Here are some of the situations to be aware of what HR can or cannot do for you if you come to them.

- If you bring a dispute between you and your manager to HR, don't expect HR to be your advocate. Many employees don't understand that HR's priority and loyalty lies with the company. Instead, they expect HR to support and fight for them when they escalate a work related issue with their management. Unfortunately, they end up walking away disappointed. Primarily, HR is there to listen and to keep management out of trouble.

- If you face harassment or abuse at work, by colleagues or managers, you need to escalate this to HR. They take this situation very seriously. Companies care greatly about public perception and don't want to be sued. Moreover, companies don't want to have the perception with their employees that they let these situations fester, and they don't want to risk causing morale issue in the workplace. HR will take action because it is in the company's best interest to have this addressed and resolved as quickly as possible.

- Don't expect HR to provide you answers to all your questions, especially if the information is sensitive or confidential. HR knows much of company's sensitive information but is not allowed to reveal to you. For example, if there's an impending change to the company organization, HR personnel would know this well in advance since they have to manage potential changes to employees' reporting structure, relocation and employment status.

- Don't expect HR to be a leader or a change agent to make breakthrough changes in the company. They are there to primarily support company management. It is more of an exception when HR played a lead role in making breakthroughs in the workplace. A common complaint many employees have had for years is the forced ranking distribution that managers have to adhere to. This type of ranking system creates unhealthy competition among employees and results in low morale in the workplace. This has been in place for decades, and only in recent years that companies have started to change to a less restrictive evaluation process.

- HR doesn't necessarily need to honor the confidential or sensitive information you share with them. In some instances, HR is required to share the information with company management such as knowledge of employee harassment or illegal actions. If you want to share with HR in confidence, disclose the nature of your topic and confirm with your HR representative whether this will be kept confidential.

How To Work With HR

If you know how to work with HR effectively, they can be a good partner and good resource. Here are some suggestions on how to work with them.

- Understand what services HR provides. When you first join the company, take a little time to learn about HR –HR services and support resources, tools you can use, different processes to follow, etc. Many companies have an internal website where you can find all or most of this out. You should also meet with your HR representative to introduce yourself and learn about their role and effective ways you can work with them.

- Have facts and information in writing when you meet with HR, especially on a controversial issue or dispute. Typically you will meet with HR representative and the person you have the dispute with. View the HR representative as a third-party witness you want there to have visibility to the information you present and to keep a record of it. Make sure you can support your position or claim with specific examples and facts. I had a colleague who felt that her manager was undermining her work and reneging on an agreement to have her work on a certain and highly visible project. She requested a meeting with HR and her manager. Since she did not have the proofs to support her claim, it became a "she said, he said" situation. Needless to say, she didn't accomplish much in that meeting.

   After that, she learned to document decisions, agreements and next steps in her meetings with the manager as well as writing down specific instances where her manager undermined her. Because her manager felt confidence the last escalation went nowhere, he did not change his style or behavior. A few months later my colleague escalated again to HR, except this time, she was well prepared and was able to back up her complaint. HR had no choice but get her manager's boss involved to resolve the situation. Her manager's boss reprimanded him. A few months later, the manager left the company.

Rely on HR as a resource to support you, to provide suggestions, counseling and guidance, but don't rely on them to make decisions for you or to be your advocate in potential dispute between you and the company.

Chapter 32

How To Tell Your Boss You Are Looking

Regardless of where you are in your professional career, you should stay on top of the employment trends in the industry and keep your eyes open to potential opportunities at work as well as outside your company. It's also a good idea to continually assess how desirable your skills and experience are. You should always have options available, be able to control your career destiny instead of having it decided for you. Even though you may not know when a great opportunity opens up, be prepared for it.

Throughout your career, you likely will be looking and interviewing for a new job multiple times. When you face this prospect, you need to deal with a sticky situation - whether to tell your manager you are looking for another job, and if yes, when and how to tell him. I have faced this situation many times in my career, and there is no one-size-fits-all way to handle this. It depends on your own situation at work, your standing in the company and your relationship with your manager. In this chapter, I'll cover some ideas and suggestions on possible approaches you can use as well as ways to handle potential responses from your manager.

When To Tell Your Manager
While no one is irreplaceable, knowing your value to your company and how much of a challenge your manager will have in trying to replace you will help you come up with the right approach to handle this situation with your manager. I will look at two scenarios: you are looking at a job inside your company and one outside your company.

- **Job opportunity inside the company**. If you are looking for or interviewing a job internal to the company, you should let your manager know early. Since your manager will likely find out soon when you inquired about the job with the hiring manager, it's better to give him a heads up and not let him get blind sighted. Typically, when the hiring manager knows you are interested and is interested in considering you, the hiring manager would check with your manager to inform him about your interest, get his thought as well as permission to interview you. Another advantage of talking to your manager early in this situation is that he may be willing to give you an objective assessment of the job you're considering. More on this later in the chapter.

- **Job opportunity outside the company**. You need to handle this situation differently. When you should tell your manager depends on the manager's personality and your relationship with him. If the manager is controlling, insecure/paranoid or a jerk, wait until you get a job offer. You may just be exploring and have not made up your mind yet. However, if you tell him early in the process, he may take it personally, be concerned whether you will be slacking off your responsibility or may get offended and want to get back at you – none of these behaviors are good. It's not worth the headaches. If you're seriously considering the opportunity and you have a good, trusting relationship with your manager who wants what's best for you, you should discuss with him prior to the formal interviews. He may be willing to share his objective opinion about the new job. Try to have this discussion in private to keep confidentiality and to avoid rumor starting in the workplace.

The discussion above is intended to provide ideas and suggestions. Since each job situation is different, use your best judgment and trust your instincts.

How To Tell Your Manager

Before you tell your manager, you need to be clear on what you're looking for in a new job – whether it's to learn new skills, to get new experience in a different job category, an opportunity to manage people, more pay, etc. When you meet with your current manager, be ready to explain why you are looking and what you are looking for that your current position doesn't provide. Avoid being negative about your current job. Rather, focus on the business opportunity and what positive benefits the new position will provide you. Avoid getting into personal issues, such as bad mouthing people at work or about the company. If you're frustrated working with people, explain about their action and not who they are. For example: "I'm frustrated with how long people take to make decisions here" or "I'm frustrated that every decision has to be consensus and that takes a very long time."

Let's look at an example. You feel stuck in your current job as a finance analyst. Most of your responsibility is getting financial data and producing financial reports for management. You have a good working relationship with your manager and believe that he appreciates your effort and values your contribution. After doing this job for a couple of years, you feel stagnant. You had given this feedback to your manager more than once and asked for more challenging responsibilities to help you grow professionally. However, you have not seen any changes to your situation for several months. You feel that you have reached a dead end and don't see a growth opportunity in your current position.

The new job you're considering is a financial analyst in Sales Organization in the same company, working with Sales Management to manage the compensation program. When you sit down with your manager, instead of saying: "I'm so bored with my current job I can do it in my sleep" or "It is a dead-end job with no growth opportunity and you're not doing anything to help me even though I have asked you several times," try saying it this way: "As you know, I have been looking for a growth opportunity where I can use my skills but also will enable me to gain new skills and experience. I learned about this opportunity that I believe offers what I'm looking for. I would love to get your feedback and advice." By saying the latter, there is no reason for the manager to take it personally or get defensive. Rather, it allows your manager to explore this opportunity with you, give his perspective and at the same time, allows him to step up and explore specific ideas to expand your current position. Moreover, you have an opportunity to ask him about the hiring manager and he may share his insight about that manager as well as any challenges you may need to be aware of. If the manager can't counter offer with an attractive alternative because he doesn't have the flexibility, then your choice is clear. If the manager makes you an offer to stay, you now have choices to consider. This is a perfect chance to use your negotiation skills. Refer to the "How to negotiate your job offer" chapter for details.

How To Anticipate And Handle Your manager's Response

You receive an offer from another company that gives you a better position with more challenging responsibilities and a slightly higher salary. You're leaning towards taking the offer but you also like working with people at the current company and are keeping an open mind. What should you do? Your knowledge of your standing in the company and your relationship with your manager is important in determining how you should handle this situation.

How do you know you are valued as an employee by your manager and the company? Evidence of this includes receiving high rankings, excellent performance reviews, employee stock awards and important and visible projects. In this situation, assume your manager values you, wants to keep you and make you a counter offer. He may ask you about the job details, what the offer includes and what it would take for you to stay. Needless to say, you have leverage here. This is a good opportunity to apply your negotiation skills. However, before considering the counter offer, you must be clear about your priorities besides the offer package, including job responsibilities, future growth opportunities, personal priorities, your working relationship with your boss and co-workers, etc. Don't look at the salary compensation only. Consider all important factors. For example, you value interesting work that also offers professional growth over getting the most money, and you value the working relationships you currently have. As a result, you would prefer to stay with the company if your job can be changed to better meet your objectives. With this assessment, you're in a good position to provide a clear response and negotiate a win/win agreement.

If you choose to, you also have an opportunity to negotiate with the new company on their offer. You must use your judgment in negotiating with both companies at the same time. You need to have a good idea on where you can negotiate and how far you can go. Consider all offers carefully and make your decision based on a clear understanding of your priorities. Keep in mind the key rule of negotiation: strive for a win/win.

If you informed your manager of the offer and he's not able to come up with a counter offer, then that makes your decision easy. No need to take it personally. I have seen cases in my career where the manager later admitted that it was a mistake and if they had a chance to do over, they would have made a real effort to keep the employee on their team. Move on and look forward to your future.

Additional Tips

- **Do not accept future promises**. Your manager may tell you he values your contributions, wants you to stay and promises that he will look into giving you more responsibilities and higher pay in the future. Don't fall for it. Future promises carry little value. Even if he means it, things can happen in the future to eliminate that possibility. Business condition can change and force the company to cut expenses or freeze salary increases. Your manager may leave the company and the promise goes with him. If your manager and the company really want to keep you, they will do their best to make it worthwhile for you.

- **Always act professionally.** Don't get personal. Focus on the job and the offer. If your manager lets his emotion get the better of him, don't reinforce that behavior. Reschedule the meeting and come back later when he calms down.
- **Never burn bridges**. The world is a small place. In the future, you may be working again with some of the same people from your previous company. When I left my company for a new company, my new manager was my former employee in our previous company. At other times, I also ended up working together again with the same people whom I worked with from previous companies. By all means, avoid the temptation to trash people and burn bridges. More often than not, it comes back to haunt you.
- **Do your job until the last day**. You may have "short timer" attitude and the desire to cruise in the final weeks of your current job. Since you have invested a lot of hard work and earned a good reputation with the company, don't risk losing it. Moreover, you will earn even more respect by being the ultimate professional. And to my earlier point – it's a small world and you never know when great opportunities will be offered to you by people who had worked with you before.

Part 7

Managing Your Career Path

Control your own destiny or someone else will.

Jack Welch

Chapter 33

How To Build, Maintain And Grow Your Network

In today's world, professionals change not only jobs but also careers. In the era of global business and interactions, we are living in a small world. People we went to school with can be our co-workers. People from a company we worked with many years ago are now our peers in the same company. Our competitors from other companies are now our partners. In the fluid world of business, it's important to build, maintain and grow our network of contacts. Our network can be instrumental in providing support and a boost to our career. They can be valuable resources and avenues for professional and career opportunities. In this chapter, I'll address a variety of networking ways to build, maintain and grow your network.

Networking Sources

- **Classmates**. People we went to school with are a great resource. As you and your classmates go different ways after graduating, they likely will be locating in different locations throughout the world. While in school, get to know as many of your classmates as you can and let them get to know you. Most schools maintain a database of each class year graduates. Fifteen years after graduating from my MBA program, a classmate and I met and discussed a business idea which resulted in a creation of a business partnership that's still going strong ten years later. You never know whom and when you may end up working with or getting a great opportunity from.
- **College Alumni**. All schools maintain an extensive list of alumni. While fund raising is a major purpose, it's also a way for alumni to stay in touch, share information and provide assistance to each other. Alumni live and work throughout the world and are a good source to identify potential career and job opportunities. An easy way to stay

in touch is to register in the Alumni Directory and include your personal and career profile for people to view. University's regular networking events such as social getting together, anniversaries, recruiting and fundraising events are great opportunities to meet, build, maintain and grow your contacts.

- **Co-workers**. People you're currently working with or have worked with in the past. If you have developed a good working relationship with them, gained credibility and earned their trust, they're a fantastic resource for finding out and getting potential opportunities. They can be great references and even better, give you endorsements. As with our classmates and school alumni, it's even more important to get to know your co-workers, develop a good working relationship with them, and maintain contact with them when you or they leave the company. If you can't get together for coffee from time to time, a simple way to keep in touch is sending a hello greeting to let them know you have them in mind. Periodically posting on your social networks is also a good way to stay connected. There have been several times in my career where I was recruited by my former co-workers and vice versa. One of my former employees recruited me a few years after leaving our company and I ended up joining his company and working for him.

- **Professionals connected to your company**. These include suppliers, partners, service providers or contractors you work with on behalf of your company. A supplier could be a company that provides your company components to build products or packaging materials to ship your products in. Service providers could be consulting companies such as Bain Consulting and McKinsey who provide consultation on different projects in a variety of areas. Contractors could be people your company hires to perform a specific task. As you work with these partners, follow the same working principle – develop and maintain a good working relationship with them. These partners are a good resource for future opportunities because they tend to have a lot of visibility of the industry. They also know many key players from their work with other companies. My colleagues have received job offers from these partners as well as recruited them to join our company.

One other source to keep in mind is your competitors. In today's world, a competitor today could be a partner or peer tomorrow. It's not uncommon for people to switch companies and go to work for a competitor. They can provide valuable information about job opportunities, insight about the company and in many cases, actively recruit people from their previous company to join them.

- **Industry organizations**. If you have industry organizations in your field of work, such as the IEEE for electrical engineers, the American Association of Finance and Accounting (AAFA) for accounting and finance professionals or the American Marketing Association (AMA) for marketing professionals, consider joining them if you're not a member. You get useful, relevant news and information specific to your field through website postings, newsletters and magazines where you get exposure to job and career opportunities. Also make an effort to attend periodic events organized by the association; these are excellent networking opportunities.

- **Head hunters and recruiting firms**. Throughout your career, you will likely receive calls or email messages from head hunters who try to recruit you for one or more job opportunities. These head hunters or recruiting firms are hired by their client companies to find qualified candidates. The service they provide to their clients includes identifying, recruiting, interviewing and selecting qualified candidates for the clients to consider. They typically get paid by successful hires or by qualified candidates, and they usually are visible at industry seminars, conferences and other networking events. You can also find them on popular sites such as LinkedIn, Monster and CareerBuilder. Introduce yourself and get their contact information. Even if you don't want to leave your company, keep in contact with them as they are a great resource to provide you up to date picture of the market.

- **Friends, family members, neighbors and social groups**. Last but not least, these could be the best ways to find out about new opportunities as well as excellent resources to help you find a right job. These people know you well, have a close relationship with you, share common hobbies or values and would likely be more than willing to help. They probably also have their own network of contacts they can tap into to give you visibility to even more people. When I graduated from college, I gave my sister, who lived in another state, my resume. Within two weeks, I received a phone interview from Honeywell Inc. They flew me in for interviews and by the end of the day, I received three offers from three different divisions. My sister was a member of her church community and through her friends there, she found out this opportunity from someone working at Honeywell at the time.

Ways To Build, Maintain And Grow Your Network

- **Use your social networking tools**. There are a number of popular social networking and professional sites such as Facebook, LinkedIn, Monster and CareerBuilder which provides a forum for all professionals to communicate and share information. If you have not, you should join, create your account and invite people to join you. Include your personal and professional profile in your account. You can find useful news and information shared by other people as well as job openings through these sites. Through your accounts, you can communicate to a vast number of people about your job interest or career opportunities you want to research.

- **Stay in touch with your co-workers**. As discussed earlier, co-workers are a fantastic resource. Having them join your social networking group is a good start, but don't forget to have face to face, direct contact with them if possible. In the age of digital communications, we tend to forget the importance of this. Remember that nothing creates a deeper bond and connection than face to face interactions. Try to find time, once every three months or so, to have lunch or coffees depending on your and their availability. I also know co-workers who have common hobbies that draw them together. For instance, people who like to ride their bike would get together for bike runs on the weekends. The group expands as more people join; this presents a good way to not only maintain, but also build and grow your network.

- **Attend industry seminars and conferences**. These events are typically organized by industry groups or by major consulting firms to have a gathering of professional people in similar fields. In high tech industry, big consulting services firms such as IDC or the Gartner group typically have at least one major event a year to discuss and share industry news, trends and to network. Of course, their goal is also to offer their consulting services to potential client companies. Since these events tend to draw hundreds or thousands of professionals from different companies, you have a great opportunity to meet with as many people as you want in one place. Over the course of my career, I have met and formed friendships with many new people and have also run into many co-workers and acquaintances whom I had lost touch with; these events allowed me to re-establish contact with them.

- **Attend social outings**. Through your social organizations, whether it's church, hobby club, sports club, volunteer or charitable organization, get together events and social outings are good forums to stay connected and get to know people better. These events allow more time for us to have longer conversations instead of the usual quick greetings and small talks we typically have at a club meeting. Through these kinds of events, I have also seen parents inquire about internship positions or potential jobs for their college children and more often than not, they would meet people who know about openings in their company or know people who are looking to hire college students.

Chapter 34

How To Deal With Changes At Work

It's a given the only thing that is constant in a workplace are changes. It was kind of a running joke in my companies that we can expect a major re-org every year. During my career spanning twenty five years, I had worked in twelve different organizations in five companies. I worked under twelve managers and experienced numerous company organizational changes. I can tell you my companies were not the exception; most of the people I talked to and interviewed also confirmed this. It's highly unlikely you will have the same manager, work in the same organization and in the same company in your entire career. Some changes will be as a result of your decision to join another department or another company while other changes will be out of your control. Company organizational changes can be unnerving and introduce uncertainties in the workplace. Many people don't handle changes well and can take a long time to adjust. However, if you're able to deal with changes effectively and adjust to the transition quickly, you will be able to not only maintain but enhance your standing in the company. In this chapter I will discuss possible changes at work and how you can better deal with them and maintain your relevance in the organization.

While it's a given that changes in the workplace will happen during your career, the first crucial rule is to recognize what you can control and what you cannot. In Stephen Covey's book "The 7 Habits of Highly Effective People," he talked about the circle of concerns and influence (Covey, 2002). As he said, many of us focus on the concerns and react to things we can't control, rather than focus on areas we can influence and proactively work on. He encourages us to focus our energy and proactively work on things we have influence over, thereby expanding our circle of influence. For example, your manager decides to leave the company and you end up having a new manager. Instead of focusing on your concerns and fear about the new manager, you should focus your positive energy on where you can influence in this new situation, such as helping the new manager get up to speed quickly with the new team. Or your company decides to reorganize and move your department to under another organization. In this case, instead of worrying about how the new organization structure will impact your job negatively, focus your positive energy on finding ways to contribute to the new organization.

Regardless of any organizational change in your workplace, the key is to first focus your time and energy on the changes that you have some control or influence over. Secondly, do your best to behave and act professionally – stay calm, keep things in perspective, focus on your work and avoid getting emotional or distracted. Just the fact of recognizing you don't have control over a particular company change will help you avoid taking it personally and keeping you sane. Thirdly, make sure your own "house" is in order – meaning your annual plan is up to date with clear job responsibilities, specific goals, results you have achieved to date as well as expected deliverables for the remainder of the year. If you have not updated the plan, work on it as soon as possible because it's an important document to demonstrate your role in the organization.

Here are several common organizational changes, key differences and ways to handle them.

- **Company changes/reorganizations**. Your team/department is moved to another organization under a new executive. An example of this move: currently you are a pricing analyst on the pricing team in the Product Management organization. With the company reorganization, the team is moved to the Finance organization headed by a Vice President of Finance. In this company organizational change, we will cover two scenarios: one where you still work for the same manager and one where you have a new manager.
  - o **You still have the same manager**. In this scenario, your manager's initial objectives are: 1) to establish her and her team's credibility by educating the new executive about her and her team's role and value to the company, and 2) establish a good rapport and working relationship with the new executive. At this point your manager should treat this transaction as a new beginning with her boss and to find out as much as she can on how to work with the new executive effectively. With your knowledge of your manager's style, strengths and weaknesses, you should take this opportunity to offer her help during this transition. Meet with your manager as soon as possible and ask

her for specific tasks you can help. Keep in mind this change is new to your manager as well and she may be feeling a lot of stress and pressure to establish her place in the new organization. For example, if your manager is unorganized and needs to prepare certain materials quickly for a meeting with her boss, she would welcome your help. Taking this initiative would further enhance your value to your manager.

o **You have a new manager**. In this scenario, the new organization's executive has chosen a new manager for your team. It's logical to assume the new manager already has a working relationship with her boss and may not know much about her new team's role and value to the company. Your objectives here are to educate your new manager about your and the team's role and value to the company as well as establish a good rapport and credibility with her. If the new manager has not already done so, seek a meeting with her. When you have the meeting, use the time to update her on the role and value the team offers. Review with her your annual plan and give your thoughts on business challenges and priorities. Although you're a member of the team, taking this initiative to discuss the team with her shows your leadership and your broad knowledge of not only your job but the overall picture of the team. In addition, ask your manager for any specific requests she may have that you can assist in this transition. Finally, take the opportunity to find out how to work with her going forward.

If your new manager came from outside the company, she probably knows very little about the company's business, organizational dynamics and about you and the team. There is a lot for this manager to get up to speed on; she may focus initially on syncing up with her boss, trying to understand the company business and as a result, may not put as much energy toward her team. Here, you have a great opportunity to make yourself valuable by proactively bringing her up to speed and sharing your insight on the team, the company and its challenges.

A friend of mine, Katie, recently went through this experience. Due to reorganization in the company, the Vice President of her group and his direct report were forced out (or "retired to spend more time with family!") and Katie was worried about whether she would be next in line. The new VP, who came from a different industry, had little experience with the new company's business and industry. Katie seized the opportunity to work closely with the new VP. She helped bring her up to speed on the inner workings of the company business and she created presentation materials for the VP's important meeting with the company's executive staff. The new VP was impressed with Katie's skills and deep knowledge about the company and its business. By taking this proactive approach, Katie established her credibility and positioned herself as a valuable asset to the VP.

Whether your manager is new to the company or not, after she has had time to digest the team information and meet her boss, you should ask to review your annual plan with her to see if it should be updated given the recent organizational change. New managers tend to want to add their own footprint to their organization and tend to make changes to their team and the team's charter. Your manager will appreciate your taking the initiative in helping her put her stamp on the team and succeed in the new role. By establishing your credibility and value, you stand a good chance to keep your job, or better yet, get a chance to be assigned to a more important role on the team. Lastly, you should proactively plan for the next step in your career; it's best to take control of your career and not put your fate in somebody else's hand or wait to see what happens next. By proactively exploring your options and planning your career, you're in control and have the confidence to drive your career. Refer to the "How to think broadly about your career growth paths" chapter for details.

- **You have a new manager replacing the previous one**. There's no change in company organizational structure. For situations where your new manager comes from outside the company or from another team, the discussion above applies here as well. The exception to the above situations is that this is less complicated since the organization structure remains the same. If you have been in this organization for any extended time, you should have a good understanding of the company business, organization dynamics and priorities. As a result, you are in a great position to help the new manager get up to speed and to influence her on the team's priorities and needs.

If the new manager is one of your peers who was promoted, it may present a bit of an awkward situation and resentment among the team members, especially if you and other members feel the promotion was not warranted. However, once the decision is made, you have no control whether that person is your manager or not. While it may be difficult, you need to do your best to be professional and not let your personal feelings influence your behavior. If you find this promotion completely unacceptable, you have a choice to explore different job options. If you choose to stay in your current position, at least for the time being, you must try your best to have a good professional relationship with the new manager and help her be successful in her new job. Keep in mind that the new rookie manager is probably feeling a bit insecure as well and would appreciate your professionalism and your best effort in working with her, even though some new managers in this situation react to their insecurity by being more hands-on and micromanaging. As difficult as it may be, maintaining your professionalism by focusing on your work will gain the respect of your new manager and people in the company. Lastly, never burn bridges. It's a small world and things tend to have a way to come back to you.

- **You move to another team and have a new manager**. In this situation, you should already have some familiarity with the new manager, whether you wanted to move to that team or were assigned to it, and that should make establishing a rapport with the new manager easier. However, you should proceed as you would in other new management situations and work with the new manager to find out how best to work with her. In addition, since you're joining a new team, use the initial time to get to know the team – how the team works together, their concerns, their needs, how they work with other teams and how you can best work with them. Many of the best practices described in the "How to start your job on the right foot" chapter apply here as well.

- **Your colleagues get laid off but you are not affected**. While this situation doesn't impact your employment status with the company, it will likely have an effect on you. In the short term, you may feel sad and sympathetic for your friends, disappointed or upset at the company's decision even while you feel relieved you still have your job. It can also be a difficult time for your manager. I have had to give the bad news to employees who were impacted and it was one of the least favorite parts of being a manager. I experienced a mix of emotions – sadness to lose an employee/friend, guilt of affecting someone's livelihood, failure that I wasn't able to keep this employee. One of the things you can do during this time is to be as low maintenance to your manager as possible. In the near to medium term, the layoff may have a real impact on the manager and the team's workload, particularly if no replacement resource is available to cover the gap left by the laid off employees. If this happens, the manager needs to prioritize and figure out how to cover the workload gap. This is where you can help your manager and yourself. Help your manager prioritize the workload, and at the same time, influence her to allow you to take on more "value-add" work and take some of the less important work off your plate.

- **Another team gets a new manager**. While this may seem to have little or no impact on you or your team, it actually can. Much of your work involves other teams and when a team inherits a new manager, that manager may change her team's priorities and the way they work with you and your team members. As a result, it would be good for your manager to hear from the new manager about any change in priorities and how both teams can best work together. Don't assume that things will continue to work as usual. Remember, new managers tend to want to put their own signature on the new team they inherit. So talk to your manager to find out if your manager has met or plans to meet with the new manager. If not, explain to your manager the importance of synching up with the new manager to avoid future miscommunications or disconnects which can derail the project both teams have been working together on. You can say: "I was wondering if you have had a chance to meet with the new manager? This project is important to both teams and it would be helpful to us to get her thoughts so we can be on the same page." Your manager understands that potential project mistakes would not reflect well on her or the new manager and would appreciate your taking the initiative.

- **Your company gets acquired or your company acquires another company**. This can be a nervous time for employees in both companies, especially if there are overlapping functions, product lines and services. This raises the likelihood of the company cutting cost and laying off people. As the companies begin the integration process and if your team is potentially at risk, your manager would likely be involved. The best you can do here is to control your own "house." Make sure your annual plan is up to date and your manager is clear about your role, responsibilities and contributions. The other area you have control over is your network of contacts, both inside and outside the company, who can help you explore options and opportunities if and when your team is impacted. Make sure you stay in contact and maintain a good relationship with your network. Refer to the chapter "How to build, maintain and grow your network" for details.

I have experienced one major company merger. When my company merged with a competitor, it was clear there were overlapping products lines and services. My product division had similar products. Once my company announced that my product division would be phased out and replaced by the other company's product line, we all knew we were going to be out of a job. Because I had maintained a good relationship with my network contacts, I was able to meet with several of them to explore job openings and opportunities in their organizations. Through these contacts I was able to land a position I liked.

Chapter 35

How To Think About Your Career Growth Paths

Whether you recently started in your professional career or have been in your current job for some time, it's never too early to think about your career growth paths and explore possible options. Many of us don't spend enough time researching possible career paths and exploring which one may best match our goals, skills and interests. Let me describe one typical career path: we see a normal career path of advancing within our current job function, from entry to senior level individual contributor position (IC). Then after a couple of years in the senior IC position, we try to get promoted to an entry level manager in our department, and from there, we hope to continue climbing the corporate ladder.

Let's take an example. After college, you start out as an entry-level finance analyst, get rewarded for a job well done with a promotion to junior finance analyst two years later and then to Senior Analyst a couple of years after that. If you continue to do well, you hope to get promoted into management rank, beginning as a first line manager in the Finance Department. Assuming you will continue to climb the corporate ladder, that growth path after first line manager is second line manager (Director level), then Senior Director managing multiple finance teams, follows by Controller/VP of the Finance Operation and ultimately CFO position. The path from an entry level Finance Analyst to VP can take many years, and twenty years or more are not unusual. You may be able to speed up this cycle by joining another company at a higher position earlier than you can by staying in your current company.

Although this path is a reasonable and logical one, it's also limited. If this is the only path you pursue and as you advance in your career, the higher the position, the more competition you face. While any career path you pursue is more competitive the higher you advance, if you have multiple paths to pursue, you at least have more chances to succeed. So why limit yourself to only one path. There are other career growth options you should consider as you progress in your career. Companies may differ somewhat in how they structure different job levels, whether they offer job rotation programs and how they manage promotions across the company. In this chapter, I will discuss generally the different career path options and how to consider them, including the option of branching out on your own. For your specific company, you should research to understand the specifics of career growth paths and the "rules," written or otherwise, you need to know if you want to advance in your company.

Career Growth Paths

As you progress in your career, some of the career path options you may want to consider include the following:

1. "Specialist" Path: becoming "Content Expert" by gaining greater and in-depth knowledge of your specific field.
2. Early Management Path: moving to management role as soon as possible to manage people in your field or function.
3. "Generalist" Path: becoming a "Jack of all Trades" by gaining experience in other fields or functions.

These three paths could lead to eventual senior management positions but in different order of priorities. Moreover, these three career paths are not mutually exclusive. Throughout your career, it's possible to change from one path to another. For example, you can go from "Generalist" path to the "Early Management" path if you have a change of heart and decide to pursue getting into management instead. However, there are constraints, requirements and implications you need to consider when you switch from one path to another. Let's discuss in details each of these three paths.

1. "Specialist" Path (Content Expert)

In this path, you're going a mile deep in your field and becoming the subject matter expert. An example of this is a "scientist" position in a company. Typically, this is a non-management path for most of the career progression. As you continue to demonstrate your capability and deliver results, you will advance to higher job level and take on more strategic "technical/technology" responsibilities. While you may not take a people management role, you may have people indirectly reporting to you. You provide them guidance and direction on specific projects but not people management tasks such as performance review or salary administration.

Let's refer to the chart below for example. Upon graduating with an engineering degree, you start your career at an entry level responsible for executing specific parts of a project. Then over time getting promoted to Junior and Senior Engineer where you focus on the planning and designing aspects of the project. Your promotional path leads you to a Technical Director (TD) and Senior Director level where you're responsible for setting technology strategy and direction. In many high-tech companies, the Senior TDs report to the Chief Technology Officer (CTO) or to the engineering organization executive.

The duration from Entry Level to Chief Technology Officer could be many years, but varies greatly and depends on your continual job performance over time as well as factors not in your control such as organizational changes. However, you can potentially shorten this duration by timely and strategically moving to other companies for higher level positions.

Job level: Entry → Junior Level → Mid-Level → Senior Level → Expert Level

Responsibility: Execution-------------Planning-----------Strategy-------Directional

Title: Entry Eng   Junior Eng   Senior Eng   Tech Director   Senior TD   CTO

Considerations For This Career Path
- You are interested and have a passion to become a subject matter expert in your specific field. You want to spend your time working on different areas of your field and developing your craft.
- This is a longer-term personal commitment. Does this path fit into your long-term objectives and priorities? Is this something you want to pursue for the long term?
- You're not interested in managing people or spending time on non-job related tasks.
- To stay in this career path, you must continue to get educated and stay up to date on your field's latest technology and emerging trends.
- As you advance progressively to higher positions, the number of top position is limited and more competitive.
- There is nothing to prohibit you from changing course and moving to another career path such as "Early Management." However, it may be a dramatic change for you personally and professionally.

2. Early Management Path
This path is more straightforward and one many people identify with: starting out as an entry level position and advancing to higher IC position as you gain experience and prove yourself. Then instead of going for the "Specialist" or

"Generalist" path, you pursue the next goal of being a first line manager and continuing to progress to senior management positions.

Refer to the example chart below on the Solution Marketing function. You start out as an entry level Solution Marketing Specialist and progressing to higher IC job positions. Then you transition to be first line manager managing a team of marketing specialist. As your career continues to progress, you look to advance to a more senior position - Senior Director, where you manage a broader marketing group such as Solutions Marketing team and Product Marketing team. Vice President would be the next promotion where you take on greater responsibilities managing multiple groups, including Solutions Marketing, Product Marketing and Partnership Marketing. Ultimately, you attain the Senior VP position where you manage the entire Marketing Organization.

Solution Marketing
Entry position → Junior Level → Senior Level → 1st Manager Level → Director level → Senior Director → VP → Marketing Senior VP

Take another example from the chart below for Finance Function. Similar to the Marketing example, you progress from entry level Finance Analyst to Senior Level (IC) position to people management position, from first line manager, Director, Senior Director and to Controller/VP position managing multiple groups, including Finance group, Op-Expense group, and Cost Accounting group, etc. And finally, attain the ultimate position as the company Chief Financial Officer (CFO).

Finance Function
Finance Analyst entry level → Junior Level → Senior Level → 1st Manager Level → Director level → Senior Director → Controller/VP → CFO (Senior VP)

Considerations For This Career Path
- Does this fit with your career objectives and priorities?
- You're especially interested in being a people manager sooner rather than later. You like to coach and develop people.
- You can juggle between handling your own work assignments as well as managing people.
- Once you become a manager, your growth path is likely to be within your function. It would be more difficult if you want to become a manager of another team in a different function in the future. You would have to compete with more experienced people in that function who also want to move into management.

- As you advance progressively to higher positions, the number of top positions is limited and more competitive.

3. "Generalist" Path ("Jack of all Trades")

Instead of going a mile deep in the "Specialist" path, you opt to go a mile wide. If you're a person who likes to learn, develop skills and knowledge in different areas, you might want to pursue this path. Many companies support and have "rotational" programs where employees are allowed to rotate from one job to another, from one organization to another over a period of time. One benefit this offers is the ability to gain a broad understanding of the company's different operations. Many executives, especially organization executives, have a well-rounded experience and knowledge of the company operations. You can pursue this path while working as either an individual contributor or as a manager, although I think it is an easier transition for an individual contributor. This path may be the best way to attain a high level executive position eventually because you can apply for and be considered among several possible executive positions in the company.

Let's take an example from the chart below. You start out as an engineer in your Engineering organization, then to Operations to work on product manufacturing process, and then to Technical Support where you work with the field to support customers. After the technical support stint, you join product management to manage a product business line responsible for pricing and forecasting. Finally, you join marketing and then business planning to work on strategic planning for the company. I have known people whose career included time spent in all of these positions.

Engineering→ Operations → Tech Support → Product Mgt → Mktg → Business planning → Etc.

Moreover, you can move back and forth between individual contributor role and management role as you move from function to function. Keep in mind it's not unusual to take a lower level position when you move to a new function. For example, from technical support manager, which is a people management position, to a product manager, which is an individual contributor. Moreover, some transitions from one function to another function are easier than others. For example, for a technical career, moving from Engineer to a Technical Marketing Specialist is much easier than going from a Finance Analyst to Technical Marketing Specialist because of the requirements involved. Technical Marketing includes both technical skills and some marketing skills. An engineer already has the technical skills and needs to learn marketing skills. On the other hand, a Finance Analyst does not have either and trying to learn the technical skills on the job would be impractical. Moreover, some positions may require higher education training. For example, Product Management position may prefer people who have technical skills as well as an MBA degree (Master of Business Administration).

Let's look at another example from the chart below. You start out as an Engineer and after a few years, move to Operations to work on product manufacturing, then onto Technical Support as an Individual Contributor. From there, you get promoted to be first Line Manager in Technical Support organization. Then you move into Product Management as a manager managing product managers. After a period of time, you get promoted to Director and eventually to Senior Director in product management group.

Your next move is to decide which organization you want to eventually become an executive of. Since you have engineering, technical support, operations and marketing experience, you can apply for an executive position in any of these organizations when the opportunities arise. Keep in mind the likelihood of a promotion also depends on your performance track record and how well you are perceived by the executive team. Refer to the "How to stand out and promote yourself" and "How to manage up" chapter for details.

Eng→ Ops → Tech Support

Tech Support Mgr → PM Mgr → PM Director → PM SD → Org VP

Considerations For This Career Path
- Does this fit with your career objectives and priorities?
- You're interested in being more of a "Generalist" than a "Specialist" and excited about learning different skills and have different types of experience.
- You're willing to sacrifice trading off higher job level to lower job level and lower job "status" for potential future benefits.
- To stay in this career path, you're comfortable and can deal effectively with new changes and ambiguity of new situations and new environments.
- Do you have at least the basic skill required for the different positions you want to take on next?
- You are a fast learner who can get up to speed quickly.
- As you advance progressively to higher positions, the number of top positions is limited and more competitive.
- The more you head down the "Generalist" path, the more difficult it will be for you to switch to the "Specialist" path because this

requires staying on top of the subject matter. If you have been away from it for any length of time, it would be difficult to catch up or regain the interest.

4. Working For Yourself

This is a fairly dramatic change in your career. As you gain more experience in your profession as an individual contributor and/or in management role, you wonder what it would be like if you branch out and work as an independent consultant. In being a consultant or contractor, you either work directly with the company or you can utilize the service of an employment agency who can help find projects and handle all the paperwork including processing payments for you. However, the agency will take a cut of your pay for their service, typically in the range of 20-35% depending on the level of service you want from them. In between my corporate employments, I had worked as a consultant for several companies, from start-up, small to large, and had firsthand experience in this area. Here is a summary of the pros and cons as well as factors to consider.

Pros:
- Flexibility. Theoretically, you can set your own schedule, choose the projects you want to work on and clients to work for, as well as having more time for yourself.
- Typically you get paid higher than the base salary of an employee, depending on your level of experience.
- Get broader exposure by working with different companies and in different industries.
- Potential attractive and permanent employment offers from client companies if you want to consider going back to a corporate position.
- Running your own business and be your own boss. You don't have to deal with company politics or put up with bad colleagues or managers as much.

Cons
- Consulting business can be unpredictable. Although there is no guarantee of permanent employment for any job, company employees usually have more job security.
- You get no additional benefits other than the payment for your work (no vacations, medical benefits, stock incentives, etc.).
- You have higher expenses such as medical and dental insurance premium.

- You may feel a bit isolated because you're not as much a part of a team as you were before.
- You don't have resources the company offers to their employees - development training, management development training, job skills training and industry resources.

Considerations For This Career Path
- Can you deal with uncertainties, not knowing where your next project will come from?
- Are you willing to spend lots of time to sell your skills and secure new businesses?
- Do you have a network of contacts you can tap into for opportunities?
- Do you enjoy working alone and not having as much "socializing" with co-workers?
- Do you have different skills and knowledge to take on different consulting projects?

Note: another path of working for yourself is going off and starting your own company. We have seen or known many people who had attempted this, some succeeded wildly and some didn't. This would be a major under taking and is not in the scope of this book. If you at some point want to consider pursuing this challenge, there are many sources and industry experts you can tap into.

Chapter 36

How To Decide If You Want To Pursue A Management Position

B eing a manager can be rewarding personally, more than the increased pay and benefits you receive. It can bring you self-satisfaction from seeing the positive impact you have on your employees. As you progress in your career, you will get to a point where you begin thinking about whether you should consider a people management role. Before you decide on this question, it would be prudent to get as much insight as possible to understand what the role entails, the pros and cons, challenges and key requirements to be a good manager. Having a realistic picture of the position helps you determine your interest and qualifications.

If you show management potential while working as an individual contributor, you may be encouraged or even asked to take on a people management role. Give it serious consideration before you decide. Once you're a manager, it can be difficult to move back into an individual contributor position. Although transitioning back to an individual contributor role from management role is not unusual, some people see it as a step down and a demotion. What I have seen is that people would rather leave the company rather than being "demoted," even if they accept an individual contributor position with another company. In this chapter, I'll lay out an objective picture of the management position – the good, the bad, the ugly and requirements to do the job successfully.

Pros:
- Higher pay, more stock incentives. As a manager, you move up to a higher job level with corresponding higher financial compensation and incentives. Companies vary on how they structure salary for managers, but a ten percent salary increase over your individual contributor's salary is not unusual.

- Title and social status. This can be a stepping stone in your career path, at your company or another company. It's a good bullet point on your resume and adds more credibility to your standing in the industry.
- Have more influence in the organization. With more responsibility you also have more influence. You participate in more strategic business meetings with company executives, have opportunities to contribute to the discussion and participate in decision makings. However, keep in mind that credibility is earned and must be demonstrated on an ongoing basis for you to be successful and continue to have influence.
- Opportunity to develop new skills. You will have a chance to learn and develop a new set of skills and experience – hiring, recruiting, coaching, developing people, managing budget, managing up, partnering with outside organizations, long term business planning and developing executive leadership skills.
- More exposure to outside world – suppliers, press, industry forums, seminars, customers, etc. In your position, you may have more opportunities to expand beyond your company and to establish yourself by interacting with other industry professionals more regularly.
- It's a stepping stone for promotion to higher management level in the future. If you succeed in this role and receive excellent performance review over a period of time, you will be in a position to be promoted to the next level. Your chances of getting promoted are also greater if you are good at managing up.

Cons:

- Additional responsibilities. As a manager in today's business world, you not only take on people management responsibilities but also specific individual work as well. Handling all these responsibilities and juggling different balls can add more stress to you.
- You probably will not be measured or rewarded for being good at managing people. You are more likely to be rewarded for business results you and your team achieved, and not on how much time you spend coaching and developing your employees.
- Dealing with more organizational dynamics and politics. Representing your team in this role, you need to navigate the organization terrain, negotiate for resources you need, fight to eliminate obstacles to allow your team to do their job, and represent them on employee evaluation meetings. All this take a significant

amount of time and require a strong ability to navigate effectively through these challenging situations.

- More pressure on work-life balance. With more responsibilities comes more stress. As a manager, you will attend many more meetings which take more time from you being able to work on your own individual work such as company-wide projects with other managers. You start cutting into your personal time to play catch up and as you spend progressively more time doing your work, you face more risk of getting stressed out.
- Emotional strain. Dealing with people issues can drain you mentally and emotionally. High maintenance employees demand a lot of your time on non-productive issues. The performance evaluation process, especially forced distribution ranking, is highly sensitive and can be controversial as it has a big impact on the employees' career.
- More administrative work - budget, employee paperwork and performance reviews, etc. Most of us don't like doing paperwork and it can take a significant amount of time. However, it's a real part of a manager's life and is a price of wanting to be a manager.

Key Success Factors To Be A Great People Manager
- **Good people skills**. Being able to listen, empower, respect, be fair and effectively communicate to your employees is absolutely important. In addition, employees are different individuals and you need to be able to recognize each employee's style, motivation and the best way to work with each one to enable them to do their best work.
- **Reward and give credit to your employees when deserved**. Recognize your team or individual team members for a job well done. Giving public recognition is greatly appreciated by the employees; even small gestures such as dinner or gift certificates go a long way to show your appreciation and motivate your employees. More importantly, show respect to your employees in public meetings and don't undermine them. Nothing is more demoralizing and demotivating to an employee than feeling undermined and getting thrown under the bus. If you need to critique an employee, do it in private, not in front of people.
- **Willing to invest significant time in your employees**. Even though you likely will not be measured or get rewarded, being a good manager requires you to spend significant time with your employees. When I became a manager for the first time, I asked my business unit General Manager during one dinner about how much time is

appropriate for a manager to spend between company business and on managing people. His answer took me by surprise. He said I should spend 80% of the time on business and 20% on managing people. I think this reflects the lack of importance companies place on the people management aspect of being a manager. I believe to be an effective people manager, you need to spend at least 1/3 of your time, depending on the number of employees you have.

- **Delegate appropriately**. As a first time manager, it may be hard to break some habits we had when we were individual contributors. We probably were high performers and did our job well, and as a new manager, we may still have the tendency to do the work ourselves or tell our employees how to do it. Either way, employees would not feel empowered or motivated. Worse, it inhibits creativity for new ideas, new solutions and does not allow them to grow in their job. By empowering our employees to do their work but being there for them to bounce off ideas and get feedback, they will feel supported and motivated to deliver results.

- **Ability to navigate organizational environments**. This requires working well with multiple key stakeholders such as peers, employees, your manager, upper management and partners inside and outside the company. Each of these groups has their own objectives and interest and to be able to get work done successfully, you need collaborate effectively with them.

- **Ability to negotiate successfully**. In many situations, you will need to negotiate successful so your team has what they need to do their job effectively. Working on your department budget, obtaining funding and additional people for your team, justifying employee performance rankings are some of the examples where you will need to earn your pay as a manager.

- **Be organized**. Without this skill, you can be overwhelmed and risk having things get out of control. For example, you need to organize effectively in order stay on top of attending all the management meetings, working on your own work responsibilities, running one-on-one or team meetings and keeping track of your employees' work individually. If this is a weakness, seek out someone on your team who has excellent organizational skills to help you.

As a manager, many of the skills important for an individual contributor are even more needed in this new role. As a manager, you will be interacting with many more people from different organizations within the company and outside the company. As a result, you must be able to collaborate, communicate and negotiate even more effectively. In addition, since you will be working more closely with your boss and other executives, you must be able to manage up – to build successful working relationships so you and your team can get work done and deliver successful results.

Chapter 37

How To Transition From Individual Contributor To Manager

Transitioning from being an individual contributor to being a manager is a significant change in your career. You're no longer responsible for just yourself because you now have a team of people that relies on you for your direction, support and guidance. When you're promoted to a management position for the first time, you have a bit of a honeymoon period to transition to your new job. You should take advantage of this opportunity to learn as much as you can and prepare to get off to a good start in your new job. In this chapter, I will describe the best practices to help you make a smooth transition to your new position.

Get A Pulse On Your Team

This can be accomplished by meeting with the key stakeholders and partners in the company who you will be working with. Also, establish a rapport and build a good working relationship with your employees.

- Meet with your manager to get feedback on your team, his view on your employees, his concerns, top priorities and expectations. This will help guide you in leading your team, developing and executing plans that will meet your manager's priorities and expectations.
- Meet with your peers to get feedback on your team, their concerns, their priorities and how to work together. This will help you assess if your team is aligned on shared goals and if there are any specific issues you need to address right away.
- Meet with your team individually to get their feedback. This helps you gauge the mindset of your team, their morale and whether they are clear on their goals and expectations. Moreover, this helps you assess any disconnect between what you learned from your team and

what you heard from other people so you can address any issue immediately.

- If you have employees working remotely, discuss ways to stay connected and to work together. Remote employees are at a disadvantage by being disconnected to what's going on and not getting information in real time. Oftentimes, information is shared via impromptu conversations and hallway talks. Moreover, managers tend to use the path of more convenience when making request to their employees. If managers need to get something done, they tend to go a team member who they trust and can get it done quickly, and as a result, they go to an onsite employee to avoid delay. It's imperative for you to be cognizant of this. While you cannot replace impromptu conversations, you can accommodate to some extent by scheduling regular one-on-one meetings with clear agenda topics. If you are a forgetful kind of person, ask an employee who is onsite to remind you to share information with your remote team when appropriate. You also need to be more organized and plan ahead to be able to delegate responsibilities across all your team members and not just the ones near you. Lastly, it's a good practice to check in regularly with your remote employees for their feedback on your working relationships and for their suggestions for improvements.
- Review employee performance review reports as well as development and annual plans from the previous manager. Before you can or want to modify any plan, you need to understand the original plan and assess whether it's still relevant.
- Bond with your team. Get to know each other. We are human beings and we crave interaction and relationship with other people, not only through work activities but also outside of work. This is a good way to build rapport and chemistry with your team. Lunch, happy hours and a short half-day team building offsite are good ideas that don't take up a lot of time. The main purpose is to do something fun that everyone on the team will enjoy and have an opportunity to bond with one another.

Familiarize Yourself With The Company Management Process

Carve out a little time during this period to learn about company processes and management tools. If you wait until you need to know, chances are you will be pressed for time as you will have been fully engaged in running your team and company business. It's much better to get familiar now and not leave it for later.

- Meet with the HR manager to understand company processes that a new manager needs to know, from employee review/ranking processes, performance improvement plans, recruiting/hiring processes, to company policies and resources available to managers. Moreover, seek to understand the role of HR in the company and when and how to engage with your HR partner.
- Sign up for management training courses to learn how to manage your team effectively – how to motivate, how to "onboard" new employees, how to exit employees, how to develop employee performance plan and how to administer salary, etc.

Develop A 90-Day Plan - Identify A High Value Priority

- Share with your manager and your team the key takeaways and information you gathered from the meetings you had. Usually, through those meetings, you discovered interesting findings and insight your team or your manager might not be aware of. This information sharing helps to get everyone on the same page.
- Based on all the meetings and reviews you completed, identify high-value priorities which have the biggest positive impact to the company. Work with your team to identify one major priority that will have the greatest positive impact to the company, enhance credibility and provide visibility to your team and you. For example, after being promoted to be the pricing manager, I conducted meetings with key stakeholders and identified several big issues in the company. I shared my findings with my team and we selected a high priority project for us to work on. Because there was no real time, up to date business performance dashboard to help executive staff identify potential business issues, they weren't able to make proactive and informed decisions. After discussing with my manager, we agreed fixing this would have a big positive impact for the executive team and the company. Moreover, it would be a big win for our team and give us great visibility and credibility.
- Once the priority is selected, develop a strategy and implementation plan in the first 90 days and get approval to execute. My team and I worked together to develop a 30-day plan and a 90-day plan. The 30-day plan would provide the business dashboard and report but would be manually created. The longer 90-day plan will automate a lot of the data mining and create graphical presentations. I got approval from my manager to proceed; we delivered the results on schedule and the Senior VP loved the results. It was exactly what he had been requesting for over a year. My boss earned a lot of credit with the

Senior VP and in turn, my team and I earned a lot of visibility and credit as well. It set us up for a really good start in my management role.

This example illustrates the importance of taking your time initially to talk to people and to get a good picture of your team and the organization environment. Many of us have a tendency to jump in and start taking action without having good insight on important business issues that need to be addressed.

Review And Update Annual Plan

Once you have met with your team and learned about them and their needs and concerns, you have a good opportunity to update your team and each team member's annual plan to align with your boss and the company's strategy and priorities. More importantly, this will ensure you and your team are clear about priorities, expected results and timeline. This task may take a little bit of time, but it's important to put in the effort. This is the basis for you to evaluate your employee's job performance at year end as well as on an ongoing basis. It eliminates potential disconnects and it helps you and your employees stay focused.

- Revise and update the team's plan as needed based on your research findings. Meet with your team to go over the plan. It should include goals/objectives, plans, expected results and timeline. Review each of these areas with your team, get feedback and revise as appropriate. It's important to get commitment from the team on the expected results and timeline because you and the team will be held accountable.
- Review and revise as needed with each employee's plan. Their individual plan is a subset of the overall team plan but also includes their own career development plan. Similar to the team plan, their specific plan should include the same categories as the team plan. Get their feedback and revise as appropriate. Get commitment from each employee on the expected results and timeline, and make sure they understand they will be measured by the results they produce.

Identify And Seek Approval For A Mentor

I didn't realize the benefits of having a mentor until later in my career. I didn't think it was a big deal and didn't want to spend my time looking for and working with a mentor. Then I had a manager who strongly encouraged and even helped identify a mentor for me. I finally acquiesced to get him off my back. After meeting with my mentor and spending time with him periodically for a year, I realized the tremendous benefits of having a mentor. Obtaining a mentor should be a priority and required item on your career checklist.

- Your mentor should not be your manager. You want someone you are free to discuss any subject without worrying about conflict of interest, awkward feelings or potential consequences. Seek a mentor who has credibility and is respected by others in the company. Your manager may be able to help you identify potential mentors. He can suggest, make the first contact and help you connect with them.
- Identify an appropriate executive level mentor. As a first time manager, I would recommend looking for a mentor at a couple of level higher than your position - Director or Senior Director. The role of the mentor is to be a sounding board for you on work matters as well as your career. Someone who can give you unbiased opinions, provide guidance to navigate organizational dynamics, help you work effectively with company executives as well as assist you in your career growth. My mentor Jay was great in helping me work with executives, from facilitating meetings with them to getting my proposals accepted. Since I have a laidback personality, he spent time showing me ways to be assertive while remaining true to who I am. He also was a good listener who gave me great insight and wisdom when I was at cross roads in my career trying to figure out my next step.

How To Deal With Sensitive Issues

For a new manager, there are a couple of specific and sensitive issues that may apply to your situation; if they do, you need to be aware of and know how to handle them.

- If you were promoted over other people from the team you are now going to manage, this could present some awkwardness. Don't attempt to speculate whether these people would resent you because they thought they were more deserving. You're not there to soothe their egos or hurt feelings. The way to deal with this situation is to be professional and establish your credibility as soon as possible. A good step to achieve this is to show that you work well with your manager and have his support. The 90-day plan is a good way to achieve this. Showing the team your manager's support of the plan will give them confidence in you and in your ability to be a strong manager for them. Moreover, by reviewing each employee's plan and revising it based on their feedback, you show them you have their best interest in mind and are sincere in helping them to be successful.

- As a first time manager, it may be hard to break some habits you had as an individual contributor. If you're now managing a team which you were a member of, you may have a tendency to do the work yourself or show your employees how to do it, especially if they're under time pressure to deliver. As tempting as this may be, resist the urge to micro-manage even if you had good intentions. Your employees will not feel empowered or motivated. Worse, this inhibits creativity for new ideas, new solutions and does not allow them to grow in their job. They will see you as a manager making rookie mistakes. This is not the way to earn their respect. You would better serve them by being a sounding board and offering feedback and suggestions.

Chapter 38

How To Conduct Yourself When Leaving Your Company

As mentioned throughout this book, most people change jobs and companies more than once in their career. It's more an exception than the norm for someone to stay in one company for their entire working life. If you had changed companies, you probably have a good idea of the steps to take in helping make your departure smoother and preparing you to start your next job on the right foot. In this chapter, I will cover a list of things to do and the best practices to follow when you decide to leave your company.

Do Not Burn Bridges

Resist any temptation to burn bridges. It's understandable if you are leaving out of frustration, anger, feeling unappreciated or being treated unfairly. Nothing would feel better than to lash out and give them a piece of your mind. While this brings you immediate satisfaction and a sense of revenge, it won't help you in the long run and may even hurt you. Trust me on this. It's not worth spending your time and energy on the people you don't care about. It's much more worthwhile to use your energy on the people you do care about and on your future job.

Moreover, it's a small world where people change companies and you may cross paths with them in the future. You may even end up working with them at some point. I had changed companies and met many people from previous companies who are now working at my new company. I also have had hiring managers asking me for my opinions on candidates who were my colleagues previously.

- **Exit interview**. Many companies have Human Resource manager or personnel conduct exit interview when employees leave the company. Don't take this as an opportunity for you to unload, to get things off your chest, even if you were told your comments will be kept confidential. It's a good rule of thumb to assume what you say is not protected. HR is there to protect the company, not you. What I would suggest is to use this opportunity to give constructive feedback and suggestions. Even if you had a bad working experience at the company, I believe you can find constructive ideas and share suggestions that will help the company. This demonstrates your professionalism and generosity even as you are leaving. If you had a good working experience with the company, by all means give positive as well as constructive feedback.

- **Leave a good transition plan**. Let you manager know that before you leave, you will complete a transition plan to ensure a smooth transition for the person who will be taking over your job responsibilities. This is especially important if there is not a replacement in place by the time you leave. When you completed the transition plan, review it with your manager to make sure he understands the details. You manager will greatly appreciate this effort since he doesn't want to be left hanging when you leave. This again demonstrates your professionalism and integrity. If you know who is assuming your responsibilities, commit to help train that person.

- **Avoid sharing negative comments**. It's a good idea to not have too much contact with your colleagues and other people at work during this transition time before you leave the company. It's human nature for your colleagues, upon hearing the news of your leaving, to want to commiserate their feelings with you. It's a chance for them to unload their feelings about the company, the people or managers. You may be "pushed" into this and may unintentionally say things you may regret later. Moreover, it may create a negative working environment that your manager and other managers may not be too thrilled with. If you're stuck and can't find ways to excuse yourself, politely listen and acknowledge their feelings, but avoid getting drawn into a downward spiral. If you and your colleagues want to get together, schedule a time after you leave the company and meet with them outside of work where you can talk more freely and feel more comfortable giving your colleagues advice.

Things You Should Do Before Leaving

Below is a list of what you should take care of before your last day. Ideally you should already have completed them and not wait until you have to, because you may have very little time to pack up. If you're leaving for a competitor you likely will be walked out the day you submit your resignation. In normal circumstance, you give the company a two-week notice. Even with two weeks, that doesn't give you much time. Keep in mind there are things your manager needs you to wrap up and prepare others to take over your job before you leave. If you have not prepared adequately, do the best you can with the following activities:

- Create a list of contacts you want to stay in touch with.
- For the key colleagues - your manager, your mentor, and people you respect and have a good working relationship, send a goodbye, thank you message and include your personal contact information. Maintain a good professional relationship since you may cross paths with them and need their support in the future.
- Make a copy of the materials, including files from your work computer that belong to you and may be beneficial to you in your next job. Make copies of personal possessions you received from the company such as stock certificates. Make sure you comply with company confidential policy on its materials and information. You most likely signed a confidentiality agreement when you joined the company and will be reminded of this at your exit interview.
- Create a list of contacts from third parties you want to add to your network, including customers, partners, industry professionals and supplier. Let them know you're leaving the company and give them your new contact information.
- Keep a record of financial items and deadline requirements. For example, if you have stock options or restricted stock units, find out when you can exercise them and when they expire. If you participated in a 401K program, find out the options you have to manage your 401K program. Typical options include keeping your money where it is, transfer to your new company or convert to an IRA account. Make sure you understand the detail clearly, especially any potential tax implications.
- Make a list of key company HR/administrative contact numbers in case you have questions after you leave the company.

Complete Personal To Do Items
- Update all your personal social media accounts with your new employment profile.
- Update your resume with your new job. This should not take much time since you probably had updated your resume when you interviewed with your new company.

- Inform your list of network contacts, who are not already on your social media account, of your new change.
- Read the "How to start your job on the right foot" chapter so you can establish a good first impression and hit the deck running. When you start a new job, you have a little bit of a honeymoon period to get acclimated to the new environment and get up to speed. Take advantage of this as it will set you up to have a better chance to succeed in your new job.
- If possible, take some time off before starting your next job to take care of uncompleted personal tasks and to recharge your battery. You want to start your new job fresh and energized. Clear your mind and do something you enjoy.
- Take stock of your financial picture. Take advantage of this opportunity to assess your financial health. With your new job, do you need to make any adjustment to your financial plan and budget? Do you need to save or invest more or less? Consult a good financial planner to help you with this as you need.
- Take advantage of your short time off to meet and catch up with people you haven't been in contact with; it's a good opportunity for you to maintain and grow your network.

About the Author

Michael Dam has over twenty five years of experience and knowledge on addressing business and career challenges. In his professional career, he has worked in many different disciplines, including Engineering, Product Management, Business/Strategy Planning, Strategic Pricing, Demand Forecasting and Business Analytics. During his years working for major multi-national companies, he has held various management positions, from first line manager to Senior Director and worked closely with many high level management executives, including serving as Chief of Staff to a Senior Vice President of NetApp, a Fortune 500 company. During his management career, he was recognized as an outstanding people manager by his employees, peers and executives. Many of his employees have gone to become high-level executives of world class companies.

To fulfill his passion for teaching, he taught college business classes as an Adjunct Lecturer at Santa Clara University. For the last several years, he has volunteered his time conducting regular workshops to help college students develop job skills and prepare for their professional career after graduation. His educational achievements include Bachelor of Science in Electrical Engineering (BSEE) and Master of Business Administration (MBA). He was selected by Hewlett-Packard Company for the prestigious Accelerated Executive Leadership Program at Stanford University.

As an entrepreneur, he has provided consulting services to several high-tech companies. In addition, he co-founded and has been managing a successful commercial real estate company since 2007. He obtained his California Real Estate Broker License in 2014.

References

Brandall, B. (2016, June 7). *How to Prioritize Tasks and Do Only The Work That Matters*. Retrieved from www.process.st: https://www.process.st/how-to-prioritize-tasks/

Covey, S. R. (1989). *The 7 Habits of Highly Effective People.* New York: Simon and Schuster.

Economy, P. (2015, August 20). *The Top 10 Ways Your Employees Waste Time at Work*. Retrieved from www.inc.com: https://www.inc.com/peter-economy/top-10-time-wasters-at-work.html

Gallup. (2017, February). *State of the American Workplace*. Retrieved from http://www.gallup.com: http://www.gallup.com/services/178514/state-american-workplace.aspx

Huth, S. (2015, June 20). *Employees waste 759 hours each year due to workplace distractions*. Retrieved 2015, from www.telegraph.co.uk: http://www.telegraph.co.uk/finance/jobs/11691728/Employees-waste-759-hours-each-year-due-to-workplace-distractions.html

Max H. Bazerman, M. A. (1992). *Negotiating Rationally.* New York: The Free Press - A division of Simon & Schuster Inc.

PayScale. (2016, May 17). *http://www.payscale.com/about/press-releasePayScale and Future Workplace Release 2016 Workforce-Skills Preparedness Report*. Retrieved from www.payscale.com: http://www.payscale.com/about/press-releases/payscale-and-future-workplace-release-2016-workforce-skills-preparedness-report

Strutner, S. (2016, August 16). *Sitting All Day Is Even More Dangerous Than We Thought*. Retrieved from http://www.huffingtonpost.com: http://www.huffingtonpost.com/entry/sitting-health-effects_us_57b4b4e3e4b095b2f5421a58

Style, H. a. (2015, August 2). *Ultimate strength-and-cardio workout: STAIR CLIMBING*. Retrieved from healthandstyle.com: http://healthandstyle.com/fitness/stair-climbing-workout/

Tolle, E. (1992). *The Power of Now*. Vancouver: Namaste Publishing.

Yate, M. (2012). Knock 'hem Dead Job Interview. In M. Yate, *Knock 'hem Dead Job Interview* (p. 256). Adams Media.

Index

Visit Michael Dam's website
www.careeratwork.com for extra topics,
additional information and helpful tools
for your career.

65378327R00190

Made in the USA
San Bernardino, CA
02 January 2018